To Hell And Almost Back

To Hell And Almost Back

Life of a Seriously Disabled WW II Veteran

Sam Jones

Drafted in 1990. Edited in 2002
after Official Records were received
Completed in 2010

To order additional copies of this book, contact:
Xlibris Corporation
1-888-795-4274
www.Xlibris.com
Orders@Xlibris.com
88119

INDEX

WHAT THIS STORY IS ALL ABOUT

These are the memoirs of a Wisconsin farm boy that grew up during the Great Depression accompanied by a great drought where many of the lakes dried up and much of the Midwest's farmland simply blew away. The Depression ended abruptly the year I graduated from high school when WW II was declared and I was drafted into military service where I spent 3-1/2 years. I was critically wounded and spent the first 30 hours in a morgue followed by almost 1-1/2 years in military hospitals before I was discharged as a permanently disabled veteran. Because of my disabilities, I could never be a farmer and had to go somewhere else and develop new skills so I would be able to support my family. Jobs were hard to get because at the end of the war in Europe, 12 million healthy veterans had just been discharged and the economy was in limbo while industry was converting from wartime to peacetime economy. The story deals with how I started out as an apprentice electronic technician, became an engineer through home study, worked and lived on all continents and finally became Chief of the Navigation Engineering Branch at the Federal Aviation Administration Headquarters in Washington DC. It is a story of how I dealt with serious wartime disabilities and managed to develop a productive career at the same time.

After I had retired from a productive career, the physical and emotional wounds of WW II came back to haunt me every night. A high school classmate suggested that I write the story of those horrible years and once I had written them, it may relieve me of having to think about those things. I am not a writer, and was reluctant to engage in such a project but I did write the story of WW II more or less to give my children and grandchildren the prospective of what war is all about. My crude factual story served as a storage place for those memories so I could get on with my life without being tortured every night.

In the last few years, the schools have become alarmed because our school system has not taught students anything about WW II. This war was the main event of the last century and the 16 million veterans were dying off at 1000 a day. Vietnam era draft dodgers and flower children that were learning to be academics in the ultra liberal colleges during the Kennedy War are the people that wrote today's history books. They devoted 5 times as many pages to Marilyn Monroe, who was Kennedy's mistress, as they did to WW II. As the last of the 16 million veterans were dying off at 1000 a day. The school system became alarmed and asked WW II veterans to come into the schools and tell the students about their WW II experiences. I had the opportunity to participate in those programs and it was immediately apparent from the questions that they asked, that they were totally ignorant of not only WW II but of the Korean and Vietnam wars as well. The Vietnam veterans of President Clinton's generation took this opportunity to omit all wars from American history probably in an effort to camouflage their own un-American guilt.

They are not even aware that this war determined such basic things as the freedom they enjoy or whether they speak English or German today. At the same time, I don't have either the time or ability to write the history of the 20th Century. Instead, I decided to use the brief unbiased history of events from the World Almanac of what happened during every American president that has served since the war as a thumbnail sketch of 20th Century history. I also briefly commented on other significant events that I personally observed and experienced during this period. Also, I am now fully aware that events like WW II don't begin and end on any particular date but have a major impact on the entire life of every combat veteran. This is especially true of physically or mentally disabled veterans, affecting the type of work they were able to do, if any rather than what they wanted to do. The war is not over for them until they die and even then it continues to affect their family if they were lucky enough to have one. My original 1990 WW II story has been expanded to cover my entire life, to provide a first person account of how my WW II experience has affected my entire life. WW II will not be over for me until the day I die.

HOME ON THE FARM

I am a farm boy from rural Wisconsin born in 1923. My Minnesota parents were married about 5 years before I was born and bought 80 acres of heavily wooded land, which they made into a small dairy farm. They lived in what they called a shanty while my father cut enough logs, and had them sawed into lumber to build a barn, chicken coop and a house that was completed enough to live in before I was born. He also had to clear the land so they would have fields to grow crops to feed a few cattle. By the time the Stock Market crashed in 1929 when my brother was born, he had cleared more land, pulled or dynamited out the stumps and everything was going well. My grandparents lived next door on an adjacent farm. They bought a new car and gave my parents their old Maxwell which was their first car. I recall my mother taking me to see President Coolidge when his train stopped in Lewis where he stayed at Seven Pines. We struggled through the Great Depression which was accompanied by the worst drought in history, where many lakes dried up and farmland actually blew away. We survived by bartering chicken eggs, strawberries and cucumbers to get sugar and other essentials that my mother needed to can tomatoes and other vegetables. We survived because my grandfather cut our mortgage payments on the farm to $10 a month. Almost all the farms had for sale signs on them because they couldn't pay their mortgage or taxes.

When Roosevelt was elected president, he did some good things such as the Bank Holiday that closed all banks until they were audited to determine if they were solvent, so people would stop withdrawing their money and burying it in their back yard. The Civilian Conservation Corp (CCC) was also a good program but the WPA, better known as the "Weary Papa's Association" was the hallmark of his administration. It was a socialist program that was the father of deadbeat's welfare as we know it today. It

9

also led to the establishment of socialist coops like the Inter-County Leader and the REA (Polk-Burnett Electric Coop) that were subsidized to the point that private industry could not compete with them and they became a monopoly. War clouds were looking down on us from every direction and these people could have been salvaged, preparing us for the war that was inevitable. This war stole the youth from 16 million American boys and the lives of 407 million of them.

Powerful Mafia controlled labor unions also went on strike so there were 2 million additional families in the US unemployed as there were, when he assumed office. Unions were powerful enough they could shut down any or all industry overnight.

You never thought of yourself as being poor because everyone was poor. Those of us that had the initiative managed to survive without government welfare. We were also the young men that were drafted into the war that would end all wars that we hadn't made any effort to prepare for.

My mother's health failed shortly after my brother was born with what they called rheumatism, which is like they now call Lyme disease. She never complained but she did have to spend the last half of her life in a wheelchair or nursing home.

I went to a one room country grade school and graduated from Fredric High School in 1941, the year WW II was declared. We didn't get electricity until I got out of high school and we never did get running water. I had to go to Chicago to get a job because once you had registered for the Draft no one would hire you because they know you won't be around very long.

OUR HOUSE WITH THE BARN IN THE BACKGROUND
AND OUR CATTLE GRAZING IN THE PASTURE

MY HIGH SCHOOL FOOTBALL PICTURE AND THE GIRL I
MARRIED 2 YEARS AFTER WE WERE ENGAGED WHEN I WAS
TRANSFERRED FROM A HOSPTAL IN EUROPE TO A US HOSPITAL.

I

BRIEF HISTORY

I. EVENTS LEADING TO AND FOLLOWING WW II

In order to understand the events leading up to WW II, we have to take a brief look back at the WW I peace treaty and events that followed. The peace treaty carved up various countries in central Europe and imposed such stringent financial penalties on Germany, it was destitute. During the years that followed, the German Jews gained control of a considerable amount of the national wealth, exercising unwelcome control over the lives of the general population. This and resentment for the war debt imposed on Germany to repay war damages, infuriated German people, causing considerable unrest that resulted in the formation of the ultra-militant Nazi Party.

After WW I, U.S. President Wilson was instrumental in establishing the League of Nations, an organization much like today's United Nations established following WW II. The U.S. became an isolationist country, more or less divorcing itself from world affairs and the U.S. Congress refused to join the League of Nations that their president had been instrumental in establishing.

About 10 years later in 1929, the U.S. Stock Market crashed primarily as a result of uncontrolled credit and runaway inflation following the war. The good life after WW I, known as the Roaring Twenties was so good it triggered off events that devastated the nation, throwing it into what was known as the Great Depression. People, who had saved money, lost it when

13

the banks failed. Factories closed leaving millions unemployed and many people lost their farms, homes or businesses because they didn't have money to pay their mortgage or taxes. During this time, there was a great drought that lasted for several years. Farmers couldn't grow crops and much of the topsoil on their farms dried up and blew away. The Great Plains became the Great Dust Bowl.

Franklin Roosevelt, an undistinguished New York Governor was elected President in 1932 in the midst of the Great Depression. He initiated some important programs like Social Security, Federal Deposit Insurance Corp. and declared a bank holiday, closing all banks until examiners declared they were solvent. Roosevelt also initiated a number of socialist programs that laid the foundation for our present welfare state. His Civilian Conservation Corp. (CCC) that set up camps for young men from impoverished families that planted trees or did other unskilled work was a good program. They no longer had to eat at soup kitchens, which were common at that, time but both the youth and their destitute parents received a small amount of money each month.

Roosevelt's Work Progress Administration (WPA) unlike the CCC was a complete failure. This was our first universal welfare program, which provided make work jobs for the unemployed, which was almost everyone at that time. The work part of the program became a national joke overnight but was the foundation for the national welfare program we have today. The more industrious people who had the pride and initiative to survive without welfare made jokes like, "How many shovel handles did the WPA crew break today?". That was by leaning on the shovel rather than by shoveling dirt. Roosevelt's recovery program relied entirely on socialized government welfare programs providing jobs rather than the private sector. Today, few people realize that 2 years after Roosevelt became President; 2 million additional people had become unemployed. When you consider the U.S. population was small at that time and women had not yet entered the workforce there was only one worker for each household, which resulted in a catastrophe of enormous proportions.

Socialism flourished, leading to the rise of powerful labor unions, coops, and a host of other social programs. Interest free or taxpayer subsidized money resulted in the failure of private enterprises that couldn't compete with subsidized coops. Powerful labor unions, like coops had the power and often used it to shut down industry and bring transportation to a standstill. Mafia controlled unions had a firm grip on the entire country. Farm subsidies and other farm welfare programs were established, which are still inexistence more than 70 years later. The drought finally ended but the new social programs were well established so we didn't emerge from the Great Depression until we entered WW II several years later.

In spite of all the socialist programs implemented, Roosevelt had been somewhat restrained by the U.S. Supreme Court. In 1937 he tried to get approval to appoint six additional Supreme Court judges, who would re-interpret the Constitution so he could overcome the objections of the present judges and expand his socialist revolution. His request was denied by Congress at that time but because of his long tenure in office, he was later able to pack the court with newly appointed socialist judges.

Radio broadcasting, which was new at the time, was rapidly becoming the primary source of information at the time that Roosevelt was elected in 1932. He used it to its fullest and everyone with a radio listened to his weekly fireside chat broadcast from the Oval Office. He was not only like Santa Claus with gifts for everyone but a great orator and almost everyone had full confidence in him. He told people only what he wanted them to know and the inevitable, approaching war was not something he wanted to talk about. People had so much trust in Roosevelt that they never envisioned him getting us into the raging war in Europe. After all, when he ran for his third presidential term, his slogan was "Keep American Boys out of Foreign Wars".

Most Americans were so engaged in their day-to-day struggle for survival that they couldn't see the war clouds on the horizon. During the second half of the 1930s, Spain was engaged in a bitter civil war, Italy had occupied Ethiopia and Germany had rebuilt its huge war machine, which was not permitted by the WW I peace treaty. Germany had occupied one small country after another in central Europe and Russia was also occupying small European countries, dividing them up with Germany. England and France had military forces positioned along what the French called their invincible Maginot Line on the French/German border in an effort to hold back the mighty German war machine. Highly mobile German armor made an end run through Holland and without any resistance entered Paris a few days later. Most of the invincible French army threw away their arms in front of the rapidly advancing German armor and got lost in the crowds.

Many of them were part of the crowds welcoming the Germans into Paris. A few who called themselves, Free French lead by General De Gaul and all British forces retreated to Dunkirk. From there, they were evacuated across the English Channel to England, leaving behind all their war material, completely abandoning the Continent. Germany and Russia, having come into conflict with each other over dividing up the small countries of Europe were now at war with each other.

Einstein advised President Roosevelt in a top-secret letter dated August 2nd 1939 that he and a group of scientists had reason to believe Germany may be developing an atomic bomb. He suggested that we initiate a research program to determine the feasibility of developing such a bomb of mass destruction before Germany. In September 1940, the U.S. transferred 50 overage destroyers to Britain. Although the U.S. pretended to be neutral, in March 1940 we started shipping massive amounts of war material to both England and Russia, under what we called the Lend Lease Program. Obviously if a German submarine would have sunk one of our ships, we would have been in war with Germany and we didn't even start drafting men for military service until 1940. The first peacetime draft was not approved until September 14, 1940.

There were also black clouds on our western horizon and the average American hadn't paid much attention to that either. The Japanese had already taken Manchuria, Korea (where they had appropriated prostitutes for solders in other theaters), and were in the process of capturing China where they raped and murdered women and children at will. The Japanese were still continuing to buy shipload after shipload of scrap iron from the United States which they were using to build ships, tanks, guns and planes to enlarge their already massive modern war machine. Roosevelt was running for his 3rd term for president at that time in 1940, using the slogan, "Keep American Boys out of Foreign Wars".

Japan was badly in need of oil to operate their huge war machine and was in the process of negotiating with President Roosevelt regarding its oil shortage problem. Finally, as a last resort, they requested a summit meeting with Roosevelt in Hawaii. Although our Ambassador in Tokyo advised him that it was of utmost importance that he honor their request, he refused. This resulted in the replacement of their more moderate prime minister with a hard line militant and Japan was secretly committed to an all-out war with the United States. Soon after that, the Japanese fleet left Japanese ports, and were not seen or heard from for more than a month. They maintained radio silence and we didn't have any idea where they were. During this period, Japan was carrying on negotiations with the U.S. State Department through their Washington Embassy.

On December 5th and 6th, 1941, a U.S. direction finder station near San Francisco picked up radio signals from what they thought was the Japanese fleet, located somewhere north of Hawaii. There was a flurry of long multipart messages being received by the Japanese Embassy in Washington, which unknown to them, we could decipher because we had broken their code. When the Japanese Ambassador finally delivered the messages to our State Department that they were declaring war on the United States, we had already decoded the messages but the Pearl Harbor attack was already underway. Information regarding the location of the Japanese fleet and the flurry of messages should have sounded a red alert to our president and his cabinet but it didn't. Our entire Pacific fleet was bottled up in Pearl Harbor like sitting ducks with most officers with authority on shore leave. None of them had been advised of the recent intelligence information and had not been alerted for a possible surprise attack that occurred early in the morning of December 7th, 1941. The attack destroyed or severely damaged the Pacific fleet about a year after Roosevelt was re-elected on his "Keep American Boys out of Foreign Wars" third term slogan. The Pearl Harbor attack also came about a month after Roosevelt refused to meet the Japanese in a summit they requested in Hawaii.

While Roosevelt was nurturing his socialist revolution, converting the U.S. into a welfare state, he failed to acknowledge that the rest of the world was rearming and it was inevitable that we would be involved. When Japan attacked Pearl Harbor, Roosevelt's socialist revolution still had not brought us out of the Great Depression and he had done nothing to prepare us for the war we were now in. He had been sending war material to England and Russia in American ships for years and now he refused to sit down and negotiate with Japan. Our country was totally unprepared for war with only a few obsolete airplanes, ships, tanks and no trained troops to fight a war with Germany and Italy in the Atlantic and Japan in the Pacific. We didn't even have the design of a modern tank or airplane on the drawing board. Any intelligent person should have had the foresight to build a war machine to defend our country, rather than providing make-work WPA jobs for the millions of unemployed. Americans could not believe that the father of our new socialist welfare society could possibly do anything wrong because after all, hadn't he provided welfare to almost everyone.

Looking at intelligence information available to the president at that time, there was considerable speculation that President Roosevelt deliberately did nothing, enticing Japan, which he considered an inferior nation to attack our fleet. This would arouse public opinion justifying our entering the war, which he was not in a position to do for political reasons. He had just been re-elected on a "Keep American Boys out of Foreign Wars" platform and it wouldn't have been creditable to get us involved in a world war, a month after the election.

II. EVENTS FOLLOWING THE WAR

U.S. President Roosevelt, British Prime Minister Churchill and Russian dictator Stalin formulated the Yalta Peace Conference in February 1945. This treaty was completed just before the end of the war in Europe, which ended on May 8, 1945. It plagued the world for the next 50 years. The war with Japan finally ended September 2nd, 1945, when Japan surrendered after we destroyed 2 Japanese cities with newly developed atomic bombs.

By the time Japan surrendered, 16.3 million had been recruited off the streets of America; 407,000 were killed on the battlefields of the world and 671,000 of us came home seriously disabled. After the war, 12 million men were discharged from military service into a society that could not provide either jobs or housing for us returning veterans. Undoubtedly, Roosevelt's failure at the peace table was the premier failure of his presidency. Roosevelt, in failing health at the time of the Yalta Conference was at the mercy of his chief advisor, Alger Hiss. In 1950, Hiss was convicted of spying for Russia before the Yalta Convention. Also when Roosevelt died on April 12th, shortly before the Germans surrendered on May 8, 1945, Truman his vice president hadn't even been advised that we were in the process of developing an atomic bomb. Truman, who was almost unknown to the American public, made a wise decision to drop the atomic bombs on Japan, ending the war and saving an estimated 500,000 American lives.

Truman a senator from Missouri that few Americans ever heard of became Roosevelt's vice presidential running mate when he ran for his 4th term as president. Few Americans knew Roosevelt's health had deteriorated to the point that it was unlikely that he would be able to serve very much of his fourth term. Even so, they needed to keep his name on the ballot to insure that Democrats would retain the White House. They wanted to replace Vice President Henry Wallace, who ran against Roosevelt on the Socialist ticket. A few powerful Democrats got together in a smoke filled room and selected Truman as their vice-presidential nominee. Finally, it came down to a choice between Harry Truman who was supported by the Kansas City Pendergast machine and Joe Kennedy who had been Roosevelt's Ambassador to England and later as the father of President John F. Kennedy. Kennedy was well known for his Mafia controlled bootlegging empire on the East Coast during Probation like Al Capone was in the Chicago area. Al Capone was convicted of tax evasion and later died of syphilis in prison. Joe Kennedy, being a powerful Democrat that had influential friends in Washington was able to avoid prosecution for tax evasion and was fortunate that none of his mistresses give him syphilis. His bootlegging fortune and the Catholic Church was later instrumental in getting his son, John F. Kennedy elected president.

TRUMAN BECAME PRESIDENT

Truman, who became president at a crucial time in history, turned out to be one of our greatest presidents. Perhaps, no president ever inherited a worse mess from his predecessor at a more difficult time in history. It would have been fortunate for all of us, if Roosevelt's death could have been timelier, permitting Truman rather than Roosevelt to represent the US at the Yalta Peace Conference. Alger Hiss, who was Roosevelt's principal advisor at Yalta also helped create the United Nations and served as its temporary secretary general when it was formally established in 1945. Although the development of the United Nations organizational plans were established before Truman became president, he formally endorsed the organization which established a homeland for the German Jews in Palestine that were rescued from the Nazi death camps. He also implemented the Marshall Plan for the reconstruction of war torn Europe, had to cope with 12 million returning jobless and homeless veterans; converting the wartime economy to a peace time economy and finally the Korean War which was a direct result of Roosevelt's failure at the Yalta peace conference. The Koran War early on established the fact that the United Nations was a farce.

Congress amended the US Constitution so a president could not serve more than two, four-year terms. This resulted from a president being able to assume so much power that he couldn't be replaced. These problems resulted from Roosevelt's failure at Yalta; the vice-president not being informed of the affairs of state when he had to assume the presidency without prior notice. Also, it became a requirement that the state of the president's health be made public information.

The United Nations was patterned after the League of Nations President Wilson tried to establish after WW I. The US Congress refused to ratify the treaty at that time because it would infringe on U.S. sovereignty. The United Nations seemed like a good idea but over 50 years of experience has proved it too is a failure. After I retired, I worked for the United Nations for 2 years and I could write a book on why organizations of this type are unworkable. Without going into detail, it involves Third World country personnel that can't manage a small program at home, taking over a world program. They fill most of the jobs, all of which are exceptionally well paid, with their countrymen who just aren't competent to do the job. Graft and corruption are rampant and there just isn't any way to control it. The U.S should limit our international support to programs that we can manage, control and support with our own people, using resources we presently give to the United Nations.

Establishment of a Jewish homeland in Palestine was and still is a very controversial program with blame and credit shared by many countries. Rightly or wrongly, the general population for a number of reasons disliked Jews in Europe. Dislike for the Jews was at least one of the principal factors that lead to the rise of the Nazi Party in Germany that was responsible for WW-II. Jews from Germany and most other countries in Europe were interned in what was known as death camps because either many or most of them were executed in gas chambers. This is accepted to be a fact but it is also a fact that almost half of those interned in labor camps or executed in death camps were not Jews. Many of them were Gypsies or others the Nazis just wanted rid of. U.S. Jewish Holocaust propaganda taught in our schools and published by the Jewish owned or controlled news media has led most Americans to believe that only Jews were involved. Through their wealth, this very small minority group in the U.S. and their Israeli brethren who also have dual U.S. citizenship, control who we elect for president and can defeat any congressman that is not sympathetic to their cause. The very people we fought and died for in WW II are now killing their neighbors, stealing their land and have made the U.S. their colony to support and protect them from their enemies. President Truman was a man of integrity and I don't think he had this in mind when he helped establish the Jewish State.

General Marshall was President Truman's most capable Secretary of State. He initiated a massive program for the reconstruction of war torn Europe. For example, major cities like La Havre were completely destroyed and not a single building was left standing. The plan included everything from food to feed the starving to the material required to rebuild their infrastructure. Germany proper had been divided into 4 parts: British, French, Russian and American. Berlin the capital city, located in the Russian Zone was also divided into 4 parts with a corridor, permitting British, French and American access to the capital. Flaws in Roosevelt's peace treaty first showed up when Russia denied other ally's access to Berlin through the corridor isolating Berlin in the Russian Sector, forcing a showdown with Russia. The U.S. established the Berlin Airlift to fly necessary supplies of food and material to rebuild the devastated city. The Russians lost the fight after an extended period of time and reopened the corridor. They later built the Berlin Wall to separate the Russian Sector of Berlin from the rest of the city, which was occupied by the U.S, England and France. The wall was primarily to keep the people in the Russian Sector from escaping to the more prosperous West.

The U.S. and countries of Western Europe formed NATO, a mutual defense organization, primarily as a defense against Russia that they already had reason to fear. Initially, NATO headquarters was in Paris but General De Gaulle who controlled France decided to get out of NATO and forced NATO to move their headquarters out of France to Brussels. General De Gaul, who had failed to defend France, escaped to England with a few French soldiers that didn't defect before they were pushed back to the sea at Dunkirk. He was arrogant and acted like a spoiled child. This was a thorn in the side of the Allies throughout the war. American forces that had fought their way from the bloody beaches at Normandy to the outskirts of Paris had to stop and wait for De Gaul's forces to parade through Paris, which the Germans had already abandoned. This was a political move made at the highest level to make him look like the liberator of Paris to enhance his prestige at home. After Allies liberated France and all the help the U.S. give them through the Marshall Plan, he kicked NATO out of France. This is how he showed his appreciation for the Americans and other allies that died on French soil, recapturing his homeland.

At the end of WW II, 12 million Americans were discharged from military service in a few months' time. Six hundred and seventy-one thousand of us were seriously disabled and the entire nation mourned the 407,000 that give their life for their country. American industry that had been engaged exclusively in production of war materials immediately came to a standstill. There were neither jobs nor housing for returning veterans until industry had time to retool and convert their factories to peacetime production. The nation was hungry for cars and other consumer goods. Cheap veteran housing projects resembling shantytowns sprang up in the far out suburbs of our cities. Newly married veterans, who had given up their youth, were anxious to get on with their life and everybody needed a place to live. Returning veterans welcomed these tiny substandard houses in the outer suburbs.

In addition to the Cold War in Europe, Russia established what became known as the Iron Curtain, isolating countries they had acquired or gained control of in WW II. These isolated countries from the rest of Europe and Asia more or less became Russian colonies which were then part of the Soviet Union. In July 1953 a Communist army from the northern part of Korea supported by Russia and China invaded South Korea. The United Nations which was established for this purpose refused to deal with this problem which clearly fell under the UN Charter. It ended up that the U.S. was the only country that came to South Korea's assistance. President Truman established the precedent of sending a large number of American troops to fight in a foreign war without obtaining congressional approval. Of the 5.7 million Americans who served in this war, 54,000 were killed and 103,000 were wounded. Many of these men had also served in WW II and as reserves or National Guard troops they were the first to be called up to fight in Korea. During the Korean War, the Railroad Union went on strike, refusing to move war material required to support our troops in Korea. President Truman ordered them back to work, threatening to use military forces to move the trains if necessary. This was also an important precedent limiting the power of the powerful Mafia controlled unions created during by the Roosevelt Administration. Eisenhower, who was the

Supreme Commander of the Allied Forces in WW II, became president in 1953 and was able to get a cease fire agreement but was unable to get a peace treaty. Not being able to secure a peace treaty, the country was divided two parts, which are still at war with each other, 50 years later and American troops are still on the ground there.

III. THE EISENHOWER YEARS

Eisenhower was not a political person and both Democrats and Republicans wanted him to be their candidate but he chose to run as a Republican. Richard Nixon, a representative from California was his vice president. Nixon received prominence as a House Un-American Activities member who forced the showdown that resulted in the Alger Hiss perjury conviction.

Eisenhower was a moderate that favored the free market system over government price and wage controls, kept government out of labor disputes, reorganized the defense establishment, supported development of the Federal Highway freeway system and promoted missile programs. He continued foreign aid, sped the end of the Korean fighting; endorsed Taiwan and SE Asia defense treaties: backed the UN in condemning Anglo-French raid on Egypt; and advocated an "open skies" policy of mutual inspection to Russia. He sent U.S. troops into Little Rock, Arkansas in September 1957 during the segregation crisis, and ordered Marines into Lebanon in July/August 1958. In general, he was very active in foreign affairs but allowed the country to stabilize on the home front, after a long hard war that affected the lives of all Americans. He was a highly respected president that was not called on to make many controversial decisions that adversely affected his popularity. His two terms in office from 1953 to 1961 were the most stable and least controversial period since WW-II.

IV. THE CONTROVERSIAL KENNEDY/JOHNSON YEARS

John F. Kennedy a former WW II PT boat commander was our first Catholic president (1961-1963) and was the first to campaign using national television. He was the second son of Joe Kennedy who had destined his oldest son to be president. Unfortunately he was killed in WW II, making John his next choice. Joe Kennedy made his fortune in a mafia class bootlegging business on the East Coast. With all his wealth, Joe was a major contributor to the Democratic Party and was given the prestigious diplomatic post of Ambassador to Great Britain as a reward. Joe called in all his Democratic Party and organized crime IOUs from his bootlegging days and dedicated his family fortune to get his son John nominated and elected president. In short, John was a handsome flamboyant playboy from a wealthy politically active Massachusetts family.

Lyndon Johnson, the powerful speaker of the House of Representatives from Texas, who was his opponent in the primary election, became his vice president. This was a marriage of political necessity, rather than one of mutual respect because they both hated each other's guts. Kennedy could count on every Catholic vote but even that wouldn't have been enough to elect him. Johnson was more pragmatic than ethical and could give Kennedy the state of Texas that he had to have to win the election. Johnson called in the IOUs he accumulated while he was Speaker of the House. They won by a slim margin but Kennedy kept Johnson at arm length, not permitting him to participate in any decision making.

The Kennedy Administration was dominated by his younger brother, Bobby who he appointed Attorney General, Bundy, his National Security Officer and Robert McNamara his Secretary of Defense. Both Bundy and McNamara were arrogant intellectuals whose judgment couldn't be questioned. Bobby Kennedy who was not an intellectual shared Bundy's and McNamara's arrogance. In April 1961, Kennedy's new administration suffered a severe setback when an invasion force of anti Castro Cubans, trained and directed by the US CIA failed to establish a beachhead on the Bay of Pigs in Cuba. At the last minute, the Kennedy Administration withdrew promised U.S. air support without their knowledge and invasion forces were killed or captured when they hit the beach. Cuba retaliated by establishing a military alliance with Russia, permitting them to use Cuba as a base for missiles aimed at the United States just 90 miles away, leading to a confrontation with Russia almost resulting in a nuclear war. The U.S on Red Alert massed military aircraft in Florida in preparation for an attack on Cuba and blocked shipping lanes to Cuba. During this confrontation, an American spy plane photographing the Russian missiles was shot down over Cuba. In October 1962, an agreement was reached where Russia dismantled its missiles bases in Cuba and stopped further arms shipment to Cuba. In return, the U.S dismantled our missiles in Turkey aimed at Russia. This is the closest we have ever come to nuclear war. Vice President

Johnson had not been allowed to participate when either the Bay of Pigs or the Cuban missile decisions were made.

The U.S. had been supporting the French Foreign Legion in Vietnam since the Roosevelt Administration, until they were defeated in the battle of Dien Bien Phu in 1954. Vietnam as well as the rest of Indochina was a French colony, occupied and strictly controlled by the French. Every official having any authority down to the mayor of a small village, who was known as the head man had to carry a French passport. Everyone that held a position of any importance was educated in France. Buddhism, the national religion was not acceptable to the French but by necessity; they allowed them to get up to two years of technical training in France. Those that accepted the Catholic religion were allowed four years of education to become engineers. In the French system, the individual with the most academic degrees is the boss, regardless of whether or not they are competent.

Vietnam was divided into two independent countries like Korea after the defeat of the French Foreign Legion in 1954. Hanoi became the capital for North Vietnam and Saigon the capital for South Vietnam. Vietnamese had one year to migrate to or from Communist North Vietnam or French Colonial South Vietnam. After that time, the border was sealed. Most of the Vietnamese in the south were not in a position to migrate but all the Catholics in the north felt it was necessary for them to migrate to the south. The Buddhists didn't like the Catholics any more than the Catholics liked the Buddhists. Most Catholics that migrated to the south were French educated with academic degrees. Once the border was sealed isolating the two countries, it was possible for the South Vietnamese Catholics to declare academic degrees they allegedly had received in Hanoi by a process similar to what we would use to notarize a document. Using the French system, all-important positions that were established in the newly established South Vietnamese government were filled by those with the most advanced degrees. When the French left Vietnam, they left all their people that did not want to return to France in key government positions. The Buddhist South Vietnamese didn't find this much different than being ruled by the colonial French.

The Eisenhower Administration sent a few noncombatant advisors to South Vietnam when it was in chaos after the French were defeated in 1954 but it was a small low key involvement. Kennedy's cocksure advisors who almost got us involved in a nuclear war decided we had to get more involved in Vietnam to keep the communists from taking over Southeast Asia. At one time, Ho Chi Minh had requested a summit meeting with President Truman in an effort to come to some agreement but Truman refused his request. Failing, he went to the communists for help and the Vietnamese war became a communist vs. capitalist war to drive out the French colonists. Kennedy has to take full responsibility for the war.

The highly publicized immorality of the Kennedy brothers was undoubtedly the hallmark of the immoral revolution in the US. While he was trying to get us involved in WW III, he also turned the White House into the national whorehouse. There is little doubt but what the Kennedy Brothers widely publicized encounters with the most glamorous Hollywood Stars glamorized immorality and had a major influence on our national morality. People were inclined to excuse Franklin Roosevelt for having a mistress in the White House because his wife, Eleanor was a detriment to his administration and her obnoxious traits were despised by every man. It was understandable why he wanted to cuddle up to warm woman at night. Kennedy on the other hand had a lovely wife who was both pretty and glamorous who stayed out of governmental affairs and knew how to act as a lady. When Americans saw the Kennedy brothers setting the national example, flaunting their power by exploiting immoral behavior, they followed their example. In addition to trying to imitate Kennedy's speech and mannerism of his young idol, Bill Clinton undoubtedly saw his unlimited sexual exploitations enticing. Our president does it so it is obviously the thing to do and the example to follow. Now one in three babies are born to teenage mothers. In New Mexico half of all the babies are born out of wedlock.

On the positive side, Kennedy was responsible for starting the Peace Corp, which was a well-accepted program, permitting young people to live and work in Third World countries. Also, even though he was pushed by early developments in the Russian space program he is credited with our all-out effort in developing a successful U.S. space program. The Alliance for Progress with Latin America was also a Kennedy program that showed promise but never got off the ground. Overall, the Kennedy Presidency was for all practical purposes a serious liability to the United States. His incompetence almost lead to nuclear destruction of our country and got us involved in a war that cost the lives of many thousands of our youth and tore our country apart. In spite of his failed leadership, he was very popular because of his youthful, flamboyant personality and young women's fantasy that they too may someday get to sleep with him or his brother, Bobby.

On November 22, 1963 Kennedy was assassinated in Dallas by a lone gunman named Oswald. Another lone gunman who claimed to be an enraged patriot assassinated the gunman in turn. Although it was never determined that anyone else was involved, there was speculation that everyone from Cuba's Fidel Castro to Vice Present Johnson was a suspect. At the time of the assassination, Johnson considered the vice president position so belittling that he was considering resigning.

Johnson automatically became president when Kennedy was assassinated. As former Speaker of the House with a Democratic House and Senate, he could call in enough IOUs to pass any legislation he wanted. He immediately went to work on welfare legislation, establishing welfare as an entitlement anti-poverty program. He also passed civil rights laws that established a quota system, requiring employers to hire employees so their workforce would be proportional to the ethnic diversity of our national population. Thirty years later, both of these programs had severely damaged the U.S. by perpetuating generation after generation of welfare dependent people that had never worked. The civil rights quota system deprived white males of jobs for which they were best qualified in order to meet minority quotas. These new laws were powerful legislation that that couldn't have passed by any other President because no one else had a black book with enough IOUs to get the necessary votes.

After completing the remainder of Kennedy's term, he was elected to a full term of his own in 1964. His honeymoon was short lived because the Vietnam War overshadowed all other developments during the remainder of his term. Facing an ever-increasing division in the nation and his own party over his handling of the war, Johnson announced that he would not seek reelection on March 31st 1968.

In early 1965, Johnson sent Bundy on a fact-finding trip to Vietnam, arriving just as the Viet Cong launched a direct attack on an American base in Pleiku. Bundy got on the phone to urge retaliation and the report he wrote became a seminal document in America's escalation of the war. His report stated; the situation in Vietnam is deteriorating and without new U.S. action, defeat is inevitable. There is still time to turn it around but not much. The international presence of the US and a substantial part of our influence is directly at risk. A new policy dubbed by Bundy "Sustained Reprisal" was born. Bundy supported the war after he resigned in 1966, telling Johnson, "Getting out of Vietnam is as impossible as it is undesirable".

President Johnson went before Congress deliberately lying to them, telling them an American ship had been attack in the Gulf of Tonkin by North Vietnam. Congress then passed the Gulf of Tonkin Resolution authorizing President Johnson to expand American military forces in Vietnam to 500,000. The program to expand both civil and military forces in Vietnam was accelerated in the middle 1960s. This required new or expanded military bases, additional living quarters for thousands of American civilians like me and all the additional support facilities required to sustaining this new American colony. When it became known that President Johnson's charges that an American ship had been attacked in the open sea was a deliberate lie which was an impeachable offense; the president's support fell even further. His lie undoubtedly accounted For most of the 58,000 American lives that were lost in Vietnam but the Democratic controlled Congress never took any action to impeach him.

Both McNamara and Bundy, the intellectuals that got us into the war during the Kennedy Administration and expanded it during the Johnson Administration had abandoned ship. Johnson directed the war himself through the remainder of his administration from the Oval Office. Bundy became president of the Ford Foundation and McNamara was made president of the World Bank. It was Bundy that brought about the end of the era in which foreign policy was entrusted to a noble club of gentlemen, secure in their common outlook and bonds of trust. Johnson left office in disgrace at the height of the war in 1969.

There was a riot at the 1968 Democratic National Convention held in Chicago. Young men had been demonstrating, burning their draft cards and rioting at college campuses all over the country. They refused to answer their draft calls and many went to Canada to avoid being drafted. Bill Clinton, an obscure admirer of President Kennedy demonstrated against the war when he was a student at Oxford in England. He also refused to answer his draft call and made illegal trips to Moscow, which was supporting North

Vietnam even though such trips were forbidden by the US government at that time. It was a very difficult period in American history, where youth drafted across America, unlike Clinton, who answered their draft calls became the villains that were responsible for the war. Men came home from Vietnam, who were drafted by their friends and neighbors, discarded their military uniforms before returning home to avoid public ridicule. The news media, many of which were draft dodgers themselves, had so inflamed public opinion that the returning servicemen, who were often called baby killers, were to blame.

President Kennedy created the basic problem and provided for college deferments for students as long as they were in college. Families with money could qualify for college enrollment, making it possible to avoid the draft as long as they stayed in school. Also, draft dodgers on college campuses rioted and burned their draft cards without any apparent repercussions. This was simply planned to be a poor man's war because anytime a young man or woman is called on to defend their country, it is their duty to do so regardless of whether or not they support the cause. On the other hand, they are entitled to fair treatment and no one should be above the law. For example, when you draft youth that may be killed in defense of our country everyone's name should be put in the hat and all those selected should serve without any exceptions. You simply don't take names out of the hat before the drawing!

V. THE NIXON-FORD ADMINISTRATION

Richard Nixon, President Eisenhower's Vice President was elected and took office in 1969 at the height of the Vietnam War. Nixon was finally able to negotiate a cease fire agreement in 1972. After removing combat troops, the country was overrun by the Viet Cong, forcing us out of Vietnam under gunfire in May 1975. We were totally defeated and American prestige was at an all-time low. America was torn apart within and laughed at by the rest of the world. Nevertheless, Nixon was credited with terminating the no win religious/colonial war that should have never happened.

Nixon was the first President to visit China and Russia. He and his foreign affairs advisor, Henry Kissinger established a detente with China, which was a major foreign affairs breakthrough. Nixon appointed four Supreme Court Justices, thus altering the court's balance in favor of a more conservative view. Roosevelt had packed the court with ultra-liberal judges during his 12 plus year socialist administration.

Nixon's second term was cut short by a series of scandals beginning with a burglary of Democratic Party National Headquarters in the Watergate Office Complex on June 17, 1972. Nixon denied any White House involvement in the Watergate break-in. On July 16th a White House aide, under questioning by a Senate committee revealed that most of Nixon's office conversations and phone calls had been recorded. Nixon claimed executive privilege to keep the tapes secret but both the courts and congress sought the tapes for criminal proceedings against former White House Staff members and for a House inquiry into possible impeachment.

October 10th 1973, Nixon fired the special White Hose prosecutor and the Attorney General resigned in protest. The public outcry, which followed caused Nixon to appoint a new special prosecutor and to turn over to the courts a number of subpoenaed tape recordings. Public reaction also brought the initiation of a formal inquiry into impeachment. On July 24th 1974, the Supreme Court ruled that Nixon's claim to executive privilege must fall before the special prosecutor's subpoenas of tapes relevant to criminal trial proceedings. The same day, the House Judiciary Committee opened debate on impeachment, charging Nixon with obstruction of justice, abuse of power and contempt of Congress.

On August 5th, Nixon released transcripts of conversations held 6 days after the Watergate break-in showing that he had known of, approved and directed Watergate cover-up activities. Nixon resigned from office August 9th after prominent Republicans went to the White House, confronting him with the evidence and asked him to resign. Unlike President Johnson's lying to Congress, which cost the lives of most of the 58,000 killed in Vietnam, this one petty burglary forced Nixon to resign or be impeached by the Democratic Congress.

Vice President Ford became president when Nixon resigned. Ford was the first president to serve without being chosen in a national election. Ford, the Minority Leader of the House became vice president when Vice President Spiro Agno resigned due to income tax evasion on October 12, 1973. It was the first use of procedures set out in the 25th Amendment. Ford's 21 month tenure following the major upheaval resulting from Nixon's resignation was an extremely difficult period in our history. He pardoned Nixon for any federal crimes he may have committed as president on September 8th, putting the Nixon episode behind us so we could get back to the business of governing. Ford vetoed 48 bills, saying most would prove too costly. He also visited China and formulated a program where the Vietnam draft dodgers that went to Canada or other countries, could earn their way back into American society through community service programs. Like Harry Truman, he had never been elected to national office and didn't have any national constituency but nevertheless he only lost the next presidential election to Jimmy Carter in 1976 by a narrow margin.

VI. JIMMY CARTER ADMINISTRATION

Jimmy Carter was a former Georgia Governor, one term Georgia senator and a political appointee to the US Naval Academy, graduating after the war was over. He had been deferred for most of the war waiting to be scheduled for a class at the Academy. He also studied nuclear physics at Union College before he was discharged from the Navy to take over the family peanut farm when his father died in 1953.

The first day he was in office, he pardoned all Vietnam draft dodgers and welcomed them back into American society. He personally played a major role in peace negotiations between Israel and Egypt but was otherwise criticized for doing a poor job handling both foreign and domestic policy. His so called human right policy lead to the fall of several friendly governments, including Iran where in November 1979 militants attacked our Embassy in Tehran and held our Embassy staff hostage for over a year. During this period he attempted a feeble rescue attempt using a few helicopters, which bogged down and were destroyed, in the desert. Following this incident, the U.S. was the laughing stock of the world because the greatest nation in the world wasn't even able to rescue their diplomatic staff from a Third World country.

Carters' failure was primarily a result of his lack of management ability, wanting to make all decisions himself rather than having a competent cabinet and staff that was capable of advising him that he was willing to listen to. It was evident that being governor of the small state of Georgia didn't give him the necessary management experience to be president of the United States. Carter was also credited with the poor state of the economy, where inflation soared and annual interest rates exceeded 20%. This was particularly devastating to the nation's farmers who mortgaged their farms to buy more farms because with the high interest rate they would be able to pay off both mortgages in a short period of time. When the following administration got inflation under control, the inflated value of farmland dropped and they lost everything because they could not pay the high mortgage rates and lost everything they owned. He also reacted to the Soviet invasion of Afghanistan by imposing a grain embargo and boycotting the Moscow Olympic Games. Reagan defeated Carter in the 1980 election and our hostages in Iran were released on the day Reagan was inaugurated in 1981.

VII. RONALD REAGAN

Ronald Reagan attended high school in Dixon, Illinois and worked his way through Eureka College. Upon graduation he became a radio sports announcer, in 1997 became a movie star making 53 movies and later president of the Actors Guild. Because of disputes of Communism in the film industry his political views changed from liberal to conservative and he toured the country as a TV host, becoming a spokesmen for conservatism. In 1996 he was elected Governor of California and re-elected in 1970.

Ronald Reagan won the Republican nomination for President in 1980 and chose George Bush as his running mate who was a former Texas Congressmen, and Ambassador to the United Nations. Voters troubled by inflation and the yearlong confinement of Americans in Iran swept him into office by an overwhelming vote.

Reagan took office on January 20, 1981 and 69 days later, he was shot by a would-be assassin but quickly recovered and returned to duty. His grace and wit during the dangerous incident caused his popularity to soar.

Dealing skillfully with his Democratic Congress, Reagan obtained legislation to stimulate economic growth, curb inflation, increase employment and strengthen national defense. He embarked on a course of cutting taxes and government expenditures, refusing to deviate from it when the strengthening of defense forces lead to a large deficit. A renewal of self-confidence by 1984 helped Reagan and Bush win a second term with a landslide victory.

In 1986 Regan obtained an overhaul of the income tax code which eliminated many deductions and exempted millions of people with low incomes. At the end of his administration, the nation was enjoying the longest recorded period of peacetime prosperity without recession or depression.

In foreign policy, Reagan sought to achieve "peace through strength" During his two terms he increased defense spending 35% but sought to improve relations with the Soviet Union. In dramatic meetings with Soviet leader Mikhail Gorbachev, he negotiated a treaty that would eliminate intermediate-range nuclear missiles. Reagan declared war against international terrorism, sending American bombers against Libya after evidence came out that Libya was involved in an attack on American soldiers in a West Berlin nightclub.

By ordering naval escorts in the Persian Gulf, he maintained the free flow of oil during the Iran-Iraq war. In keeping with the Reagan Doctrine, he gave support to anti-Communist insurgencies in Central America and Africa.

Overall, the Reagan years saw a restoration of prosperity, and the goal of peace through strength seemed to be within grasp.

VIII. THE FIRST BUSH ADMINISTRATION

George Bush had served, as a fighter/bomber pilot in the Pacific Theater during WW II having 2 planes shot out from under him, in one case being rescued by a US Submarine. After graduating from Yale University in 1948, he settled in Texas where in 1953 he helped found an oil company and was elected to the US House of Representatives in 1966 and 1968. He was Ambassador to the United Nations from (1971-73), headed the U.S. Liaison Office in Beijing (1974-75) and was director of Central Intelligence from (1976-77). Following an unsuccessful bid for the 1980 presidential nomination, Ronald Reagan chose Bush as his vice presidential running mate. He served as U.S. Vice President from 1981 to 1989.

In 1998 Bush was elected president and took office faced with the ongoing U.S. budget and trade deficits as well as the rescue of insolvent U.S. savings and loan institutions. The savings and loan problem was linked to what was known as the Keating Five Scandal, which involved 5 U.S. Senators with one or more getting a kickback from a savings and loan association. Bush annually struggled with military cutbacks in light of reduced Cold War tensions and vetoed abortion-rights legislation, a minimum wage law and an anti-discrimination bill that did not reflect his own views.

Bush supported Soviet reforms and the development of Eastern European democracies. He was criticized, however for keeping US policy tied to Mikhail Gorbachev as the Soviet leader lost power and under-reaction to the Chinese government's violent repression to pro-democracy demonstrations in 1989. In 1989 Bush sent military forces to Panama, which overthrew the government and captured military strongman Manual Noriega who had become a drug lord.

Bush reacted to Iraq's August 1990 invasion of Kuwait by sending U.S. forces to the Persian Gulf area and assembling a U.N backed coalition, including NATO and Arab League members. After a month long air war in February 1991, Allied force retook Kuwait in a 4 day ground assault. He was recognized internationally for his diplomatic initiative, bringing together the international military and financial coalition that not only helped fight the war but also paid for it. This coalition was made possible only by his even handed, unbiased peace initiative in the Middle East. Bush forced Israeli Prime Minister Shamir out of office because he refused to enter into good faith peace negotiations with his Arab neighbors. Bush's Secretary of State was making good progress in his effort to broker an Arab/Israeli peace treaty at the time that Iraq invaded Kuwait. The quick victory gave Bush one of the highest presidential ratings in history but his popularity plummeted by the end of 1991 as the economy struggled through a prolonged recession. The US Israeli community was a small minority but with unbelievable financial and media control, objected to the restraints Bush placed on Israel in his effort to negotiate an Israeli/Palestinian Peace Treaty. His Democratic opponent, notorious draft dodger, Bill Clinton in the 1992 election assured the Jewish community that they could count on his support if he was elected. Clinton's mentor, Senator Fulbright a popular highly respected Senator from Arkansas, had previously been defeated by the Israeli lobby because he wanted to cut US Aid to Israel. Clinton was a good politician and wasn't about to make the same mistake so he pledged full support to Israel at the expense of their Arab neighbors.

IX. THE CLINTON ADMINISTRATION

Bill Clinton attended Georgetown University, Oxford University in England as a Rhodes Scholar and Yale Law School. He worked on the 1972 McGovern presidential campaign, taught at the University of Arkansas from 1973 to 1976 when he was elected State Attorney General and became the nation's youngest governor in 1978. He was defeated for re-election in 1980, but returned to office from 1982 to 1990. Despite personal attacks on his character resulting from: being a proven Vietnam draft dodger; Making a trip to Moscow from England, which was forbidden by the US State Department during the Vietnam war, demonstrating against the Vietnam war while he was in England; Smoking Pot at Oxford, which he initially denied and when caught said he didn't inhale, Multiple sex scandals while he was governor of Arkansas.

Clinton won most of the 1992 Democratic presidential primaries. He moved the Democratic Party toward the center, broadening his appeal and became the party nominee. He received overwhelming support from both the American and Israeli Jewish communities in return for his promised restraint in developing an Israeli/ Palestinian peace treaty.

Immediately after he took office he initiated an unsuccessful high profile effort to open up the military to the gay/lesbian community. Unbeknown to the general public they were major supporters in his election campaign. In 1993 he narrowly won congressional approval of a 500 billion-dollar tax increase and spending cut to reduce the federal budget deficit, which was opposed by the Republican minority. His wife Hillary led a healthcare reform legislation initiative but it died in the legislator for the lack of support. He received a measure of success getting congressional approval of the North American Free Trade Agreement negotiated by the Bush Administration even though his Democratic Congress openly opposed it.

Following the 1994 midterm elections, Clinton faced Republican majorities in both houses of congress, which clashed with him over the scope of federal spending. He pursued a centralist course on most domestic issues, winning passage of a major anti-crime bill in 1995 and with reservations supported another Republican measure to overhaul the welfare system and end federal guarantees of support. This in effect ended President Johnson's

Great Society program. Among other measures, he approved an increase in the minimum wage.

Clinton sustained limited political damage in a real estate deal called Whitewater while he was governor; obtaining FBI files of Republicans so he could blackmail them; Firing all personnel in the White House travel office, replacing them with an Arkansas travel firm; Renting out the Lincoln Bedroom for campaign donations; Accepting illegal campaign donations from China, which was speculated to be payment for military secrets or equipment that it was illegal to export. This broad based activity known as China Gate included but was not limited to selling admission on official Department of Commerce trade missions to China.

The Clinton Administration was plagued by numerous scandals starting when he was governor of Arkansas and his wife's work for a controversial law firm. During his first campaign, they both went on national TV together; denying Bill had a well-known, long term sexual relationship with Jennifer Flowers an Arkansas TV personality. Although he had relationships with numerous women, he denied that they ever took place, accusing the women of lying. In one case, Caravel one of his pit bulls made the statement about Paula Jones one of his victims who lived in a trailer park, "When you drag a $100 bill through a trailer park, she is what you get". Later, the press publicly accused him with overwhelming evidence of having a long time sexual relationship with a young woman in the Oval Office. Later, when interviewed on public television, he made the emphatic statement that, "I have never had sexual relations with that woman". Later he got so entwined in lawsuits, giving conflicting testimony at two different courts and was convicted of perjury. The Republican congress held a formal impeachment hearing and he was impeached. The U.S. Senate, who has the option to determine whether or not an impeached president is removed from office, refused to remove him from office. This was the second occasion when Democrats refused to remove their president from office when he had either lied to Congress or perjured himself in a U.S. court. In Lyndon Johnson's case, his lie probably resulted in the loss of most of the 58,000 American lives lost in Vietnam and in Clinton's case his lying to a grand jury along with multiple other illegal activities destroyed not only his creditability but the office of president as well. The Republican Party removed President Nixon from office without going through the long complex formality of impeachment.

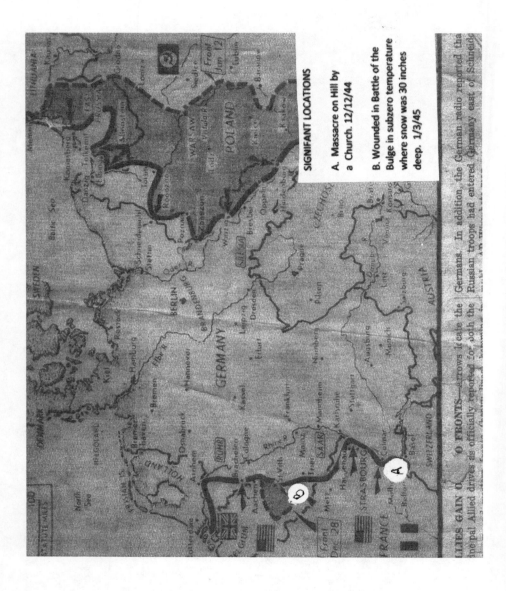

SIGNIFANT LOCATIONS

A. Massacre on Hill by a Church. 12/12/44

B. Wounded in Battle of the Bulge in subzero temperature where snow was 30 inches deep. 1/3/45

LLIES GAIN O 'O FRONTS—Arrows lr cate the the pal Allied drives as officially reported fo, 3oth the

Germans. In addition, the German radio reported tha Russian troops had entered Germany east of Schneid

II

WORLD WAR II

MY PERSONAL WAR EXPERIENCE

This is the story of my experience and those that were massacred on a hill by a church during WW II. It is the story of the wounded, the dying, the dead and the personal hell that every combat infantryman went through. It is not a story for the squeamish or those that cannot or will not face the realities of life. It may not be a story for those who lost family or loved ones in combat because any fantasies they may have developed over the years probably are not as bad as it really was.

I was critically wounded in the Battle of the Bulge on January 3rd, 1945 and was taken to a field hospital where they abandoned me for dead in an enormous morgue. The next day, I regained consciousness and my mind was alert but by body was helpless. More than a day later, I was rescued by a Catholic chaplain who was going through the morgue administering last rights to those of Catholic faith. He located a medic who gives me blood plasma that saved my life.

Some weeks later, I developed a severe case of hepatitis and for two weeks I was again at the threshold of death. Finally after about a year and a half, I was discharged from the hospital permanently disabled with half of one leg paralyzed but was eventually able to live a productive life.

I have always believed my life must have been spared for some purpose but I searched in vain to find out what that purpose was. I took a job in

Vietnam, which was both dangerous and challenging primarily because of a career setback resulting from reorganization at a time when I had ever-increasing family obligations but I never overlooked the possibility that that could be my purpose. This assignment resulted in the failure of a good marriage of 26 years, loss of my home and everything that was dear to me as well as my physical and emotional health. The news media had created an atmosphere where anyone that had worked or fought in Vietnam was treated as a social misfit. I also took challenging jobs in South America, Washington D.C. and southern Africa where I had also been successful but never had a feeling of satisfying my obligation to society.

Forty years after I regained consciousness in a Belgium morgue, my life took on a whole new dimension. During the long nights when I couldn't sleep or woke up long before dawn and couldn't go back to sleep, memories of an earlier battle came back to haunt me. Memories of the Battle for the Rhineland were so horrendous; they had been shut away in the innermost sanctuary of my mind because they were just too awful to deal with. I remembered things that happened before and after that were also unthinkable but when I got to that period in my life it simply had no admittance or keep out sign on it and something in me said don't challenge it. After all the gruesome details unfolded over the next two years, I realized that I had also been involved in a violent massacre on a hill by a church and my life had been spared 3 times rather than the 2 that I previously remembered.

The sleepless nights became a dialogue or debate with or about those who were so violently massacred on the hill by the church. It was like sitting in a circle talking informally with those boys or young men, as they looked that day in the churchyard where they were massacred. They talked about their parents, wives, sweethearts and children they had never seen. None of them ever suggested their country wasn't worth whatever price they had to pay.

They insisted that I write their story of the "Battle of the Rhineland" and I simply said "No. I just don't have the ability to do justice to your story." They all responded in unison, "Don't worry we will all help you". The argument was, "If you don't, who will?"

There are so many disturbing aspects of this battle. A few German tanks simply massacred thousands of American Infantrymen who had no protection against tanks. There has been so much written and so many movies made about the Battle of the Bulge where 10,276 American boys were killed, 47,497 wounded and 23,218 missing in action during this 6 week battle of the 3-1/2 year war in which 407,000 Americans were killed. When you equate that to the Vietnam War where only 58,000 men were killed in the 10-year war, it is difficult to understand why there was so much concern about the very few that were missing in action. The Battle of the Rhineland was also a major battle, so why were the wounded left to die and the dead left on the battlefield for days? Their bodies became covered with snow so they wouldn't be recovered until the snow melted in the spring. Their families probably received a postcard in their mailbox, advising them that their loved one was missing in action, as mine did. However, the families wouldn't be notified of their death until the snow melted in the spring. My family was relieved when they received a second postcard over a month later, telling them I was critically wounded, which let them know I was still alive.

I felt relieved that the spirits of the dead seemed to give me peace, when I agreed to write their story for whatever purposes that it might serve. Now as time goes by and my health is failing, their voices cry out with ever increasing urgency. I have to get on with their story because they will not allow me to rest in peace.

Note: This story was written while I was recovering from my second of three major back surgeries in January 1990. It was such an emotional issue, I didn't even consider editing my rough draft and writing the story of the Vietnam War until 10 years later.

Note: I an engineer, not a literary scholar and I deal with hard facts that I don't have the ability to express in flowery literary language. You may find some misspelled words or grammar errors but this is intended to give factual background data on how military combat affects the entire life of a combat infantryman. For us survivors, the war did not end at the edge of the battle field.

"The object of war is not to die for his country but to have the other Bastard die for his"
GENERAL GEORGE PATTON
(1895-1945)

1. TRIP TO THE FRONT

It was late October 1944 when we were going through the slums of Paris on one of several troop trains that were transporting the 87th Infantry Division from the Port of Le Havre to the German front. The tiny boxcars were so small they were known as the 40 or 8 in WW I because they could only haul 40 men or 8 horses in each car. After WW II they were known as holocaust cars because they were used to haul Jews and others, the Germans considered society misfits to the death camps. There was a decided difference because the holocaust trains had an outside toilet on the back end of each boxcar and infantry trains didn't have any toilet. In the crowded infantry boxcars without seats, only a few of us could sit on the floor at one time and one corner of the boxcar had to be used as a toilet. Obviously, they had used this boxcar to transport infantry for a long time because the stench was so overpowering that it was nauseating. The door was locked from the outside when we left Le Havre early that morning. So, even when the train stopped from time to time along the way, we couldn't get out until we reached our destination sometime that night in Luxemburg.

Everyone was in full battle dress primarily because there wasn't any place to store our gear. We were wearing thermal underwear, wool OD pants and shirt, a waist length jacket and a full-length wool OD overcoat. Long wool socks, leather GI shoes about 8 inches high and a pair of rubber galoshes protected our feet. The only clothes we had were what we were wearing. Our backpack contained an oilskin sleeping bag with just one thickness of OD blanket lining that could be rolled up in a 3 by 12-inch roll, a mess kit we never had a chance to use and a flimsy folding shovel to dig foxholes in the frozen ground. There was also room for a shelter-half, which is half a pup tent that you and a buddy put together to make a tent that you both shared. The gear also included a wide woven belt for your canteen, first aid kit, hand and rifle grenades and the rest of the space was used to carry ammunition clips for your rifle. An infantryman's first aid kit included sylph powder for open wounds, a large compress bandage, tape and a very large vile of morphine, which you could inject yourself once the protective glass covering was broken off. Since we never had any first aid training, this was obviously intended to be available for a medic, which you were not likely to see near the front line in a combat zone. Last but certainly not least was your rifle or weapon as they called it. There was so much emphasis on the care and use of your weapon that once you were assigned to an infantry unit, you could not get a pass to leave the base until you could completely disassemble, clean and reassemble it blindfolded. With all this gear the tiny boxcars were both crowded and smelly. Even on this late October day, they were uncomfortably hot and it was difficult to hold your head up with your heavy steel helmet.

As we looked through the cracks in the aged wooden boxcar, we could see Frenchmen sitting on their patios or at a sidewalk café drinking wine and soaking some early afternoon sun. Certainly, no one could guess from their carefree attitude that the greatest war in history was being fought in their country and the frontline was less than 200 miles away. It seemed like such a short time ago when Dan Dykstra, our distinguished and highly respected social science teacher at Frederic High School lectured us on the invincible French Maginot Line that would keep WW II from ever happening. It was a fortress of huge gun turrets near the French/German border that simply could not be penetrated by the German war machine. A few miles to the east, the Germans had also built an equally impregnable Siegfried Line to protect them against the French forces. It seemed like only a few days after his convincing lecture that mechanized German armored units made an end run through Holland, his ancestral homeland and in just 4 days occupied France. The fleeing French soldiers couldn't throw away their arms fast enough in front of the rapidly advancing German army. The invincible Maginot Line was defenseless when hit from the rear because their gun turrets couldn't be turned around in the opposite direction. Most of the British and a few of the so called, Free French managed to evacuate the continent on whatever boats or ships were available from Dunkirk, across the channel from England, leaving all their war material behind for the Germans. The French whores welcomed the advancing Germans on their knees as they entered Paris and the invincible French army got lost in the crowds. That day they were enjoying a leisurely afternoon at the sidewalk cafes in Paris while we were fighting their war.

After entering the war crippled by the barbaric Japanese attack on Pearl Harbor, American had built a land, air and sea war machine from scratch and fought our way back across North Africa to the European continent. Now as part of the Allied forces we fought our way from the beaches in France and Italy to the outskirts of Paris. Here politicians halted the American armies, waiting for General Charles De Gaulle and his Free

French army so they could parade down the streets of Paris, which had been abandoned by the Germans and officially, liberate Paris. After the French festivities, the American armies continued fighting their dirty war and we are now pushing up against the Rhine River where we undoubtedly are headed. There was a sober mood as we stood in that stinking boxcar almost hypnotized by the noise of the rails and occasional train whistle. It was a very private time for each of us, with our own private thoughts as if we were about to act out our last will and testament. We concentrated our thoughts on the loved ones we left behind and about how we ever got into a situation like this. Why were us innocent boys that were not yet men being sacrificed for events that we had no control over?

Although jobs were plentiful at that time in war industries, no one would hire those of us that would be drafted. The only young men that had jobs at that time in our area were those who took over the family farm and were commonly referred to as wartime farmers. Families bought useless land so their son who had never milked a cow could qualify for a farm deferment. It was also astonishing that health of so many fathers suddenly failed, making it necessary for their son to take over the family farm. Most of the farms in the area weren't productive enough and couldn't survive without government subsidies. A t that time, there were probably more corrupt politicians on the draft board than in Washington.

After some time, I found a job working for the Aircraft Radio Lab in Chicago, inspecting new radio equipment at the radio factories where they were manufacturing radio equipment for the military. The pay was hardly enough to survive so I had to share a sleeping room in a private home with another young man about my age. We got a hot beef sandwich at the nearby bowling alley every night but there wasn't any money left for social activities. We shared the second floor in a private home with another man from our group who had his own room. He was a professional radio technician from Iowa who had to close his business because it couldn't survive under the wartime economy. We spent considerable time together and he was like a private tutor, teaching me more radio theory in a few months than I learned during the rest of my life. Chicago was a very unfriendly, lonely place for a farm boy from Wisconsin and I didn't get paid enough so I could enjoy most activities that could have been available to me. After a couple months, a girl that was a friend of one of my roommate's acquaintances arranged to meet me and we developed a great relationship. She was a senior in a Catholic high school that under different circumstances, I would have considered marrying after the war.

Her father was an adamant supporter of the Irish Republic Army, a radical organization whose primary objective was to kill Protestants. It was something that we could have worked out ourselves, if her father could have accepted me. We parted the best of friends with mutual respect and admiration for each other when I was drafted into military service.

Military service had never been one of my priorities but I had been brought up with a sense of responsibility so when I received a draft notice, there wasn't any question but what I would go. Also, I don't believe a system, called draft deferments that remove names from the hat before the lottery is fair. This simply eliminates individuals from the list of people that may be executed. I was drafted into military service and took my Army Air Corp basic training in St. Petersburg, Florida and went to Hammer Field at Fresno, California where I was assigned to the Signal Corp. Those of us that were classified as radio technicians were promoted to Cpl and transferred to nearby Camp Pinedale where we would wait for the next opening in radio school. The camp was little village of tarpaper shacks where the Japanese that lived on the West Coast were interned after the attack on Pearl Harbor but the Japanese were no longer there and it was now an Air Corp signal camp. One day a Signal Corp officer called me in and said, "I see you have had some radio experience and I am going to give you some exams to see which school would be best for you." When I completed the third exam he said, "You missed one of the questions on the last exam." and spent the next hour explaining my error. He told me that this was the equivalency exam for their most advanced radio school and they wouldn't be sending to school. A few days later, I was assigned to the 324th Signal Company Wing, a company of 68 officers and men that provided radio and telephone communication for a forward airbase that was located just behind the front lines. I was pleased with the assignment but was disappointed that I couldn't spend a year in radio school at Scott Field in Illinois with the rest of my group.

A few days later, I joined the Signal Company that was on maneuvers in the High Sierra Mountains. I liked the Signal Company and was satisfied with the mission it was supposed to accomplish. I soon discovered that a Cpl wasn't allowed to do very many things because military rank, like civilian job descriptions rather than ability, limits what you are allowed to do. After about a month, I was called in to see the Company Commander who was called the Chief Signal Officer. He showed me a message he had just received from Training Command Headquarters that said, "Some men had been promoted because they were going to school and for some reason they didn't go. If they had anyone in that category, they should be reduced to their previous rank". He told me there wasn't anything he could do to help me because he already had almost twice his authorized complement. He had to reduce staffing down to what was authorized because they were going overseas in the immediate future. This was disheartening because it meant that I couldn't succeed unless I went through the normal school routine and they had refused to send me. It simply was not possible for me to succeed in the Signal Corp even though that was where I could make the greatest contribution. A few days later, I went back to Hammer Field in Fresno, took the required examinations and was admitted to the Aviation Cadet pilot training program. I had always wanted to be pilot and was excited about my new opportunity.

My new assignment resulted in me being transferred back to Florida, where I would spend a few weeks at Miami Beach, waiting for college training classes to start at the University of Florida in Gainesville. It was also an opportunity to spend a few days at home on the way to Miami. In this short but significant leave, I got engaged to be married to the girl that that I met when she was a high school freshman and I was a junior. I met her when I took my grandparents to visit their old friends and neighbors in a Minnesota community where they used to live and my parents grew up. While my grandparents were visiting, I saw a pretty girl sitting on the lawn and went out to talk to her. Her aunt, who was her father's sister and her husband were the son of the neighbors that my grandparents were visiting. They had raised her since she was about a year old. I was impressed with her country style charm, which is evident in people that don't have many material things but are proud and grateful for everything they have. Our relationship had developed over the years and even though I was not in a position to marry her at that time, I wanted her to look forward to our life together when I returned.

I spent about a year in the Aviation Cadet training program at the University of Florida and Preflight Training in San Antonio, Texas and it all ended on July 1, 1944 when I was half through primary flight training at El Reno, Oklahoma. They called a special all hands meeting and told us, effective immediately, the entire national Aviation Cadet training program was cancelled in its entirety and we would all be reassigned in a couple of days. On July 4th, we changed trains in Memphis on our way to Ft. Jackson, where we would receive infantry basic training in the newly formed 87th Infantry Division. The division was made up exclusively of those of us from the terminated Aviation Cadet and Army Specialized training programs. The war had progressed to the point where they needed infantry rather than pilots and engineers. You simply can't have a war unless there are infantry to shoot at.

The spell was broken as the train screeched to a stop in Luxemburg. Finally, they unlocked the door of our stinking boxcar and we stumbled out trying to straighten out our cramped legs and get a breath of fresh air. In Luxemburg we were temporarily assigned to guard Ft. Dreon, an underground citadel that was previously bypassed by American armies because too many lives would have been lost in conquering it. It was a self-sufficient fort built in a hill with large gun turrets on top, like a battleship that could survive without support for an extended period of time. The Germans in the fort knew escape was hopeless and were probably happy to sit out the remainder of the war in relative safety. In reality, this was probably a keep busy mission to keep us occupied until a convoy of trucks arrived to transport us to the front, we later found was the Battle of the Rhineland.

2. THE BATTLE OF THE RINELAND

A convoy of 2-1/2 ton trucks picked us up a couple days later to take us to some unknown destination. There were trucks as far as we could see both to our front and back on this narrow 2-lane road or trail in the flat farming area that extended out for several miles from the Rhine River. We skirted around Metz, a transportation hub near the Rhine where a major battle was currently underway to capture it from the Germans. We continued in a southerly direction, not knowing where we were headed but we did cross an east/west road which had a sign that showed Strasbourg was 20K (14 miles) east. Perhaps 10 miles further south, we saw what appeared to be strips of snow in the fields. The cold November wind blew against our faces in the back of the open truck as it sped down the road, which had now become a trail through the open farmland. The spots in the snow were no longer a mystery as we could see it was only on the north side of the bodies of American dead where the sun had not melted the snow that fell some days ago. As we continued down the trail, we could see the fields were littered with American dead as far as we could see in every direction. There were thousands of them and it was apparent that they had been there for quite some time. We were all shocked, each of us thinking, "Is that all I am worth".

About 20 miles south of the Strasbourg sign, the convoy came to a screeching halt. Our truck stopped by a large oak tree, which was the only tree within miles, which of course had dropped its leaves because it was already winter at this higher elevation in the foothills of the Alps. Obviously we were in France, in the vicinity of the Swiss/German border. As we started to disembark, we saw the worst sight any of us could imagine at the time we were just going into combat ourselves. A group of American infantrymen, thinking they were far enough from the front to be careless, had been sitting around in a circle. Possibly they had a little fire to heat up the frozen stew in their C rations, when a German artillery shell landed right in the middle of the circle. The lower part of their bodies were still, sitting around the shell crater and bits and pieces of their upper bodies, including their intestines, were hanging from the tree branches like Christmas decorations. Our unit the 2nd platoon of Company L, 345th Infantry fell into formation and marched off in the direction of the front. Not one word was spoken, but everyone understood.

That night we bivouacked about 100 yards in front of our artillery, which was probably located about 3 miles from the front line. Lou Stein, my best buddy and our first scout took our shelter-half out of our backpack and set up our pup tent that night as we had many times before. Jim Sousores had also been in our squad but, being an expert marksman, the Company Commander had pulled him out, to be his personal bodyguard. Shortly after dark the artillery started firing their big guns over our head and this continued all night. We were so close to the guns that the concussion from their muzzle blast lifted us right off the ground. The next morning after a sleepless night, our ears hurt and we were nearly deaf. That was the last time I ever slept in a pup tent since front line troops have to sleep in foxholes for both warmth and security. The profile of the tents, illuminated by flares, kept the battlefield lighted up bright as day identifying your position and drawing enemy artillery fire. A foxhole also provided protection from fragments of artillery shells that might explode in the area. We were up before daylight, stowed away our gear and were on our way by the first light of day.

We no longer marched in any type of formation but spread out over a wide area so no 2 men were closer than 30 feet apart. An infantry company is made up of 3 line or rifle platoons and a so-called heavy weapons platoon. Heavy weapons include a 30 caliber machine gun and a few mortars that are heavy only by infantry standards because men have to carry them and the ammunition on their back for perhaps 10 miles a day. When an infantry company advances, 2 platoons are out in front or on line as they call it and 1 is in reserve, perhaps 100 yards back. The heavy weapons platoon is broken down into units and deployed at the discretion of the company commander. Rifle platoons consist of 3 squads of 12 men with 2 on line and 1 in reserve, perhaps 100 feet back. The entire company advances under cover of an artillery barrage which keeps moving up so the shells fall about 100 yards in front of the advancing infantry troops.

One day when we were advancing on a frontal attack with infantry units lined up as far as you could see on either side, we heard what sounded like an airplane. We looked in the direction the noise was coming from but it was traveling so fast it had already passed overhead and was almost out of sight before we realized what was happening. It was a strange fighter type aircraft flying less than 100 feet above the ground with fire shooting out of the back. Being former Aviation Cadets, most of us had considerable training in aircraft identification, but none of us had ever seen or heard of such an aircraft. It was undoubtedly a new type of reconnaissance plane that was gathering intelligence information on troop movements as it strafed the area.

We advanced up to 10 miles a day, making our way from the flat plains where the trucks dropped us off to what appeared to be the beginning of the foothills of the Alps. We didn't know where we were but we must have been within 20 or 30 miles from the German/Swiss border. At dusk, we stopped to dig in on top of a barren hill. We had to dig a slit trench long enough to lay in and deep enough so shrapnel form an artillery shell that might explode nearby wouldn't hit us. The trenches were far enough apart so a single artillery shell couldn't get more than one of us. It was difficult to dig with the little folding shovel; we carried in our backpack because there was a thin frozen layer on top of what would otherwise be mud. The ground crunched when we walked on it from breaking the layer of thin ice that had formed on top of the snow that had melted during the day.

I had almost finished digging my slit trench, which would provide some warmth and security for the night when Cpl Bell came and asked me to help with a detail. Cpl Bell, like Sgt Diekman was a former cadet from Minneapolis. Both were married and had a baby they had never seen. If Cpl Bell had been able to continue in the Cadet program, I am sure he would have ended up as a Wing Commander because of his outstanding leadership ability. His detail consisted of taking a half a dozen of us a couple miles back, over terrain we had just covered to pick up ammunition, because the trucks didn't dare come any closer to the front line. We set out in single file, with Cpl Bell in the lead, trying to keep far enough apart so a well-placed artillery shell wouldn't get more than one or two of us and close enough together so we could see the man in front of us in the dark. It was a very dark night and we constantly stumbling over frozen bodies of American dead. We picked up more cases of ammunition than we could reasonably carry for such a long distance, often falling flat on our face, hurriedly getting up and catching up with the group before we got lost in the dark. We weren't very sturdy on our feet because they had been cold for so many days that except for being miserable they didn't have any feeling left.

Cpl Bell had a good sense of direction and just as it appeared we were almost back to our bivouac area, we heard a single German artillery gun fire one round. In a few seconds, a flare ignited high above the battlefield, lighting the entire area brighter than day. As soon as we heard the muzzle blast from the big gun, we all hit the ground and laid there like we were dead. The flare was so bright the Germans could have detected the slightest movement from their position across the valley. If they had detected any movement, they would have laid down an artillery barrage, which would have killed many of us. These were tense moments, waiting for the flare that floated down with a parachute to burn out so we could get back to the relative safety of our slit trench, which couldn't be very far away. That was wishful thinking, because before one flare burned out, another one replaced it. After lying on the frozen ground for what seemed like an eternity, I was getting so cold; I had to do something because I would freeze to death before morning. I carefully surveyed the area, paying particular attention to the bodies of two American dead who were less than 10-feet away. I speculated that one had been wounded and when a buddy went to help him, they were both killed by another artillery shell. All of a sudden a replacement flare failed to ignite and in the seconds of darkness before they replaced it, I crawled over between the two frozen bodies. The long wool OD overcoat on one of them was soaked with frozen blood but I managed to unbutton it so I could lay one side of it on the frozen ground to lie on. The other man's overcoat was not frozen and I was able to pull his frozen body close enough to me so I could cover myself with his unbuttoned overcoat. Throughout the night, I could hear the cries of the wounded and dying, which must have been there for some time since there hadn't been any shelling since we moved into the area the night before.

Morning finally came. The Germans had not detected any movement so there hadn't done any shelling during the night. At first daylight, our artillery resumed firing and we moved out in the direction where the flares were fired from the night before. After weeks of advancing over the frozen bodies of Americans whose weapons had been taken, eating frozen stew and filling our canteens with water that had seeped into shell craters, we were cold, fatigued and weary from loss of sleep. My feet had been cold for so long, I no longer had feeling in them. I hadn't had my shoes or galoshes off since we left Luxembourg and I was having trouble walking. I knew from the American dead and an occasional burned out German tank, we saw along the way, that they had been here, but we had yet to see our first German. Evidently the Americans had occupied all this territory, the Germans had counterattacked, killing thousands of Americans and now we were trying to take it back again. If they knew what was going on they weren't about to tell us. One night as we dug in on a hill overlooking a wide valley with a ridge on the other side, someone commented that we hadn't seen any American dead that day. There was also something unusual because our Platoon Sgt who usually hung out about a half a mile back was up front to make sure half of us were awake and on guard that night. Long before daylight, he said in his roaring voice, everybody up and get ready to move out at daylight. It didn't take that long to get ready because we didn't brush our teeth or wash our hands and had been fully dressed with our overcoat, shoes and galoshes for weeks. All we had to do was roll up our sleeping bag into a 3 X 12-inch roll and put it in our backpack. Sometime later after it warmed up a little, we would eat a can of the frozen stew that we carried in our backpack. There was something unusual happening because Sgt Spencer was not only up front, but he was also shook up. As we sit around waiting for daylight, I was shocked to see 4 medium sized tanks parked behind the crest of the hill with fire shooting out of their exhaust. We had never had tank support before and didn't know what to make of it. We moved out at daybreak and never saw or heard about the tanks again. They were evidently our artillery support that dropped shells on our position later that day. In the early morning light, we moved down across the wide deep valley looking at the profile of two buildings on the hill which was still two or three miles away. The building on the right was evidently a country church and the other building approximately 100 yards to its left, appeared to be a long warehouse type building. Soon, we were down in the valley and couldn't see anything except an almost vertical incline, rising up approximately 75 or 100 feet to a flat ridge, where the buildings we had seen previously were evidently located. The flat wide valley was probably a dry riverbed that had been cut through the foothills by erosion over millions of years and if we followed it to the east it would undoubtedly end up at the Rhine River. We had to stop and rest several times before we reached the top of the incline and could see the flat area on top of the ridge.

That day our platoon was on line and the second and third squads were up front with Sgt Dekman and Cpl Bell's first squad in reserve. Lou Stein, our first scout was the first one to see across the flat ridge above the steep incline and I was about ten feet behind him. The ridge was perfectly flat and about 100 yards across, dropping off into a valley on the other side, where there might be a village. The flat ridge extended as far as we could see to both our left and right. The warehouse building was directly in front of us and the church, with a fairly large cemetery was approximately 100 yards to our right. It wasn't just a country church as one would expect in a rural area where we hadn't seen a single house, making it safe to assume it must be associated with a village on the other side of the ridge. In this area, farmers lived in villages and drove their cattle out to pasture each day when they worked their land. The church with its large cemetery had massive grave monuments, that faced what we now assumed was a village below the hill.

After several tries, our artillery zeroed in and dropped a shell through the roof of the warehouse type stone building. Being Christians, the church was spared because it apparently didn't occur to anyone that the Germans might have a lookout in the steeple of the church. After the warehouse type building was secured, the heavy weapons platoon was deployed in the cemetery, taking advantage of the cover provided by the massive gravestones. We advanced, crawling on our bellies through grass that was about 2 feet high, as we approached the other side of the ridge. I was about 20 feet behind Lou Stein when all hell broke loose. He raised his head to look over the far side of the ridge, when a German tiger tank just over the crest of the hill opened up on him with a 50-caliber machine gun at close range. The impact of about 25 rounds was so great that it lifted him up on his haunches and he fell back on his face when they stopped firing. The tracer bullets that made up about every 3rd or 5th round in a machine gun magazine went through his chest, setting his backpack on fire and continued to zing over my head. At that instant my system was flooded with adrenalin, my first instinct being to rush over and hold my best buddy in my arms while he died. Fortunately, common sense prevailed before it was too late, and I realized he was already dead. Also if that tank moved ahead a few feet, it could also see me and I too would be dead. It took a few moments to recover enough to crawl back to the protection of the steep incline on the other side of the ridge. I crawled into a shallow ditch where the water runoff had eroded the soil, which was now covered with native grass. I was just below the top of the ridge and could see the front of the church at an oblique angle. I watched the huge tiger tank pull up from behind the ridge to the edge of the cemetery, where it fired many rounds with its 88mm gun at the grave stones our heavy weapons men were using for cover at a range of less than 100 feet. The stones exploded into a cloud of fine sand that along with bits and pieces of bodies rained down over a wide area. The elaborate above ground marble or granite burial vaults located in a prominent location in front of the church had been reduced to rubble and bits and pieces of the bodies that were in them covered the entire area. The shells had so much impact that parts of buried coffins were blown out of the ground. Pieces of the old dead, recent dead and today's dead were impacted into the white wood siding on the front of the church. Once our heavy weapons platoon was annihilated, the big tank turned to join a companion tank on the ridge. The tank which was using its big gun as artillery, firing on our reserve forces as they tried to retreat across the wide, open valley. As the tank made its way from the cemetery in my direction, it went out of its way to run over bodies. Perhaps they got satisfaction, seeing the blood from the mashed bodies squirting high in the air like a garden hose or maybe they just wanted to make sure they were dead. Finally, it stopped about 30 feet from the steep incline where I was hiding and joined its companion firing at our retreating troops. I could see the wide intimidating tracks a few feet in front of me, as I looked up at the long barrel of its huge gun. Although they kept the hatch closed on top of the tanks, they continued to spray the area with machine gun fire even though their visibility couldn't have been very good, because they couldn't see over the edge of the steep incline. An artillery observer in the church steeple was evidently directing fire on our retreating troops.

I looked up at the sky behind me and saw what looked like a flock of birds approaching just over the horizon. It was immediately apparent that cluster of dots was not birds but an incoming artillery barrage fired by our own artillery to destroy the tanks. A direct hit is necessary to destroy a tiger tank and then it may only disable it by knocking off one of the tracks. When artillery shells started exploding around us, both tanks took off at high speed for cover behind the ridge. Whoever called for the artillery either didn't know we were there or they were willing to sacrifice us to get the tanks? Once the artillery started shelling our position, they continued for some time because they evidently didn't get the word that the tanks had left. Our artillery claimed as many or more lives than the tanks did in the cemetery. After the shelling, only three of us were left. One of them was laying on the steep incline with his legs spread to keep a low profile. About 10 feet from me, he had a shell burrow in the ground between his legs, which fortunately turned out to be a dud and didn't explode. He was afraid to move and the other survivor and I had to drag him away, in case for some reason it might still detonate. The man's name was Allen, neither a former Cadet nor ASTP, who should have been on limited, non-combat service because he had heart trouble and other physical problems. When our artillery stopped firing, the tanks pulled back up from behind the ridge and were again firing at our troops, as they retreated across the valley. Obviously, the Germans had an observer in the church steeple that was directing fire.

Two American planes appeared out of nowhere, a P-47 and a P-51 with a single bomb hanging under their fuselage. All firing stopped and the planes again disappeared behind the ridge. We heard the two bombs detonate but don't know whether or not they knocked out the tanks and weren't about to wait around to find out. By this time, most of our surviving troops had retreated across the valley and were out of sight, giving us the opportunity to make a run for it. I felt sick as the three of us were trying to escape across the valley pock marked with fresh shell craters, steaming from the recent explosions and the dead and dying Americans along the way. Although, I hadn't had anything to eat for more than a day, I was sick to my stomach, vomiting green bile that got in my nose making me even sicker. I told my two surviving buddies to go ahead rather than wait for me because; I was too sick to walk and had to rest before I could continue. I stopped twice to fill my canteen from shell craters that rapidly filled with explosive tasting water, to wash the terrible taste out of my mouth. I got further and further behind but I wasn't concerned because I knew the way. Unfortunately, by the time I reached the other side of the valley, everyone had left. Not knowing what to do, I continued in the same direction until I was startled by the muzzle blast of a big gun that was fired in my immediate area, literally shaking the earth. The smoke from the muzzle of the big gun rose up above the bushes and small trees like Indian smoke signals. I crawled around the bushes, not knowing whether it was theirs or our and to my relief, it turned out to be an American antitank gun. The lone gunner pointed out the tank he had just fired at, as it sped along the ridge across the valley by the church. Perhaps, the fighter planes had destroyed one or both of the tanks and this was a replacement rushing in to close the gap in their front line. I asked the gunner if he knew where I could locate an infantry unit that was in this area. He said, "No but there was a transportation company down the hill in the woods." The company actually consisted of two ammunition trucks and a few lost infantrymen like me that stumbled into them by chance. I felt secure sleeping under one of the ammunition trucks, perhaps 2 or 3 miles from the fluid front line, which for all practical purposes had been abandoned. I had not been that far from the frontline for well over a month.

I was sick, tired, exhausted and my feet were numb. The day seemed like an eternity and I couldn't get the events of the day out of my mind and go to sleep. I had lost my best buddy and 50 or perhaps a hundred others that I spent months in training with and my thoughts were all about death and dying. My first experience with dying was when I was a little boy about 4 years of age when, I went with my mother to take some food she prepared to the home of Mrs. C. A. Carlson of Frederic after she died. Mrs. Carlson and my mother both belonged to the "Bee", a close knit organization of only 12 women and even as a small child I liked her a lot, because she always paid so much attention to me. I will never forget when we went in the front door of the big Carlson house and saw her lying propped up in her coffin surrounded by a room full of flowers. I thought she was sleeping but my mother tried to explain that she had died and gone to heaven. I was obsessed about this business of dying and ask my mother questions about it for weeks. During this time, some other lady who was either a friend or relative of the family also died which further complicated the problem. Her husband had died some years ago and was buried in the Frederic cemetery where they also had a grave for her. As it turned out she was Catholic, whatever that was, and the priest would not conduct her funeral, unless she was buried in what they called the Catholic Cemetery. Finally, the priest consented to conduct her funeral, if her family paid him to bless the grave so it would be a suitable place to bury her. I didn't understand the procedure but it must have been something like having to fumigate our house after I had been quarantined for scarlet fever for 6 weeks. I didn't know preachers did that type work but thought a lot about it, hoping my dad or mother never get Catholic, because if they would ever die my family was to poor to pay a priest to bless the dirt in their grave. I couldn't envision them ever dying, but if they did, I wouldn't want them to be buried in different cemeteries. I was obsessed with that for years and every time we went to the cemetery, I asked my parents to show me where they buried the Catholics. I couldn't understand how the Catholic Cemetery was better than the one where ordinary people were buried, because it didn't look any different to me.

Lying under that ammunition truck, I couldn't envision how that French Catholic parish on the hill where all my buddies were killed that day would react when they saw what happened to their church and cemetery. Obviously, a Frenchmen's concern would not be for the Americans that perished that day on their holy ground or appreciation for not destroying their church, which could have saved the lives of so many Americans. Instead, they would accuse us of contaminating their sacred burial ground with bits and pieces of non-Catholic American flesh, blood and bone. Perhaps the United States would give the French government more welfare so they could hire enough priests to cleanse the area so it would again be suitable for their Catholic dead.

I was bitter that we were fighting the war while the French were sitting at sidewalk cafes in Paris leisurely slopping up wine, while we were fighting their war and mourning the massacre of our buddies. There were just so many things on my mind that night and tired, exhausted and miserable as I was; I simply could not go to sleep. I was also preoccupied about how combat infantrymen were treated. Officially, you were entitled to a combat infantry badge and $4 in addition to the regular $50 a month you received before they took out $6.50 for life insurance which you would never collect. Of course, the $4 premium pay didn't start until you had been on the frontline for a month or were wounded or killed in action. Certainly, no one wanted to be a combat infantryman, but this was a naive approach because my experience indicated few infantrymen survived on the front line for a month without being wounded or killed. I had lost track of time but even though I probably hadn't been there much more than a month, I had gone through hell, and more than the lifetime of most of my buddies. Perhaps it would be more appropriate to define a combat infantryman in terms of how many days or weeks he had been under artillery fire as he advanced so many miles with so many of his buddies being killed along the way. Also, how many wounded, crying out for help had been abandoned because of rapidly shifting artillery fire. The people that made the rules had obviously never been there and didn't have the slightest idea what it was all about.

Although my company was still in the immediate area, I wasn't able to locate them and get back for 3 days. When I returned, they were in the process of loading the remnants of the 87th Division into a small convoy of trucks, which were heading north to another unknown assignment. As we departed, I took one last look across the valley at the church on the hill. It was like a private memorial for those whose frozen bodies we left back there on the hill, across the valley and the thousands we had seen along the way. I said a special prayer for Lou Stein, my best buddy. These last weeks had been worse than being condemned to hell for eternity. These were real people; boys that were not yet men that we had lived trained and socialized with for the last 5 months and not just mutilated bodies left lying in the frozen mud and snow. They had mothers and fathers, wives or sweethearts and some of them had children they had never seen. Perhaps one of them would have become our president. I will see the tracer shells passing through Lou Stein's body with his burning backpack the rest of my life. I envisioned his body frozen to the ground with the blood that gushed from his massive chest wounds and the bits and pieces of the human remains of our heavy weapons platoon plastered all over the front of the church. I thought of the hundreds of dead that had been killed by our own and enemy artillery as well as tank machine guns. They were among the finest and brightest young men America had to offer, who could have made major contributions to the entire human race.

I was personally troubled trying to make sense of it but somehow it had something to do with that church on the hill. I know the artillery observer that directed the massacre had to be in the church steeple, yet I can't blame the church building because it was nothing more than brick, mortar and wood like the warehouse we blew up. No, it wasn't the church building but our Christian attitude toward the holiness or sanctuary of churches that told our company commander to destroy the warehouse but save the church, as if the church building was more important than 100 American lives. Somehow, we have to separate worship from the building where we worship. The act of worshiping has nothing to do with where it takes place. I would have to take on the Church later when my thoughts were clearer; this was a time to honor the dead and not a time for vengeance. They were Catholics, Protestants and Jews whose prayers and their family's prayers had fallen on deaf ears. God had abandoned these men who have nobody left but their families, who won't even know they were dead until the snow melted the next spring. Protestant chaplains were thicker than hair on a dog back in the U.S. but I hadn't seen a single one since we left American shores. Perhaps they are allergic to blood or the sound of gunfire.

Before Christmas 1944, their families would receive a preprinted postcard saying your son or husband is missing in action, as mine would because I was also missing in action for 3 days. If you are lucky enough to get back to your unit, they don't bother to send them another postcard saying you are no longer missing. The following spring when the snow melted, they will pick up their body and notify their family that they were killed in action. These men had been human sacrifices in what President Roosevelt called the war to end all wars. We were totally unprepared, even though it was hardly a surprise, because he had been shipping war material to Europe for years and refused to attend a summit meeting requested by the Japanese in Hawaii. How could he be considered a great president, when he turned the country over to the Mafia controlled unions, resulting in 2 million more Americans, being unemployed 2 years after he too office. He failed as a leader because he wasn't willing to sacrifice his popularity to get America prepared for the inevitable war, which was rapidly approaching. He elected to initiate more popular make work welfare programs like the WPA rather than prepare for the war which was at hand. The net result was that we didn't recover from the Great Depression, until we formally entered the war, totally unprepared with inadequate obsolete equipment.

There was simply too much to sort out at such a troubled time but I was greatly disturbed by the Battle for the Rhineland. Why did we send thousands of infantry troops in to a major battle where the Germans were using nothing but tanks without any defense against tanks? From my observations, it appeared that the Germans didn't commit more than 25 or 50 tanks on a wide front where they killed thousands of American Infantrymen. During more than a month on the front, we hadn't seen any Germans and not more than 2 or 3 burned out tanks, which appeared to have been destroyed by aircraft. Perhaps it was because General Patton relished getting involved in high visibility tank battles where he could get a lot of publicity to feed his ego. He was quoted more than once of saying, "Keep the infantry out in front of the tanks because tanks are hard to get". Perhaps that says it all.

3. THE BATTLE OF THE BULGE

The word was out that we were on our way to Allied Supreme Headquarters located in Reams, France. That was welcome news. We envisioned hot food, a warm place to sleep and being able to warm our frozen feet. In a few hours, the skyline of Reams came into view and we couldn't wait to get there. Unfortunately to our disappointment, the convoy stopped about 2 miles outside the city and they said," This is it, everybody out." We put up our pup tents, which don't have a bottom, in a muddy field along the road, which had about four inches of snow on top of the muddy ground and as usual ate our frozen stew. I had to find a new buddy to share my pup tent with because my buddy Lou Stein who I had always shared a tent with was no longer with us. I thought a lot about Lou that night. The next day they took us into Reams for a shower at a portable army unit where perhaps twenty of us were in the shower at the same time. We took off all our clothes as we went into the building and threw them into a huge pile at the entrance. This was the first time we had even had our shoes off since we left Luxemburg, well over a month ago. They didn't let us stay in the shower, which wasn't very warm nearly long enough to even get our feet warm but it felt good anyway. We got dressed in new clothes and went back to the bivouac area where we slept in the mud with the cold water from the melting snow soaking all our new clothes.

The next day we got replacements for the men that we had lost bringing our company back up to authorized strength before leaving for Belgium, where we would take part in what they called, "The Battle of the Bulge". We arrived in some little town just as it was starting to get dark and appreciated, being able to sleep in a house that night even though the

Germans had slept there the previous night. It was actually the second time we had slept under a roof since we left England, which seemed like such a long time ago. The first time was the night we arrived in Luxemburg from La Havre, when we slept on the floor of a German military school that the Germans had recently abandoned. Four or five people, including two or three girls lived in the house but we couldn't talk to them because we couldn't speak French and they couldn't speak English. They treated us nicely and I am sure no one molested them. This was a typical Belgium village where the farmers lived in the village and drove their cattle out to the countryside for pasture every day during the summer. The barn and the house were in the same building, connected by a door between the barn and the kitchen. They kept their cattle in the barn during the winter, piling the manure between the barn and the main street that went through the village. I slept on the wood floor of the unheated living room in my sleeping bag that night.

Early the next morning, we had a company formation out in the street in front of the manure pile where they called the roster of those of Catholic and Jewish faith to be excused for religious services. Initially, I thought those rosters, which were called periodically, were for some detail. One day, I got in a group by mistake, only to find out it was a Catholic religious service. There was a lot of turnover and I didn't know a new man had been assigned to our company that had the same name as me, who happened to be Catholic. By this time, I didn't know very many men because most of them were replacements and no one knew or cared whether or not I belonged there. Anyway by the time, I found out what it was all about, it was too late not to go along with whatever it was. I spent a couple hours in a nice warm house where it was more of a fellowship than a prayer service. Now that I knew what it was all about, I recalled numerous previous instances when the Catholics and Jews were excused for religious services, while the rest of us were loaded into trucks and taken out to some ungodly location on what was a miserable, dangerous assignment. When I was a high school senior, I was president of the youth group at my church and I was upset by the sneaky anti-Protestant bias. Obviously the Catholic priests and Jewish rabbis, who were supposed to be chaplains for all denominations, were only looking after their own and to hell with the rest of us. It would be interesting to know how many Protestants were killed while their clergy were sheltering Catholics and Jews from danger. We were loaded into the familiar 2-1/2 ton trucks and taken several miles down a deserted road where each of us and a new buddy were dropped off to establish new guard posts about 100 yards apart. We were going to be there for an extended period and one of us had to be up, alert and on guard 24 hours a day. Together we dug a slit trench about 50 feet back from the road where one of us could sleep that was both secure and warm enough so we could survive the subzero temperature. The trench was both deep and wide enough so we could line and cover it with pine boughs, which were plentiful in the heavily wooded forest. We covered the top with snow for camouflage.

We were actually replacing the American infantry troops that were guarding the southern flank of the front line where the Germans broke through. This was not an enviable assignment because a few days ago German armor and infantry that broke through on a wide front overran the infantry outfit posted along this same front, and either killed or took them prisoners. The bodies of those prisoners were later found where they had been herded into a ravine and killed by machine gun fire. They put an extra bullet in the head of those that they thought might survive because they couldn't be bothered with prisoners. The idea of having two guards together was that one would always be up on alert and the other could keep from freezing when he wasn't sleeping and he was available if need. We had a standard procedure for challenging anyone that may approach and everyday someone came and gives us a new password. Instructions were, if they didn't know the password, shoot and ask questions later. You would undoubtedly be killed in the process but the shots would alert other guards up and down the road so they wouldn't be taken by surprise. No, this wasn't an enviable assignment and most of us would have preferred to be in church.

One night while I was on guard, I heard footsteps of several men approaching through the forest in the darkness. I squatted down behind a large tree and waited quietly. I was scared half to death as they approached because my buddy was sleeping and I didn't dare wake him up because it would alert them to my presence and I wanted to surprise them. In all the excitement, I had forgotten the password and as hard as I tried it wouldn't come to me. When they were about 20 feet away, I could just see their outline in the darkness and I said in a loud demanding voice, "Halt who goes there?" The most welcome voice I ever heard came back to me saying; "This is Corp Bell with a patrol." He had also recognized my voice and I was so relieved.

We stayed in the woods for about a week before we moved to a central location where we slept on the floor of a large covered building and stood guard about 12 hours a day or night. Soon it was Christmas Eve, 1944 and a package of cookie crumbs and two candy bars arrived from my family. I hadn't received any mail for well over a month, making it even more of a surprise to get a package from my family. By now most of the men were total strangers, and I didn't feel obligated to share any of the cookie crumb powder with them. I slipped the two candy bars into my sleeping bag and that night I pulled my head down inside of my sleeping bag and savored one of the chocolate candy bars for a very long time. Christmas is the loneliest time to be far from home in a place like this, especially when you can't be optimistic that you will ever be home again. As I ate the candy bar bit by bit, it was as if I was having Christmas dinner with my family. I later learned that it wasn't a very happy time at home either because they had just received a preprinted post card telling them I was missing in action about two weeks ago and they didn't know whether I was dead or alive. At a time like that, when you feel the entire world has abandoned you, it is so important to know you still have a family.

January 1st was payday. They give us a hand full of French francs that we knew couldn't be worth much because we didn't make much and whatever it was there was neither time nor place to spend it. Actually, now that we were officially combat infantrymen we were paid $54 a month but after they took out $6.50 for life insurance that we would never be able to spend and $25 for a War Bond, there wasn't much left. All we had was a handful of useless paper that we couldn't even use to start a fire because it would draw artillery fire. They also paid us what we would have been paid on December 1st if we hadn't been advancing on the front line at that time. When you stop and think about it, that wasn't a bad deal for them because less than 25% of us were still alive. Obviously, our objective was not money but survival. We were there for the duration of the war plus 6 months which meant that we would be there until we were either killed or wounded badly enough that we couldn't return to service. Most infantrymen with minor wounds returned to service after a few days.

On January 3rd, the 87th Infantry Division went on the offensive, moving into positions the Germans had strongly fortified and booby trapped as well as zeroed in their artillery on key positions. Company L was concentrated in a heavily wooded wedge shaped area, with the point, extending out into an open meadow where a single large oak tree stood about 200 feet out beyond the point of the wooded area. I had never fired a machine gun or didn't even know how to load one but I became the assistant gunner in a two-man squad that day. We got a replacement gunner in Reams who was going into combat for the first time and needed someone with experience to help him survive. I wasn't thrilled with the assignment but since I had survived under constant fire for over two months, I was probably a logical choice. The machine gun was set up at the point of the woods where you could see across the meadow because it had more firepower than any other weapon in an infantry company. The two of us spent most of the day digging a gun emplacement about six feet square and 30 inches deep with our little shovels that folded up so they would fit into our backpack. It was fortunate that there was so much snow on the ground so the ground wasn't frozen under the snow. There was enough room for the gun, several boxes of ammunition and enough space so we could both lay flat on the bottom in event of an artillery barrage.

Early that evening, they sent word for us to take turns, coming back to the rear area because we were going to have a hot meal. This was quite a treat because we hadn't had a hot meal since we left England well over two months ago. The meal consisted solely of the same stew we had lived on but it had been heated up in large galvanized garbage cans that were brought in on a jeep. While I was taking my turn, eating in the rear area, the Germans started laying down an artillery barrage that covered the entire wooded area where Company L was dug in. They started in the back and covered the area in a systematic pattern; dropping shells about 50 feet apart, making a horizontal sweep across the back. Each pattern was a little closer to the front until they had covered the entire area. When the shelling started, I quickly made my way back to the gun emplacement, approximately 200 yards in front of the mess jeep, only to find someone else in the gun emplacement where I was supposed to be. It probably was a buddy of our new gunner but I never found out who it was. I crawled in between them the best I could but this left me exposed from the front and both sides. Artillery in a wooded area is devastating because a shell detonates when it hits the trunk of a tree above and there is little I could do to protect myself because shrapnel flies in every direction.

Shrapnel from an artillery shell that exploded in a tree directly above hit me but I didn't have any pain and had no idea how bad it was because the lower part of my body was totally paralyzed. Fortunately, this was about the last shell in the barrage, making it possible to get me out right away. Sargent Dekman and Corp Bell, two special friends that I had crossed paths with so often these last six months were there in no time with a stretcher. I was alert and could move my arms but my legs were completely paralyzed so I didn't feel any pain. They and two others carried me back through waist deep snow to a jeep ambulance that had a rack for four stretchers that was parked where the mess jeep had been. When the jeep was loaded with four stretchers, they took us back about a mile or more to the battalion aid station. There was a long line of stretchers with wounded lying in the snow waiting to see the lone medic. There was another area close by that I guess you would call a morgue where they lined up the stretchers of those that had already expired. When I got to see the medic, he removed my first aid kit that I carried on my belt and injected me with the large vile of morphine. He said he didn't have a compress large enough to cover my wounds so they just loaded me into one of the waiting ambulances that hauled four stretcher patients back to the field hospital which are better known today as MASH units. The morphine took over soon after we left the aid station and I didn't wake up until sometime the next day.

4. RECOVERY IN EUROPE

When I woke up, my mind was sharper than any time in my life. I was still lying on a stretcher with my wool overcoat on, wrapped in a blanket with my arms by my sides, just as I was when they put me in the ambulance. My teeth were chattering and I felt like I was freezing to death but I wasn't in any pain. I knew I was in shock because most of the men on the battlefield died of shock rather than their battle wounds so the symptoms were familiar. I wasn't sure whether or not I had any feelings in my hands but the only thing I could move was my head so for all practical purposes, I was helpless. First, I reasoned that this was the next day because there was light coming in from somewhere and I was wounded in the evening. As I moved my head a little up and down and side to side to survey the situation, I could see that I was in the center of a very large warehouse type building with stretchers laying head to foot on the floor, the full length of the building in rows less than a foot apart. My first thought was that there were hundreds of stretchers in here but when I counted the overhead wires or cables between every other row of stretchers, there were obviously many more. The wires that would normally be used to hang plasma bottles extended the full length of the building but there were only a few bottles in the far distant corner of the warehouse. After checking and rechecking my calculations, I concluded there had to be over 1000 stretchers on the floor of the building. I couldn't see anyone standing or walking in this enormous building. Also, there wasn't any sign of life on the stretchers around me that I could see so well. I had to accept the dim reality, they thought I was dead when I arrived at the hospital and put me in the morgue. Also, I had been there for some time because the way stretchers were packed so close together, they had to be put in one row at a time and at least 500 stretchers had been brought in since I arrived. Perhaps this wasn't the day after I was wounded but some day or days later. The situation was hopeless, I knew I was going to die but I wasn't in pain even though my teeth were chattering from the cold but in a way after all the pain and suffering I had been through, it would be a relief. I said what I thought was my final good bye to my loved ones and drifted off to sleep.

Sometime later, I woke up, hearing someone moving around a couple rows from me. My mind was no longer clear and I couldn't see very well but I could make out someone going from one body to the next checking their dog tags. I tried to cry out but nothing came out and I drifted back to sleep. I woke up and opened my eyes when someone lifted my head up to check my dog tags. It was a Catholic chaplain going up and down the rows administering last rights to those of his faith. When I woke and looked at him with my teeth chattering, he said that he would get someone to give me some blood plasma to warm me up. I was very weak and as soon as he left, I drifted back to sleep. Sometime later, I woke up feeling warm and comfortable, noting that the plasma bottle hanging on the wire above me was still 1/4 full. I knew I was going to live and went back to sleep. More than 50 years later, I received a copy of my medical records from the 107th Evacuation Hospital that shows, I was admitted to the hospital at 0030 on 5 January 1945, received 500cc of plasma at 0130 and went into surgery at 0500. Based on the official records, I would have been in the morgue from the evening of January 3rd until 0030 on 5 January 1945. I was wounded the evening of January 3rd, the first day of the offensive and was taken directly to the morgue, where I spent more than 24 hours.

About 5 in the morning, a doctor tried to awaken me by shouting, "Can you feel this; can you feel this?" I regained consciousness enough to know I was on an operating table and doctors were sticking pins in my body to see how much of it was paralyzed. Sometime the next day, I woke up in a body cast that covered me from my toes to my armpits. My legs were spread apart with a crossbar between them so they would be able to lift me. They give me an apple, a candy bar and the personal things that were in my pockets when I was wounded and loaded me into an ambulance with three others to take to a hospital in Reams. They had trouble getting me in the ambulance because my cast was so big one of the other patients had to lie on the leg of my cast. I don't remember whether or not I ate the apple and the candy bar but I do remember the German POWs that carried my stretcher took my personal effects, which included the useless French francs that I received on January 1st. The elevator at the Reams Hospital was so small that the German POWs that carried my stretcher had to almost stand me up so my cast cut into the flesh where I was wounded and I screamed with pain. I couldn't talk to them and was relieved to get a private room.

A woman who was probably a nurse's aide must have thought I was the dirtiest person she had ever seen because she kept washing my hands. The dirt was so engrained in my chapped skin; it wasn't about to come out. She tried to feed me my first meal since I was wounded but I couldn't talk to her or anyone else at that hospital and it just didn't work. Finally, I motioned for her to sit the tray on top of my body cast above my chest and even though I couldn't see what was there, it still worked better. The hospital was evidently a collecting station because a few days later, we made our way down that same miserable elevator and they loaded us on a hospital train staffed with British nurses that wore uniforms that resembled Catholic nuns. Until this time, I hadn't even talked to a doctor and didn't have any idea what was wrong with me. The body cast covered my whole body and I wasn't sure if it was still all there. They left our medical records in an envelope, lying on top of my cast and I couldn't resist the temptation of finding out what was wrong with me. The envelope contained 3 pages of brief hand written notes from the 107th Evacuation Hospital, which were difficult to decipher. The note on the 0500, January 5th surgery was as follows: "Litigation (tied off) of severed femoral vein in upper 1/3 of thigh. Artery intact but extremely traumatized." The portion of the sciatic nerve affecting the rear half of my right leg was completely severed and tantalum wire marking sutures were placed on the severed ends. There was also "loss of sensation present over foot and medial aspect of right leg, paralysis of plantar flexing and other leg muscles present". They probably weren't aware that my left leg was also totally paralyzed because there weren't any shrapnel wounds in it that would have alerted them to a potential problem.

We were transferred from the train to a hospital ship, which appeared to be a converted ferry because it had hospital beds all over the deck. We crossed the English Channel on this small boat staffed with American nurses and went by ambulance directly to an American hospital somewhere in the southern English countryside.

I was in three different hospitals in the same general area, which were all identical, each having perhaps a dozen wards in Quonset type buildings. Each building was large enough for about a 50-bed ward, a nurse's office, and 2 private rooms where they moved patients into before they died so they didn't upset other patients on the ward. The wards had a blacktop floor and a sidewalk that connected all wards, surgery and other support buildings. In my ward, all of us were bed patients except one; perhaps half were unconscious because of head injuries. The man in the bed next to me had part of his skull missing and was unconscious. There were several large pieces of shrapnel the surgeon had removed from his head lying on his little bedside stand. One day I recognized the only ambulatory patient in the ward, who had a cast from his waist to his neck, covering his arms if he still had any, was from my company. At first, I thought I was seeing a ghost because he was the platoon sergeant of our heavy weapons platoon that was annulated in the massacre on the hill by the church. We exchanged enough words that I was sure he knew who I was but he didn't want to talk to me. Many evenings we had sat around talking at the base back in the U.S.A. so I was somewhat offended that he chose to ignore me. Perhaps he was afraid, I would say something about the massacre on the hill by the church where everyone in his platoon was killed and the very sight of me reminded him of what he was trying to forget.

I was not in great pain because both my legs were still paralyzed but they insisted on giving me pain medication, which impaired my ability to think clearly. I received a penicillin injection every three hours, day and night so my open wounds wouldn't get infected. They saved the urine from all patients receiving penicillin because it was a new drug that was in short supply and they had developed a process of recovering the penicillin. The huge open wound large enough to run my fist through from my upper thigh to the cheek of my buttocks was constantly draining into the cotton lining of my body cast and smelled terrible. Days all ran together so my pickled mind could only think in terms of milestones. For example, the second time they changed my cast they didn't put my left leg in the new cast and the doctor told me he thought he would be able to save my right leg. Both my legs were totally paralyzed at that time and I remember, telling him," Doctor. does it really make a difference". He went on to the next bed without saying anything. Every time the doctor or nurse went by my bed they said, "Think about moving your big toe." The next milestone was a couple of weeks later when I thought I could see a slight movement in my left big toe. That was 6 weeks after I was wounded. The next 6 weeks, while the feeling was coming back in my legs was the worst 6 weeks in my life. I didn't think I could stand it but there wasn't anything they could give me to control the pain. The pain medication they insisted on giving me when I didn't need it was not effective and the hypos, which they gave sparingly, offered little help. The skin in my feet and legs was so sensitive; they had to put a wire cage over the lower half of my body because I couldn't stand to have a bed sheet touch my Legs.

Before the pain subsided, I got a severe case of yellow jaundice that was later known as hepatitis B. There were several patients in the ward that had yellow jaundice but they didn't know how contagious it was at that time. That was before they had disposable needles, when the ward nurse sterilized the needles in her office every night. I was very sick, had an extremely high temperature and they moved me into one of the two dying rooms where I stayed for a couple weeks. All the doctors had extensive experience in surgery but very little knowledge of general medicine and none of them knew much about yellow jaundice at that time. The doctor kept cutting into a large bedsore on my right heel, trying to get it to bleed because he thought I had gangrene in my paralyzed right foot. They did extensive emergency laboratory work, including spinal fluid tests but it was obvious the doctor didn't understand my problem and in my weakened condition, resulting from the major trauma that I was still going through, it was apparent he didn't expect me to survive. It was a long slow recovery, which undoubtedly prolonged my stay in overseas hospitals for at least a month.

My mother wrote, saying they had received a preprinted postcard with a blank line where they wrote, "Critically wounded in action". She didn't tell me about a similar postcard they received just before Christmas saying I was missing in action. Even this last postcard was welcome relief because it

```
        #501  01-19-2016 12:00AM
   Item(s) checked out to p1063320.

TITLE: To hell and almost back : life of
BARCODE: 30483000264780
DUE DATE: 02-09-16


      Do you love your library?
 Join the Friends of the Balsam Lake PL
```

was the first indication they received that I was still alive. I wasn't physically able and was too medicated to write a letter for quite some time and there wasn't anyone there that could help me. The staff was overworked because there was only one nurse and two orderlies for a 50-bed ward of seriously wounded bed patients. The ward nurse worked 16 hours a day and slept in the office at night to cover emergencies. She was also the duty nurse, perhaps one night a week, which meant she had to give all the 3-hour penicillin shots on all the wards, during the time the other nurses were sleeping. The two orderlies worked 12-hour shifts but often had to overlap, during busy periods. There weren't any chaplains, or volunteers like Gray Ladies in U.S. hospitals that came to help patients write letters read their mail or do other personal things for them. The staff had all they could do to keep as many of us alive as possible until we recovered enough so we could stand the long trip back to the U.S.A. as a bed patient on a hospital ship.

Finally, after about three months, I started to emerge from what seemed like a bad dream where I was floating around in space somewhere between life and death, nurtured by drugs and tortured by pain. When pain subsided to a level I had learned to live with and my head cleared, I looked around the ward and tried to assess what the future had in store for all of us. Obviously, many perhaps half, had nothing to look forward to and would have been much better off if they could have joined their buddies that were left behind on some hill by the church in this far away cruel land. Finally, what about me, what do I have to look forward to? It appeared at this juncture that I would probably survive. One day they will remove my cast and I will go back the U.S. as a bed patient on a hospital ship. Once I get there, they will cut me open again and I will undergo major reconstructive surgery where they will repair as much as the state of the art permits which unfortunately won't be enough. My flesh wounds will eventually heal, no one knows how much permanent liver damage I will have from hepatitis, and it is definite that half of my right foot and leg will be permanently paralyzed. It is difficult to see how a cripple could succeed in a society where hard work is usually associated with success. Would I be able to get married and have children, if so, how would I support them? The future didn't look very bright from that lonely faraway place.

When I started to recover, I wrote to Lou's girlfriend Flo and my dad's cousin in Wales. As it turned out, neither of them lived that far away and they both came to see me. I just happened to remember their address or

I couldn't have written to them because the German stretcher-bearers stole my address book along with all my personal effects that I carried in my pockets. In Flo's case all I could give them was her name and near the intersection of two major roads in Manchester so I was surprised she received it. The only address, I could give them was my APO number so they had to check with the Red Cross to find out where the hospital was located. My dad's cousin that I visited in Wales before I went to France the previous October was about my dad's age and she had four children: A girl Rowena, about a year younger than me that was in nurses training; a girl Megan, about 2 years younger than me that just finished school; a boy Mike and a younger girl Gwyneth. They treated me so nicely when I went to visit them in Wales; I really appreciated her coming to see me. She wrote to my dad and mother and told them about everything. They were so grateful to hear from her because they knew so little about what happened to me.

It was also a pleasant surprise when Flo came to see me because I wasn't expecting her either. When I wrote, I simply told her that Lou was killed and thanked her for what happiness she had given him. She sat on the edge of my bed because beds were so close together there wasn't room for a chair between the beds. When I was holding her hand, I felt the softness of her skin, making me immediately aware that I had either forgotten or never really knew how soft girls were. I hoped the open wounds that were still draining in my cast didn't smell too bad but it was one of those things I had gotten used to, and couldn't really tell any more. She told me her husband had been killed in the war and she had a 2 year old son but I could see she didn't want to talk about it and I didn't push her. She was a beautiful woman with charm and dignity and I could see what Lou saw in her. As she leaned over to kiss me good bye, I put my hand on her bare shoulder exposed by her sleeveless dress and it found its way down to her bare breast when she give me a long passionate goodbye kiss. I had been depressed and lonely but now for the first time, I realized there might still be something in life to live for. What a difference a breast makes.

Finally, the day came when I was going home or more correctly back to the U.S.A. It didn't happen all that fast because the Queen Mary, which had been converted to a hospital ship, was very big and it took so many stretchers to fill it up. There were convoys of ambulances extending out miles from the ship. We were bed patients so it wasn't much different from being in a hospital ward. It was Easter Sunday and they were playing Easter music over the ships P.A. system. When we docked in New York they took us to the Army hospital at Staten Island. I remember the New York skyline as they carried me down the gangplank to a never-ending convoy of waiting ambulances. It was great to back in the U.S.A. but I knew all too well that it was still a very long way home.

5. RECOVERY IN USA

After a couple days at the Staten Island hospital we left on a hospital train going to Percy Jones General Hospital in Battle Creek, Michigan. Percy Jones General Hospital located on the north edge of Battle Creek was an impressive 22-story building more than 15 stories above any building in the little city. In reality, Battle Creek was a major hospital center, which also included the Percy Jones Annex that was the former base hospital for Ft. Custer, and the base itself was the convalescent hospital. The general hospital seemed like a luxury hospital after being in hospitals overseas. I arrived about the time Roosevelt died and just before a hospital train arrived, bringing in Bataan/Corregidor prisoners of war that had just been released from Japanese prison camps. Any one that saw these men could not have anything but hatred for the Japanese people. About half of the beds in the 16 bed ward that I was in, had been reserved for the prisoners of war, coming in on this train. They didn't talk about it, but what you couldn't tell from their swollen stomachs, yellow skin and sores all over their body, you could tell by their screams in the night. They were in effect abused Japanese slaves that had to work hard for long hours, living on fish heads and potato peelings. They were on a very strict diet and would continue to be until such a time as they would be able to eat American food. I had what they called major reconstructive surgery around "Victory in Europe Day" (VE Day) which happened to be both President Harry Truman's and my birthday. It was a very long complex surgery which not only involved extensive neurosurgery but other major surgery, involving the tissue and muscles, resulting from a shell fragment wound that made a hole between my upper right thigh and buttocks large enough to put your fist through. Before WW II little was known about nerve or brain surgery and every medical center wanted to take advantage of the opportunity to experiment and develop new technology where they had an abundance of healthy young patients. The Chief of Neurosurgery at Percy Jones Hospital was from the Mayo Clinic. Most of the first generation of neurosurgeons got their training and experience at similar hospitals. They put me in another body cast for 6 weeks which again started under my armpits and included my right leg which was bent backwards 90 degrees at the knee, making it necessary to rest my foot that was in the cast on a chair beside my bed. It wasn't too bad once you got used to it until the 30 inches of sutures from the back of my knee to my waist started itching and I didn't have any way to scratch it.

The doctor told me I should be able to walk again but things weren't going to be the way they once were and I was going to have learn to walk all over again which would take both time and patience. He explained he had repaired everything, making it functional except the nerve, which controls feeling sensation and controls the muscles in the bottom of my foot and back of my leg. There were also some significant things that he should have told me, that should have been passed on along to neurologists and neurosurgeons that treated me in future years that would have been most helpful. When I finally got a copy of my military medical records more than 50 years later, it was too late to do anything about them. He was right when he said that when they take off my cast, I would soon be able to do what he called stumble around. If I am willing to devote the necessary time, effort and patience, learning how to walk without a pronounced limp, I should be able to do so. He explained that patients were often able to develop what he called a parasitic nerve, which was something like crossed wires on a telephone line, where one nerve can be trained to energize an adjacent muscle. In my case, the nerve that produces sideways or turning motion of the foot would also control downward motion of some of my toes. I decided if it could be done, I would do it. He told me that I would get a 30 day leave or furlough from the hospital as soon as I could walk well enough to get around while I was recovering from my surgery. There would be more treatments and other leaves until they were satisfied they had done everything they could do for me.

Although, my cast wouldn't be coming off for over a month, I was so enthused that I called the girl I had been engaged to for almost 2 years and asked her to come and see me. After a two day train ride from Minneapolis via Chicago, she waited in a block long, 6 foot wide waiting line to get into the huge hospital lobby, when they opened it up during visiting hours. The lobby was filled with patients in wheelchairs with no legs, others that couldn't move were, being pushed around on carts normally used to take patients to surgery and there was a menagerie of patients with parts of their arms, face or skull missing. All of them were waiting to see what normal people looked like and some of them may have been expecting visitors. When she came into my ward, she was sick to her stomach. She thought it was food poisoning but I was reasonably sure it was the sudden realization that there was a real war where so many young men were killed or maimed which people in Minneapolis weren't really aware of. After almost two years, I was happy to find that our relationship had not changed. Although I was a cautious person, so much had happened, I knew how fragile life really was and I wanted to get on with my life while I still had some left. We had time to talk about what life had in store for us and didn't neglect the obstacles we had to overcome. We decided to get married on my first 30 day leave after my cast was removed and I learned to walk well enough to get around. Wedding plans were somewhat complicated because her mother and her aunt that raised her from a baby hadn't spoken to each other since she started school. Her mother's Catholic priest intervened and a feud developed that destroyed both families and lasted a lifetime. There wasn't anybody that had any money to pay for a wedding. We decided to bypass all those problems by just getting married and visiting the family later.

Finally the day came when they cut off my cast, one piece at a time with what appeared to be a large pair of tin shears. I soon discovered after spending almost six months in bed and six weeks of that with my right leg being bent back 90 degrees at the knee, there was more to getting up and walking than just removing the cast. I tried to stand on one leg while holding on to the foot of the bed but just the weight of my skinny bent leg was unbearable because I couldn't straighten it out. Obviously, this business of walking was going to be far more difficult than I anticipated. In a week's time, I managed to get the leg straightened out and develop enough muscle to stand but not walk on crutches. Three more weeks went by before I could walk well enough to go on leave.

I stopped in Minneapolis to see my bride to-be, on my way home. Next week, we were going to be married but this week was for my family. My family and friends welcomed me and I was happy to see them after these most difficult two years. It was immediately apparent that this had also been a most difficult period for both my mother and dad as their health had deteriorated and they had aged many years. It comforted them just to know that I had come home which seemed unlikely only a few months ago. We spent most of the time just sitting around the house visiting. My mother's arthritis had gotten much worse and it was very difficult for her to push herself around the house in her wheelchair with the foot that was still somewhat usable. My father had lost a lot of weight and had difficulty trying to do less and less farm work. I told my parents that I could only stay for a week at this time. But after we were married and had the opportunity to visit Vi's family, we could be back and stay longer before I had to go back to the hospital.

One thing I had to do was try to breathe some life in my old 1934 Plymouth coupe that I abandoned as junk out behind the barn when I was drafted. Not having any priority, the ration board wouldn't consider allowing me to buy a new set of tires so I had to buy four recaps at $10.50 each, which was a lot of money to me at that time. The first one lasted 50 miles and the last one blew at 250 miles because the casings were either rotten or they capped over holes in the casings. Finally, I got a pair of recap truck tires with liners which were to big but usable, from my former boss and two more from a wartime farmer that had been blessed by the ration board with a new set of tires for his car. I bought the car in 1941 for $65 with money I earned in the North Dakota harvest fields. I had the crankshaft and bearings replaced once but remembered it was past due again. I couldn't have bought a car even if I had money, so I had to do what was necessary to keep it running.

The wedding wasn't exactly a gala affair but Vi had made the arrangements with a former pastor of her home church, who was then in Minneapolis. We were married in his church even though no one was there except my cousin and her husband that stood up with us. We visited Vi's relatives for a few days before going to Frederic where my church had an unexpected shower and reception for us. I had been active in the church and was president of the youth organization when I was a senior in high school. But hadn't seen or heard from anyone from the church all the time I was in the military service. It was nice to see my family and friends again and have them welcome my new bride. We were also grateful for all the gifts we received at a time when we had nothing. It was important that this special group that had played a special part in my life accepted her.

We went back to Battle Creek where we rented a one-room apartment on the third floor of a very old house with a kitchen just big enough for one person to stand for $50 a month. We shared a second floor bath with two apartments on that floor and a refrigerator located in the stairway between the two floors with one of the apartments on the second floor. When I wasn't at the hospital, we slept on a roll away bed that we set up in our one room which we called the living room every night. Vi got a job as a secretary to the doctor who was in charge of one of the locked mental wards at Ft. Custer Veteran's Hospital. She recorded all the patients' medical records and typed up all the doctors' periodic consultations with the patients on the ward. We made friends and had a limited social life provided it didn't cost very much. I was in and out of the hospital and at one time I actually got a job working in an electric motor overhaul shop. That ended abruptly after about three weeks when I burned my paralyzed foot against a heat radiator while I was laying on my cot at the Percy Jones Hospital Annex, where I had been transferred when I came back from leave.

My right leg was always cold because of poor circulation resulting from my femoral vein being cut and tied off so I lay down on my cot with my shoe on the end next to the steam heat radiator. Not having any feeling sensation in my foot, I didn't realize that I had burned my foot until I took my shoe off that night. My shoe was half full of water from a large blister on the sole of my foot that had broken without me even knowing it was there. I was in bed for more than two weeks with an infection they were not able to control and my leg swelled up like a balloon all the way to my hip. The doctor warned me that if they couldn't control the infection they would have to amputate my leg. After having several reoccurrences of a similar infection, I have since learned it is now called cellulite which is a very serious flesh eating disease that can now be controlled by a new type antibiotic if it is identified soon enough. If they are unable to control the disease, amputations are not uncommon. They put me in a paraplegic ward because it was the only bed patient ward at the annex where none of the patents were ambulatory. That was an experience in itself; because it is impossible to understand how those patients live or exist would probably be a better word, unless you have lived with them. Patients ranged from those that had their spinal cord severed in their neck that couldn't do anything but possibly turn their head to those whose spinal cord was severed somewhere in their back and were able to pull themselves up on a trapeze and swing around like a monkey. Those in the first category were completely helpless and slept on special beds where a new top with a thin mattress fastened on top of them could be turned over every three hours so they didn't get bed sores. I knew about bed sores because, I had a large one on the heel of my right foot from lying on my back in a cast for a long period of time. These patients were undoubtedly the most serious victims of the war because their mind worked normally and they knew what was going on but couldn't even end their own life if they wanted to. Those that had use of their hands and arms could swing themselves from their bed to a wheelchair and get around quite well in the hospital environment but undoubtedly would have trouble in the 1945 world which didn't have much concern for the disabled. I learned to understand the problems of the seriously disabled and realized how well off I really was.

As soon as I recovered from my burned foot and things seemed to be going well, we had more problems with our old car. The crankshaft had to be machined and the bearing replaced again but that wasn't the end of it. One of the pistons broke and made a hole through the cylinder wall, making it necessary to get the cylinder wall machined, a new sleeve installed and of course the piston had to be replaced. We scraped together every cent we had to pay for it but we were happy and I seemed to be recovering well. In fact, a couple days before Christmas 1945 we were homesick and decided to go home for Christmas. It was a very cold winter with lots of snow in Battle Creek and we had to get our car pulled to get it started that morning but we set out for Wisconsin. Even though I put a card in front of the radiator the heater didn't work and we almost froze. When we went through Madison, Wisconsin, U.S. highway 12 was covered with ice and we had trouble getting up a hill. When we stopped that night we almost froze because the cheap motel was so cold. Nevertheless, we were home for Christmas and it seemed important to me. I hadn't been home for two years and last year I was on the front lines, during the Battle of the Bulge. Also, I felt bad and almost guilty that my family had just received a postcard telling them that I was missing in action just before last Christmas. In spite of all the problems we had a nice trip, and under the same circumstances, I would do it again. In January we found that we were going to have an addition to our family. The little one would be welcome and we both knew that somehow everything would work out.

Jim Soures had been discharged from the Army and was now working at their family restaurant in Detroit. After some correspondence, I decided to spend a weekend with him in Detroit, which was only a two or three hour train trip from Battle Creek. My wife didn't want to go but she took me to the train station and Jim picked me up in Detroit. After all we had been through together; he seemed kind of like a stranger in this new environment. We had so much to talk about and yet we didn't feel comfortable talking about any of those things that troubled us both so much. We didn't stop at their restaurant on the way to his home because it was closed on Sunday. We just talked about trivial things as he drove to his home. It was somewhat awkward because although we were close buddies in what seemed like another world, neither of us wanted to even think about that. His house was like a huge mansion that reminded me of a castle, where his entire extended family, including, aunts, uncles and cousins all lived together. I slept in an extra twin bed in Jim's room with him across the hall from a huge dinning or banquet room. The dining room table was at least twenty feet long with so many people sitting around it for Sunday dinner; they had trouble squeezing in another chair for me. It was a sumptuous meal where they had everything you might expect at the most elegant banquet and one person more or less was of no consequence.

That night, we finally broke the ice and sat down together in Jim's room and talked about all the horrendous things we had been trying to forget. Jim initially was in the second squad of the second platoon in L Company and stood on my left side while Lou Stein, our first scout was the first man in our squad that stood on my right. We didn't talk about Lou's tragic death. Jim was an expert marksman and the Company Commander pulled him out of our squad to be his personal bodyguard as soon as we got in combat. Jim told me he was discharged at the time he was injured somewhere in Germany shortly before the war ended. I ask him what happened to Sergeant Dekman and Corporal Bell because I always felt quite close to them and they were the ones that carried me out of the woods the night I was wounded. He told me the night after I was wounded, they took a six man patrol out to see if they could find where the shelling came from the night before. They hit a trip wire about 200 feet in front of our machine gun emplacement where I was wounded that detonated a shell camouflaged in the big oak tree and all six of them were killed. Both of them were married and had a baby they had never seen in Minneapolis and it affected me deeply. He also told me that Sergeant Wood; Platoon Sergeant of our first platoon was among many that were killed the night I was wounded. That night, I remembered briefly, stopping to talk with him when I went back to get our first hot meal and commented, "That is quite a fortress you have here". He had dragged in every log he could find to cover his slit trench and it did look like a fortress. He had been a Staff Sergeant in Army

Air Corp supply and came into the aviation cadet program as an Aviation Student rather than an Aviation Cadet so he could retain his grade and not have to take a pay cut. He was married with two children in addition to a new baby he had never seen, so I could see his motivation for building a fortress. I told Jim, I saw our heavy weapons platoon Sergeant in a hospital in England but in addition to being seriously wounded, he appeared to be shell shocked. Even though it was apparent he knew who I was, he wouldn't talk to me. He was as surprised as I had been, because we all understood that everyone in his platoon had been killed in the massacre on the hill by the church. Between the two of us, the only survivors we could identify in L Company were he and I and the heavy weapons platoon Sgt. It was obvious that there would never be any thought of a reunion!

I was discharged from the hospital in at the end of May and the only thing we could do was move in with my family on the farm. Fortunately, Vi got along well with my mother and dad and we were happy even though I was preoccupied with getting a job. It wasn't easy as 12 million service men had just been discharged. Employment was not a problem for over 400,000 men that were killed but it was a serious problem for over 670,000 of us seriously wounded veterans that survived. The wartime economy had come to a halt when the factories that were making airplanes, ships, and tanks and guns shutdown to convert over to peacetime production. Our society had never accepted disability in the workplace and there wasn't any reason to change now when millions of healthy men were looking for jobs. Things were so bad I even made 3 trips to Chicago, which was my least favorite place to live in search of a job. I received $25 a week unemployment and $46 a month disability compensation from the Veterans Administration but I had no intention of trying to raise a family on that.

Much too every one's delight, our little girl arrived at the end of October and we called her Joy. Her grandfather thought she was the greatest thing on earth and dreaded the day when we would take her away. I was proud to have her baptized at the church where I had watched my father dig the basement, using horses and a scraper. A few days later the pastor hit me up on the street for a contribution. I simply told him, I didn't have anything to contribute and never went back to that church as long as he was pastor. Some years later, my church stock dropped even further when he was made a bishop. After all, where was the Church when I needed it? Probably the other small town pastors stayed home to politic the influential members of their community, during the war so they could become bishops rather than support the young men that were suffering or dying of wounds in the hellholes of the world. During my third trip to Chicago, I again stopped at the Regional Office of the Civil Aeronautics Administration looking for a job. The Chief of Electronic Maintenance opened a file drawer to show me my application was on top of the pile but he didn't know when or in which of the six states in the region that the next vacancy would occur. After those words of encouragement, he said because of my disability, I would have to sign an affidavit that I could do two things that that the job required:

1. In whatever state that I might be assigned, I would have to obtain an unrestricted driver's license that certifies that I can drive a car or a small truck without special equipment.
2. That I can climb 120 foot free standing radio towers to replace obstruction lights.

I signed the affidavit, not telling him I had reservations about the second one. I couldn't quite visualize how anyone could climb a 120-foot tower without feeling in his foot but if that was necessary, I would find a way to do it and I did.

III

CAREER DEVELOPMENT

CD-1 CINCINNATI, OHIO (MY FIRST JOB)

On January 7th, 1947, I started a new career in Cincinnati, Ohio but I had to leave my wife and baby daughter with my family in Wisconsin until I earned enough money to rent an apartment and pick them up. I only made $2644.80 a year before taxes and 7 1/2 % of that was taken out for retirement. The $46 a month disability compensation, I received from the Veterans Administration was helpful but all together it was hardly enough to survive. It was a month before I received my first check, which was just enough to pay back room and board at Mrs. Carter's place. She gave me credit because two of my coworkers were also staying there. It seemed like it would be a long time before I could save enough money to get another engine overhaul on my old 1934 Plymouth and rent an apartment so I would be able to pick up my family.

I started my new job at a defining point in history when civil aviation was new. Civil aviation, almost unheard of before the war was progressing with unprecedented speed, utilizing technology and equipment developed during the war. The Greater Cincinnati Airport, like so many WW II military airports all over the country became a civil aviation airport. Cincinnati, like Rome is the city of seven hills, just across the Ohio River from Covington, Kentucky. They had to go several miles beyond the city of Covington to find a location where they could build an airport on the flat land above the Ohio River Valley. Even though they had three bridges across the river, it was not readily accessible because they all crossed the river in the busy downtown area and it seemed like every spring the river flooded so you couldn't cross anyplace. The new airport terminal building with a state of the art air traffic control tower, communication station and weather bureau had just been completed. The week before I arrived, airline passenger and freight operations had moved from the little Sunken Lunken Airport, located in the Ohio River Valley near downtown Cincinnati to the new airport on January 1, 1947. We still maintained the control tower and some other equipment at the old airport for use by smaller private or corporate aircraft. The Ohio River flooded every spring, covering the entire airport with water rising up to the second floor, just six steps below the tower cab. That is where the airport's Sunken Lunken name came from.

The Greater Cincinnati Airport terminal building had all airport offices, communication station, weather bureau and our electronic/electromechanical office and workshop on the second floor. The control tower was above the second floor but elevators weren't considered necessary so we had to carry heavy test equipment up/down stairs. The airport was also equipped with the most modern communication, navigation and instrument landing system equipment with some navigation facilities being located as far as 50 miles from the airport. We also had an air traffic control center with an associated teletype communication station on the fourth floor of the Provident Bank building in downtown Cincinnati. I knew this would be an exciting place to work.

My boss, A. Stanley Kasper was a very distinguished looking man that always wore a starched white shirt and a black bow tie. He looked and acted like a dude, hardly the type of person that I expected would supervise a maintenance staff of four electronic technicians and a secretary. As it turned out, he was a good supervisor as well as a taskmaster. Technically, he was very capable but he didn't get his white shirt dirty unless he had to. I started as an apprentice so it was comforting to know that help was available when needed. Every time I called him, he came to my rescue regardless whether it was day or night.

The three journeymen level technicians weren't all that competent and like me, they hadn't had any specialized equipment training. Each of them worked 5 days a week, on a six-week rotating schedule. During this period every technician worked on every facility and every piece of equipment in it. Being an apprentice, I was assigned to work with each technician for 6 weeks, learning how to maintain all types of facilities and equipment. Although I was still a trainee, after this 18-week period I took my place along with the three journeyman technicians on the rotating watch list. It was a great training experience, where I learned each technician's techniques, making it possible for me to pick and choose what I considered the best each of them had to offer, in developing my own techniques. At that time, I was also assigned emergency duty every fourth week. We were required to take home the 1937 maintenance vehicle for emergency transportation. The technician on emergency duty was on call to make emergency repairs on any facility that failed, during the night or on weekends when other technicians were not on duty. It was very restrictive because you had to stay home waiting for telephone calls which averaged about three a week, some lasting all night. There wasn't any such thing as overtime, nor did you get time off for the extra hours you worked. It was all part of the job and I was delighted to have one, making it possible to support my family.

Emergency maintenance was extremely important because the navigation and communication facilities that we maintained made up the airways system, which were like highways in the sky between major U.S. cities. They not only provided guidance so airplanes could follow the airways, but essential air traffic control communication, delivering clearances required to maintain separation between aircraft so they didn't run into each other. If one of our facilities failed it was often necessary for an aircraft to land at some undesired out of the way destination or if they had enough fuel, fly hundreds of miles out of their way to get around the section of the airway that was no longer useable. Instrument landing systems were particularly critical because once an airliner arrived at its destination it was unable to land.

By this time, I had saved enough money to get my old Plymouth overhauled and rent a two room furnished apartment on the third floor of another old house. We had to go through another apartment to get to ours but it only cost $50 a month, which was all we could afford. I picked up my family on a 3-day weekend because I didn't have any leave and couldn't afford to lose a day's pay. It was a difficult 1600-mile round trip in the middle of winter, with an old car and a little baby. We made it back with everything we owned in the 1934 Plymouth coupe. I was happy to have a job so I could support my family and have a productive life because it was more than I had realistically expected. I looked forward to seeing my young daughter and her mother wave to me from the window of our third floor apartment when I came home from work each night. My evenings weren't all free because I was taking college courses at the University of Cincinnati a couple nights a week. I needed to supplement the college training I received at the University of Florida under the Aviation Cadet training program because the field of electronics was in its infancy and I had to be ready to grow with it.

My job was a temporary war service appointment but as a disabled veteran, I was entitled to take the civil service examination after six months. Passing this exam would lead to permanent status after an additional year's probation. Unfortunately, after I passed the examination, I had to spend a full year in the same position, which only paid 2644.80, before I could be promoted. Times were tough and recreation or entertainment was limited to a walk in the park overlooking the Ohio River or a trip to the free zoo, taking our daughter in her stroller. We never complained but we had been longing for an apartment where we had our own furniture and didn't have to go through someone else's apartment to get to our own. Our apartment was on Price Hill, just west of downtown Cincinnati, which was so steep they previously had a cable car from the city to the top of the hill. They were now erecting the first television tower in Cincinnati at that location, in the opposite corner of our block. The road that went by our apartment was on a very steep grade, going down the hill to the road that runs along the north side of the Ohio River. The park where we spent many hours on nights when it was too hot to sleep was at the bottom of this hill, overlooking the river.

The job was going well even though I had early indications of pending health problems. I was having more lower back pain and occasional reoccurring hepatitis attacks where I became very ill in less than an hour's time. Finally not knowing what to do, I went into the Cincinnati Veterans Administration Regional Office, which was, near our air traffic control center in downtown Cincinnati and asked for their advice. This was before the massive network of Veterans Hospital was up and running and it happened that there were three Veterans Administration doctors stationed there. The team of three doctors gave me a comprehensive orthopedic/ neurological examination, which determined that the extent of my war injuries was considerably worse than previously known. The permanent damage to my right foot/leg was severe enough that I was classified as having lost the use of my right foot. This is equivalent to having my leg amputated and having to use prosthesis. This new classification increased my disability compensation; retroactive to the time I was discharged from military service. The additional money made it possible to buy enough basic furniture and rent a three-room apartment in another old house. Also, unknown to me at that time, the loss of use of my foot classification also made me eligible for a $1600 grant toward the purchase of a new car. Although used cars were still hard to get at that time; I was lucky to sell my old Plymouth for $25. The new furniture, apartment and car were a terrific moral builder for my family and me but there was no denying that I had medical problems I didn't know how to deal with. Our new apartment was on the first floor in Ludlow, Kentucky that was across the river from our old apartment but much closer to the airport. After my required additional year of probation, I got permanent civil service status and a couple promotions in a relatively short time, putting me in the same pay grade as my boss, by the time I left. They were opening up new stations all over the country and wanted to send me to Chicago Heights, which was a hot spot in the airway's system at that time. After working in Chicago a few months before the war, the word Chicago turned me off and I accepted a position at Redwood Falls, Minnesota.

CD-2 REDWOOD FALLS, MN

I opened a new airways technical field office in Redwood Falls on July 1st 1949, where the Civil Aviation Administration also opening a new airways communication station with a staff of five. I was the chief of a new technical field office headquartered at that same location, which reported directly to the regional office in Kansas City that covered 13 states. At age 26, I was the youngest of 70 sector managers in the region. Setting up a new office and workshop for this new field office was a challenging job. I was the only technician in the field office, which maintained two airway communication stations and a variety of air navigation facilities within a 50 miles radius. The first year was particularly difficult because of inherent problems with newly installed equipment and deterioration of other facilities I inherited that had not been adequately maintained. It was extremely important to keep all equipment in the best possible condition to minimize failures. I alone was on call to make emergency repairs anytime during the day or night seven days a week. Again, I didn't get overtime or even time off for the time I spent on emergency calls but I could adjust my work schedule to some extent to accommodate my health problems. As long as I kept things shipshape and had a minimum number of facility failures, the regional office didn't complain. I had to schedule my vacations carefully because the regional office had to send in a relief technician when I went on leave or had to go to the hospital. Moving to a new location involved more than problems directly related to the job. Housing was a problem everywhere after WW II and it was especially bad in small rural cities like Redwood Falls. After living in a small apartment, which was half of the main floor of a house, we were fortunate enough to rent an old farmhouse on the edge of town. About a year later our daughter, Joy who was almost four got a baby sister, that we called Jackie. This emphasized our need for better housing but there just weren't any houses for sale and if there had been we wouldn't have had enough money to make a down payment. Finally, we bought the first lot in a new undeveloped addition and against my wife's better judgment; I decided to build our house myself, more or less one board at a time as we got a few extra dollars. Since I wasn't an established carpenter, banks wouldn't give me a loan without security and I didn't have anyone to cosign my loan. It was a slow process because during the next couple years, I had to attend specialized electronic equipment courses for 5 months in Oklahoma City, where civil aviation had their technical school. In reality, this probably expedited completion of our house because I was able to save enough on per diem while I was attending school to buy more boards sooner. I also saved considerable money by buying birch and oak lumber back home in Wisconsin and having it made up into trim and flooring. Working evenings until long after dark, weekends and vacations, it took almost three years to finish the house so we could move in and we would complete the breezeway and garage the next year. The people I worked with helped generously and about the time our house was finished, new houses were springing up all around us. We had our pick of all the lots and ended up with the best lot in the new subdivision. Living through the Great Depression, I was apprehensive of long-term debts, even if I could have gotten a 30-year loan. My health problems cast a long shadow on how long I could be productive enough to adequately support my family. My father worked hard all his life and was never able to pay off his farm mortgage. My mother became an invalid in midlife and we lived in poverty from one bank note to the next. Sometimes, this is unavoidable but if possible, I wanted to do all I could, while I could, to spare my family what my parents went through.

By 1954 my chronic hepatitis problem had deteriorated to the point Dr. Flynn, my local physician arranged to have me admitted to the Veterans Hospital in Sioux Falls, South Dakota. My eyes and skin turned yellow in less than a half hour and I was very ill, vomiting green bile. In most cases, he had to come out to my house and give me an injection so I could stop vomiting. He told me he didn't understand my case and just didn't know how to treat me. This created somewhat of a problem, being the only technician in Redwood Falls it meant my Regional Office had to assign a relief technician for an undetermined period of time. I was released from the hospital after two weeks, not knowing any more than when I was admitted. The old Veterans Administration doctor speculated that either I had imaginary or marital problems. I knew that neither was the case and this was the first of many instances that caused me to lose all faith in the Veterans Administration Medical System. Regardless of this, I was called in for further evaluation about two months later. Although they still didn't find anything, having to bring in a relief technician again cast further doubt on my fitness to hold this particular job.

Reluctantly, Dr. Flynn give me some powerful medication, I could take with me and administer myself when and where such an attack occurred. I would have to lie down where ever I could and sleep for a couple hours before I could drive a car or continue what I had been doing. The attacks came less and less frequent and finally stopped altogether about ten years after I had a severe case of hepatitis in the Army hospital in England. I wasn't aware of any permanent liver damage, caused by this almost fatal hepatitis B attack until I had a comprehensive preoperative physical examination before my second spinal surgery in 1990. At that time they found my liver was grossly enlarged but was apparently functioning normal.

Redwood Falls was an ideal place to live and raise a family. People were friendly in this small town atmosphere and they had an excellent school system. As a government employee, I didn't have any intention of getting involved in local civic affairs. Nevertheless, I woke up one day realizing that I had been elected President of the Redwood Falls Junior Chamber of Commerce. After that, it seemed like my phone never stopped ringing. That year we joined the other civic organizations in starting the Minnesota Inventors Congress, moving the Railroad Depot from North Redwood to the county fairgrounds in Redwood Falls and establishing a nonprofit organization called Redwood TV Improvement Corp. The Minnesota Inventers Congress turned out to be a very successful organization that brought inventors together with companies that may be interesting in manufacturing their product. Now, almost 50 years later it is still a successful nationally recognized organization.

The North Redwood Railroad Depot was the home of Sears Roebuck & Co. While Sears was the depot agent there he started sending out flyers, which soon became catalogs, selling watches and other items by mail order. This was the initial stage in establishing the huge national mail order company. When the railroad lines were discontinued in the early 1950's, the North Redwood Depot located 3 miles from Redwood County Fairgrounds was given to the county to be used as a historical museum. The depot was not actually moved until after I left in 1960 but all the money for the project was raised by civic organizations in Redwood Falls rather than state or federal grants. Unfortunately, this historic building burned a few years after it was moved and restored.

Redwood Falls is located in an area where Minneapolis television reception is extremely poor. The city council was approached by a company that wanted to install cable TV in the portions of the city where it would be economically feasible, at a cost of something in excess of $1,000,000. They were enthused with the idea and called the head of all the civic organizations together to meet with the company representatives. After they explained their proposition to us, I asked one question, "What would be the difference in cost between your proposed cable system and a translator system (which is a rebroadcast system)?" Obviously, it was an unwelcome question, but they admitted a translator system would only cost about half as much but there wasn't any way to finance such a system. A few days later the city council again called us all in but this time it was to meet with a company that sells and installs translator systems. They quoted us a rough estimate of $35,000 to install a system that would rebroadcast four Minneapolis channels, not just to the city of Redwood Falls but also to some of the rural community as well. From then on it was full speed ahead. The city council and their legal staff decided we could finance the system by selling $50 shares of stock in a nonprofit organization. Dick Wilding, a former Green Bay Packer and I were designated to sell the project to the community. The local newspaper gave us good publicity and we were called on to talk to almost every church and civic group within 20 miles of our proposed station. The entire community was enthused and wanted to get on the band wagon. I already had a FCC license and was able to obtain a license for four translator stations and construction of our 450-foot tower got underway without delay. The system was very successful and some small towns behind the broadcast tower not covered by our radiation pattern went out and raised another $100,000 to increase the power and expand the coverage area. Now, over 45 years later, they have installed a cable system in the more populated part of the city utilizing TV signals from the tower we installed. The original system is still used by those that don't subscribe to cable in the city and those in the rural community. The cable company provides free Minneapolis television programming for the translators in return for antenna space on the 450-foot tower.

Every year after we finished building our house, we took a good family vacation, going to an exciting new place every year. We went to such places as the Black Hills, Yellowstone, Estes Park and Dallas where the entire family could explore these exciting places together for a couple weeks. It was nice to get away from day to day activities and be alone with my family.

I liked my job, the community and my family was very content in Redwood Falls. Our house was just two blocks from the community swimming pool and one block from the athletic field that I flooded every winter to make a skating rink. Every winter, our house was like a community-warming house for our girls and all their friends. The kitchen floor was piled with skates, snow suits and boots while the two different age groups of girls played in the basement and combination living/family room. Yet, I had to sit down and have a long talk with myself. I was 37 years old, had already turned down several real good jobs at other locations, and with rapidly advancing technology, I probably wouldn't be able to continue doing what I was presently doing the rest of my life even if I wanted to. Life was good, we had so many friends, my daughters were doing well in school and I hated to move. Yet, I wasn't making enough money to pay for college and eventually two weddings. My deteriorating health problems also made it more urgent to be in a location where medical assistance was more readily available. Without a doubt, I was going to have to take a hard look at any new jobs that might come up.

CD-3 MINNEAPOLIS, MN DISTRICT & AREA OFFICES

In the summer of 1960, just 11 years after I arrived in Redwood Falls, a new position opened up in the Minneapolis District Office. I had already declined an assistant chief position in another district office when these positions were first established a few years earlier. More recently, I had also declined an exciting position in the Kansas City Regional Office as well as a similar engineering position in this same office. Already, many technicians I had trained had moved up where they were now my bosses. At age 37, I felt that this could very well be my last chance for advancement and accepted the position.

It was a summer of turmoil, selling our house, buying one in Minneapolis and getting our family moved while I was trying to perform the duties of my new job. Fortunately, we were able to buy a new house for about the same amount of money we had received for the one we sold in Redwood Falls. We bought our house in Richfield, a southern suburb because it was both close to work and had one of the best school systems in the Minneapolis area. It was an easy adjustment for our youngest daughter, going into fifth grade that fall but it was difficult for our older daughter going into ninth grade. She went from a school with about 100 students in the graduating class to one with 800.

Once the family was settled, I was able to get on with my job in earnest. It was a small district that supervised and provided technical assistance to several field offices or sectors as they were called in Minnesota, part of Wisconsin and Iowa. Not being a graduate engineer, I was hired as an engineering technician, who was one pay grade lower than an engineer. If I were able to establish professional engineering status, I would automatically be promoted because I had been hired as an engineering technician, in lieu of an engineer, which the position called for. There were two positions of this type in this office, the other being filled by a graduate engineer at a higher pay grade.

It was exciting work because every day we were challenged by problems on old and new state of the art electronic navigation, communication and air traffic control facilities and equipment. Although, performing technical evaluations was our primary job, we spent most of our time solving technical problems throughout the district. It was important to keep all facilities operating as much as possible in order to guide aircraft and keep them separated so they didn't run into each other. The navigation aids provided radio beams like highways in the sky to guide aircraft flying on instruments from one destination to another. When a navigation aid fails on any airway, it is like closing an interstate highway making it necessary to reroute aircraft flying on that airway. It was a challenge to keep these unreliable, 1940 vintage, tube type facilities operating and we made an all-out effort to assist our field office technicians in event of major breakdowns.

I had hoped to be able to take some night courses at the University of Minnesota but it wasn't possible because of so much unscheduled travel throughout the district. It was becoming apparent that somehow I was going to have to achieve engineering status, not just to progress but to hold my present position. Fortunately, at that time there was a shortage of engineers and they came up with a method for people like me to achieve full engineering status. Anyone that could document an established combination of education and experience would be permitted to take the national, "Engineer in Training Examination". This examination utilized by states, gave graduates from accredited engineering colleges, the opportunity to establish engineer status in their state. It obviously was a long-term goal because I had a lot of studying to do before I would be able to take such an examination. The examination would be given in two parts by the Civil Service Commission: The first 4 hours, given in the morning covered higher mathematics and all the engineering principles covered in a four year college engineering course. The second 4 hours, given in the afternoon of the same day was exclusively on your engineering specialty, which would be electronics, in my case. If you didn't pass the first part, they didn't even grade the second part.

Although, I had years of studying to do before I dared to even attempted to take the examination, I started putting a portfolio together. I validated the formal college credits acquired at the University of Florida, during my aviation cadet training and night courses at the University of Cincinnati. All told, this was less than two years college but it was weighted heavily in physics, science and mathematics. I also started a file on the high profile engineering projects that I had worked on and made provisions to add future projects. There wasn't a study guide for the examination, making it necessary to purchase study guides for mathematics and all the basic engineering disciplines involved. I set aside a room in the basement as a study and established a disciplined study program, studying a few hours each night. If I was traveling, I took a study guide with me. After 2-1/2 years, I had met all the qualifications and actually took the examination. I failed the examination but learned more about what I needed to study and passed it on my next opportunity six months later.

Much was happening during these three years and there was more to do than study for an examination. Until this time, all equipment design was based on radio tube type technology, but now transistors and computers were coming into use and we had to learn a whole new technology. This required formal specialized training at Palo Alto, Ca. and Philadelphia, Pa. My first major project was in connection with the relocation and establishment of the new Minneapolis Air Route Traffic Control Center (ARTCC). This was one of 20 being established to control all instrument air traffic between airports in the continental United States. I was involved with the communications network, used by air traffic controllers to talk directly with aircraft, utilizing automated remote communication stations along thousands of miles of airways. Having maintained one of these remote communication stations at Redwood Falls, I was already familiar with the remote facilities. This was around the time when President Kennedy was on the verge of an atomic war with Russia, making it necessary to install a secure coded telex system between Washington Headquarters and all 20 ARTCC facilities. The U.S. military provided special training and CRYPTO security clearances for everyone that had access to the new secure communication system. Air traffic controllers also had access to radar displays so they could see the location, altitude and identification of aircraft along the airways they were controlling. The most difficult part of my job was coordinating the transfer of telephone lines with the local telephone company, from the old control point at the Minneapolis airport to the new facility about 20 miles to the south, keeping both in operation during the transition.

Perhaps my most challenging job was during President Kennedy's Cuban Missile Crisis. The Duluth, Minnesota airport was a military airport, which was shared with civil aviation. The instrument landing system (ILS) originally installed by the military had been turned over to civil aviation but was still essential to the military. An ILS primarily consists of two principal facilities, the localizer and the glide slope. The localizer provides a radio beam down the center of the runway that an aircraft can fly in on from approximately 20 miles from the airport. The glide slope produces another radio beam from a point on the localizer beam about 1000 feet above the ground a few miles out to the touchdown point at the approach end of the runway. The two beams and a couple markers make up a system to guide aircraft to the touchdown point on the runway during instrument weather conditions. Geographically, the terrain at this airport doesn't meet established criteria for a conventional glide slope, because of rising terrain beyond the approach end of the runway.

The glide slope had never functioned properly but the Air Force made it a crisis during President Kennedy's Cuban Missile Crisis. I worked with Federal Aviation Administration (FAA) research and development engineers and a consultant from Ohio State University, who were trying to develop a new design for a glide slope that would function in this environment. About the time winter set in, it appeared they had succeeded but the complex monitor system they designed was not reliable enough to use. They all left for the Christmas/New Year's holidays and they no sooner had gotten out of town than the system failed again. Needless to say, I spent the entire holiday season in Duluth. One night between Christmas and New Year's, during a terrible blizzard, I was sitting out in the middle of the airport in the little glide slope building trying to decide what to do next. Periodically, the air traffic controller on duty in the control tower called me on the intercom to see if I was still there and was all right.

I had been working with some of the best engineers in the country and fully understood the design of the new glide slope as well as the reason why their design for their prototype monitor system would never be reliable. I started from scratch, trying to design a new monitor system, adapting and piecing together a variety of concepts, used on other types of facilities that I was familiar with. This glide slope had been a research and development facility for months, leaving miscellaneous unused parts lying around the building, which were immediately available. During the night, I assembled what appeared to be the portion of a workable prototype that was located inside the building. During the wee hours of the morning, I called the controller in the tower cab, telling him I was coming in and to watch for my car lights coming down the runway. I ventured out in the blinding blizzard, hitting the hard packed snow drifts that had piled up across the otherwise bare runway with enough speed that I could make it through.

By the next day the blizzard had subsided and it was a very cold, 20 degree below zero, calm day. I removed the two lower antennas from the lower 30 feet of the antenna tower taking them inside the building where it was warm enough to work on them. I installed a small loop in each antenna that I had designed specifically for this purpose and put the antennas back up in their original position on the tower. Once I installed the required connecting cables to complete the installation and made the necessary adjustments the monitor system functioned as I had anticipated. Certifying any navigation aid and an instrument landing system in particular is very complex because the consequences of even a minor error can result in a catastrophic aircraft accident. Certification of a new experimental facility is far more complex because it is necessary to fully document that the monitor system will respond to every conceivable unsafe condition and shut the facility down so an aircraft cannot use it when it is unsafe. I painstakingly made a record of all monitor parameters and left the facility operating on a test basis even though it could not be used because the monitor system had not been officially certified. The next day the facility was still performing as it was left but I again rechecked all the monitor parameters. Satisfied that it was functioning properly, I caught a plane back to Minneapolis, just in time for New Year's Eve. I was unable to contact the Washington engineers that I worked with because they were still on their Christmas/New Year's holiday.

I filed a detailed engineering report, providing design, construction and performance data. When the Washington engineering staff returned after the holidays, they approved full unrestricted use of the glide slope, using my new prototype monitor subject only to the standard flight check, which is always required. Federal government employees cannot patent anything they develop but I did get an $800 employee suggestion award. I'm sure they were disappointed because the consulting engineer from the University of Ohio, brother-in-law of FAA's Chief of Research and Development could have patented the new monitor system. The new type "capture effect" glide slope, utilizing my monitor system soon became an international standard, used extensively at sites where less complex facilities would not function because of the terrain.

Organizationally, it seemed like we were always in a state of flux. The Kansas City regional office cut the number of district offices in half, doubling the size of our district to include all of Wisconsin, Upper Michigan and more of Iowa. I was then the navigation aids program engineer and had another engineering technician to assist me.

During the first week after taking over this additional territory, we had a major failure at a Marquette, Michigan facility, which as usual happened on a Friday. I had never been to Marquette or even seen a Doppler Visual Omni-Directional Range (DVOR), which at that time was one of two in existence. One of our flight inspection aircraft that was there on a routine inspection found the facility didn't meet standards and shut it down. I caught North Central Airlines DC-3 to Green Bay Wisconsin that went north along Lake Michigan to Marquette. The ceiling was low and the winds were strong, making it the roughest flight, I was ever on. As we were landing at Marquette, our flight inspection aircraft, also a DC-3, was parked on the ramp with its engines running. Apparently they were waiting for me to arrive so I could press some magic button to fix the problem. The local technician took me out to the facility located on the airport to get my first look at a DVOR. When I looked inside the building at this strange unfamiliar facility, immediately I knew that I was in trouble. Obviously, it was going to take a lot of studying to see how this strange facility was supposed to operate before I could determine what was wrong, let alone fix it. I told the flight inspection crew that it would take some time and they just as well return to Battle Creek, Michigan. I would call them when we were ready for another flight check

The local technician hadn't had any formal training in this type facility but he had managed to maintain it for some time and could tell me what it as supposed to do and to some extent how it did it. Obviously, if he had understood how the facility was supposed to function, he would have been able to determine what was wrong and repair it. If that was the case I would be spending a leisurely weekend at home with my family. He gave me a short course on what the thing was supposed to do, and showed me where to find the technical manuals and gave me a truck for transportation. I excused the technician until Monday to give me the opportunity to read the directives and become familiar with the facility. I worked at the facility late into the night, becoming familiar with this strange equipment and understanding how the overall facility was supposed to function. By Monday morning when the local technician returned, I had identified several potential problems. Going over them with the technician, we determined what had always been that way and what hadn't. A week later, we were ready for another flight inspection and we must have done the right things because everything was all right. What I learned on this project turned out to be very valuable at a later date. I never dreamed 12 years later, I would be a FAA Headquarters, Branch Chief, supervising the team of engineers that designed a new type of DVOR power distributor, the principle component of this type facility.

My daughters were growing up and were preoccupied by school activities but we still took time for a good family vacation every summer. We bought a boat that we could tow behind our car to the many lakes in the Minnesota area. Both girls got to be expert water skiers and we went out to Lake Minnetonka a few nights a week, after I got home from work. We got so proficient; we could navigate around the huge lake, through the many bays and channels at night, using a spotlight to identify the buoys. In later years we took our family vacation every summer at a lake in northern Minnesota. There was also modeling school for both girls and we were very proud when our oldest daughter was one of the top five contestants in the Miss Minneapolis contest which is one of the major pageants in the Miss America pageant. Later, we were very proud when our other daughter was the only majorette in the Richfield High School marching band. It was quite an honor to lead the very professional marching band in this school with 1200 students in her graduating class.

During these five years, I was having more and more pain and paralysis in my left leg, which was particularly troubling, because the back half of my right leg was permanently paralyzed. By 1962, I was going to the Veterans Hospital Outpatient Clinic near my office for treatments but the problem kept getting worse. Finally in 1963, I had lost all the feeling sensation in my left leg and they had me admitted to the VA Hospital. It was a bad experience. I didn't see a doctor for a week after I was admitted and after a migraine, two weeks later, I went home with such a bad headache that I couldn't hold my head up. Two weeks later, I went back to work but my activities were limited until I was admitted to a private hospital for emergency spinal surgery in July 1965. Surgery was very successful and I was able to go back to work.

By this time, I had passed the engineer in training examination, qualifying me for promotion to the engineering position; I had been filling as an engineering technician for a couple years. Unfortunately, all promotions were on hold because of another pending reorganization. The Kansas City Region was consolidating three district offices like mine into an Area Office so they would be eliminating two of the three positions like mine. The one that already had his engineering status in the higher grade was selected for the new position and I was caught in a situation where it was unlikely there would be much chance for advancement in the foreseeable future. I was counting on this promotion because with a growing family and I already had college expenses and there would be much more to come. I had encouraged and assured my daughters that they would get a four-year college education if they so desired. I knew from experience that a college degree would have made my life much easier and would do anything possible to give my daughters such an opportunity. Also, my family had been deprived of too much for too long and after I passed that examination, I expected to be able to make up for it.

Tan Son Nhut Control Tower
Mortar destroyed office/maintenance shop at
base of Tower

New Tower Building

One of many 4 prop jet aircraft destroyed in their flight line bunkers
when VC captured part of Tan Son Nhut during the TET Offensive

Civil Aviation Electromechanical Workshop Hit by Mortar

You can see the anxiety on the face of some of our CAAG Group as they
watched Saigon burn from the roof of our building

Quin Nhon Extended Range Communication Facility that
opened the Saigon/Taiwan Airway and had longer range
coverage than any in the world.

IV

THE VIETNAM WAR

VN-1 THE VIETNAMESE ADVENTURE

In 1964, President Johnson created a phony incident, alleging North Vietnam had attacked an American ship in the Gulf of Tonkin. He deliberately lied to Congress, resulting in them passing the Gulf of Tonkin Resolution. This gave him the authority to escalate the scope of Kennedy's limited war into a major international conflict. By the summer of 1967, Johnson decided to send 500,000 U.S. military troops to Vietnam in order to get Kennedy's war over in a hurry. South Korea and Australia supplied a few military troops while, the Philippines and Taiwan provided other support. With the exception of Australia, the U.S. paid all the costs, one way or another.

Unlike previous wars, there were thousands of U.S. civilians working alongside of our military and the government of South Vietnam, providing direct support to our military. Civil support was provided primarily through the U.S. Agency for International Development (USAID), other U.S. Government Agencies, U.S. contractors and contract personnel from other countries, all paid by the United States. On the civilian side, the U.S. provided assistance in everything from rice farming to commercial aviation. With President Johnson's escalation of the war, the technical assistance program became so integrated with the military assistance program; they were one of the same. Finally, on July 1, 1967 the U.S. Military took over funding for all activities, including those that were administered by USAID. I was one of thousands of additional U.S. civilians that were sent to Vietnam at that time.

The Federal Aviation Agency (FAA), one of the participating agencies was assigned responsibility for all air traffic control activities in Vietnam. This included all air navigation, communication and radar facilities in Vietnam as well as radio and sea cable links with surrounding countries. Under an agreement with USAID, FAA already had some personnel in country, providing technical assistance to the Vietnamese Department of Civil Aviation. Now, FAA was also responsible for controlling military aircraft and only American FAA personnel were allowed to do that.

In June 1967, FAA started recruiting to fill a combination of about 25 additional engineer, technician and air traffic controller positions. With those already in the country, this would increase our Civil Aviation Assistance Group (CAAG) staff to 50 Americans. A tour of duty was 1-1/2 years but since married employees couldn't take their family with them, they got a three week family visitation in the U.S. every 4 months. Those that arrived before July first when the military took control of the program could bring their family to Manila or Bangkok, which they called safe haven posts. This made it possible for those working in Vietnam to visit their families more often. In my case, I would also get a promotion and 25% hazardous duty pay. At first, I thought, no way. My youngest daughter would be a high school senior in the fall and I certainly didn't want to miss that. Then, I had to remind myself that she would be going to college the following year which was expensive and that would be the reason for going in the first place. I knew my wife could manage because we had a strong marriage and had made lots of sacrifices in the past. My oldest daughter had just started work as a flight attendant for American Airlines and was now on her own. I thought about it for several days before I even mentioned it to my wife. After a few days discussion, we thought we could work it out but needed to find out what our daughters thought about it. We had a family conference, discussing the pros and cons and even though none of us were thrilled about it, no one could come up with a compelling reason why I shouldn't bid on the job. From my position, there were three basic reasons for considering this position:

1. It involved a promotion plus 25% hazardous duty pay and we needed the money.
2. Career enhancement became important when I failed to get a promotion during the recent reorganization.
3. I always felt guilty, surviving WW II on three separate occasions when the odds were overwhelming and so few of my buddies

survived. I vehemently disagreed with Presidents Kennedy and Johnson getting us involved in this war, but I wouldn't be going out of respect for them but to help as many young American youth as possible survive. I felt I had the necessary skills to accomplish that.

I wasn't comfortable with John F. Kennedy and hadn't voted for anyone during the presidential election. While I was trying to decide who the worst of the two evils was, I was assigned to computer school in Palo Alto, Ca. at the last minute and didn't have the opportunity to vote for anyone. Kennedy was elected by overwhelming support of the Catholic Church and his father's bootlegging fortune, accumulated during the probation period. Joe Kennedy was one of the shadiest characters in U.S. politics. He was notorious both as Al Capone's East Coast Mafia counterpart and President Roosevelt's controversial Ambassador to England during WW II. The only difference between Joseph Kennedy and Al Capone was that Joe had enough political friends in high places to protect him from income tax evasion, keeping him out of jail and unlike Al Capone; none of his mistresses gave him syphilis.

Jack Kennedy's lack of leadership initially became apparent by the type of people he appointed as key members of his cabinet. McNamara, Kennedy's Secretary of Defense was solely an academic, without any real life experience who as a youth was one of several TV Whiz Kids. They were given problems on a TV show, which they solved with lightning speed, indicating it was a fraud because they obviously already knew both the question and the answer. Bundy, his Secretary of State never impressed anyone with either his intellect or ability. His brother, Bobby who he made Attorney General was an arrogant know-it-all, whose primary claim to fame was his ability to keep the women on his brother's campaign staff sexually pacified in the notorious Kennedy style. He accepted Vice President Johnson as his running mate, only because he had to carry the state of Texas to be elected. Johnson like Truman was kept totally ignorant of administration policy.

Kennedy's inexperienced, infallible, know it all team made one decision after another that had serious negative impact on the U.S. Almost immediately, he withdrew promised air support from the Cubans when they tried to take back their country. Those that hit the beach at the Bay of Pigs invasion were either killed or captured because unknown to them, Kennedy withdrew air support at the last minute. Once Castro had secured Cuba, the Russians moved in, setting up atomic missiles aimed at the U.S. mainland, less than 100 miles away. This major confrontation almost resulted in an atomic war with Russia. We had to make major concessions, removing our missiles from Turkey in order to defuse the rapidly escalating probability of an all-out nuclear war.

VN-2 ARRIVAL IN VIETNAM

We were met at Tan Son Nhut Airport by a number of people that we would be working with but Ed Vie, who I would share an apartment with, was the one I remembered best. Ed was the only airport engineer in our CAAG group. I had never met Ed even though we had both worked out of offices in the old Minneapolis Airport Terminal Building. We had many things in common because we knew many of the same people and had worked at the same airports that fell under the jurisdiction of the Minneapolis Area Office. Unlike the rest of our group, I was filling the position vacated by an electronic engineer who had completed his tour of duty and returned to the U.S. A. The apartment he previously shared with Ed had been reserved for me. Ed, having been in Vietnam for almost a year, was on a two-year tour of duty, making it possible for him to have his family in Manila. When the military started funding the entire Vietnam program, tours of duty were reduced from 2 to 1-1/2 years but dependents were no longer allowed to live in nearby safe haven posts like Manila or Bangkok. Instead, those of us with families got a ticket to go home and visit our family in the U.S. for about 3 weeks every 4 months.

Ed had acquired the use of a WW II jeep from the Vietnamese Directorate that he worked with. Used jeeps that had been stored in Belgium warehouses since WW II were shipped to Vietnam for general use. Although, there apparently weren't any spare parts or mechanics that knew how to install them, most of them were still usable. After I cleared customs and got my luggage, Ed took me to our apartment near the Imperial Palace that was several miles from the airport, near downtown Saigon. Although I was exhausted and confused from jet lag on this sultry afternoon, the trip down town was like entering a New World. The little people looked so much alike and their features were so strange, I could not recognize one from another. The strange buildings or storefronts with their pull down metal curtains, like you see in downtown Chicago alluded to security problems. The hot humid air had the aroma of decaying garbage.

We had a very nice apartment on the second floor of a small modern apartment building located across the street from what had once been a beautiful park, which had fallen into hard times. It was a rather large apartment with a combination dinning/living room, a kitchen in the center and a bedroom and bath on each end. We had a Vietnamese man and his wife as our cook and maid. They had previously worked for the French, and he was a pretty good cook. It was a nice place to live, but it was far from work and the traffic was horrendous. Traffic consisted of bicycles, motorcycles, scooters and cars, all with undisciplined drivers that disregarded traffic rules, if they had such a thing. The other members of our group were not so lucky, as they had been put up in French villas all around Saigon. Tensions were high with 4 to 6 men sharing a villa, there was considerable discontent. The next day, Ed took me out to our CAAG office at Tan Son Nhut airport located a few feet from the perimeter fence of MACV, often referred to as the Pentagon East. Our office building appeared to be long and narrow but once you got inside, it was not as long as it appeared from the outside and was very narrow. The CAAG Chief, a former Navy Captain had the only private office and everyone else was in the large room that made up the remainder of building. It was so crowded; desks were arranged on both sides of the building, with two people facing each other with the ends of their desks against the outside wall. In order to make room for those of us that just arrived that would also be working in the office, it was necessary to add additional desks in the center aisle on one side of the building. The back of these extra desks butted against the ends of the two desks facing each other. As a latecomer, I inherited a desk in the narrow center aisle and had to move every time someone went down the aisle to the rest room.

I met my new boss, a tall well-built, low-key man who was previously stationed in Panama for quite some time. Our mission had changed since his arrival and his primary objective was to finish his 1-1/2 year tour and get back to his wife and twin daughters in Panama. He assigned our new supervisory technician from the Washington Office to supervise ongoing maintenance activities. We had a number of technicians standing watches, maintaining equipment at the Saigon Air Route Traffic Control Center (ARTCC) and others that provided technical support for Vietnamese technicians maintaining navigation, communication and other facilities throughout the country. We also maintained direct radio or sea cable point-to-point voice and telex circuits with Manila, Hong Kong,

Singapore and Bangkok that were used for air traffic control purposes. Although the military maintained separation from other aircraft during air strikes, we assumed control as soon as they dropped their armament. At that time, Tan Son Nhut Airport had more landings and takeoffs than any airport in the world. It was a complex mixture of American air carriers bringing in men and equipment, military cargo planes, fighter aircraft on air strike missions and both international and domestic air carriers. American controllers controlled all traffic between airports and Vietnamese controllers at all airport traffic.

My job was programming, planning and installing new facilities as well as upgrading existing facilities. This required close coordination with the Vietnamese government, Department of Civil Aviation. A couple weeks later, a Bird Colonel and a Lt. Colonel showed up, joining us in that little building to make sure our military funded group was giving military requirements the necessary priority. Every day, the Col came back from his early morning MACV briefing with a list of the facilities that was either inoperative or not performing properly. Vietnamese technicians in remote parts of the country maintained most of these facilities, where Americans weren't allowed to go. Considerable coordination and follow-up was required with those remote facilities that were difficult or sometimes impossible to contact. All contacts had to be made by point-to-point radio. Sometimes we had to go out in nomad's land where Americans were not allowed to help them out.

During my first week on the job, W.W. Christine, our CAAG Chief who I had not formally met as yet, waddled down the crowded aisle, putting a stack of papers about 8 inches high on my desk and said, "I would like for you to take care of the program". Without any discussion, he made his way back down the crowded aisle to his office. I didn't have any idea what the program consisted of or what purpose it served. I still didn't understand what is was all about after I went through the massive pile of paper. I did recognize it was a massive project that had already missed the June 30 deadline by over two weeks. That night after dinner, I sat down with Ed in our apartment to learn what he knew about the program. He told me he had provided input to the airport portion of the program the previous year and might be able to help me some. He explained the program was in fact the entire CAAG budget that had to be backed up by programs, justifying all our requirements. In other words, it was an outline of all the programs, equipment and personnel requirements that were necessary to accomplish the CAAG mission and coming up with a dollar amount, which would be the CAAG budget. Obviously, I had to first learn what we were supposed to accomplish what if anything we had on hand and start from there. It was going to be a difficult job and time was not on my side.

VN-3 THE 1968 CAAG PROGRAM

I had done some budget work back in the Regional Office and understood that the budget which was already 2 weeks overdue had to be supported by projects you planned to accomplish and at this point I didn't even know what was required. First, I had to learn what we were supposed to accomplish and I hadn't even got out of the office yet. At this point, all I knew was there was 25 new FAA people on the plane that I arrived on. Ed, the man I shared an apartment with unlike the rest of us worked with the Directive of Air Bases, knew what his mission was. I talked with my boss, Chief of the Electronics Branch who considered up until that time, that maintenance of air traffic control equipment at the air traffic control center was our reason for being there. Now that we had significantly increased the size of our electronic group, he didn't know what we were supposed to do with the extra people. My predecessor, who had already been gone for three months, prepared last year's budget. That apparently was not based on existing programs but an informal off the top of his head, dollar estimate. My boss really didn't understand what I was talking about nor did he have any idea where I might locate information on any projects. He was aware that we had a warehouse full of equipment that some predecessor had ordered but didn't have any idea what is was or what project if any that it was intended for. The CAAG Chief thought they had submitted a budget last year, but perhaps they were late and just sent in a dollar estimate.

I found Mr. Dao, a Vietnamese in our office who I had not even been introduced to, was in charge of the CAAG warehouse, which I didn't know existed. And had a list of what was in the warehouse. It seemed that I was Mr. Dao's supervisor or at least he thought I was and it turned out that was more or less the case. Mr. Dao and I got a car and driver to take us to the nearby warehouse so I could survey the situation, giving me a better idea of what we had to work with. The warehouse was a building roughly 25 by 40 feet with a perimeter fence about 8-feet high approximately 20-feet from the building. The area between the building and the fence was piled high with large cable reels and goodness knows what, making it impossible to walk around the building without climbing over all this material. The inside of the warehouse was much the same, making it impossible to identify any of the equipment on Mr. Dao's list. I examined the list of equipment that was supposed to be in the warehouse to determine what we may be able to use in the near term as well as future projects. The next day, Dao got some laborers, located specific pieces of equipment that I wanted to look at and had them moved to the front of the building so I could examine them to determine if it was something that we could use. This to a large extent would determine the makeup of our new program. My supervisor hadn't established any relationship with the Vietnamese Department of Civil Aviation (DCA), which under the U.S. Aid (USAID) program we were supposed to be assisting rather than replacing. I ask Mr. Dao whom I should contact at DCA and he told me Mr. Peterson, my predecessor used to work with Mr. Quong and Mr. Lang. We only had a couple telephones in our office and there were several different phone systems in Saigon, making it practically impossible to dial from one system to another. I didn't know where the DCA office was so I got a car and driver and just went down to meet them. The huge, almost empty office was on the second floor of an old building about half way between the airport and Saigon. Mr. Quong, my counterpart was not in the office but Mr. Lang was happy to meet me. He was a short man about 2-1/2 feet wide and I was happy to find he spoke excellent English. He told me Quong and his wife had a pharmacy in Saigon so he wasn't at the office very much but he would probably be able to help me. I soon learned that Ouong was the boss because he had 4-years of college in France, making him an engineer whereas the rest of them had only 2-years technical college in France. In the French system, the man with most degrees is always the boss. Those that pledged their allegiance to the Catholic Church got four years of college but the Buddhists only received two. It was apparent why the Catholics that came down from the north in 1954 held all the high-level government positions.

I tried to explain to Lang that we had to come up with a list of projects that we needed to accomplish next year, determine what type equipment would be needed, prepare plans, schedules and determine the costs so we could prepare a budget. He had a vague recollection that CAAG had some equipment in their warehouse but didn't know how or where it was supposed to be used. I told him, I would do some preliminary work and we could work out the details together. Unfortunately, even though we were under time restraints, I couldn't even talk to him about the budget until we had identified what projects were required and determined how much of the required equipment we had on hand.

About that time, an U.S. Air Force Bird Colonel and a Lt. Colonel moved in our CAAG office, which was now funded by the U.S. military. They wanted to make sure we provide the necessary support to carry out their military mission. We pushed the desks even closer together, crowding them into our small building along with everyone else. They arrived at the time President Johnson was introducing an additional half million military troops in Vietnam and air traffic control system improvements were their highest priority. The sudden influx of air traffic on the airway across the South China Sea from Taiwan to Vietnam resulted in long delays. There was a vast area where aircraft could not communicate with either Saigon or Taipei control centers, making it necessary to use time separation that significantly reduces the number of aircraft that could use the airway. This delayed President Johnson's rapid buildup of military troops and war material that was brought in by U.S. commercial aircraft. Saigon would be the busiest airport in the world for the following 2 years.

American air traffic controllers also alerted me to what they considered was a serious problem. The Saigon Control Center was using an inadequate locally fabricated radio control system, which they weren't familiar with. Some years ago, USAID contracted with Western Electric to install their WE-301 telephone key system, similar to the ones they installed and maintained at all U.S. Air Route Traffic Control Centers (ARTCC). The system was somewhat complex and had never been used because it wasn't interfaced with the ARTCC radio circuits. Obviously, the Western Electric installer or the FAA technicians that were there at that time didn't know how to interface the two systems. Although both systems were electronic, box numbers rather than schematic drawings, which electronic technicians understand were used to identify telephone systems black boxes. Telephone system black boxes are connected together by the numbers with other boxes in that same system without any knowledge of what is inside. Electronic technicians have to know what is inside the box in order to interface it with a system that is not compatible with that particular telephone system. Two of our best technicians were assigned the time consuming laborious task, of disassembling one of each type of the telephone black boxes. They traced the circuits and made a schematic drawing of it so electronic technicians could see how it is supposed to function. Once we had the schematic drawings, we were able to interface the two systems so it was similar to the U.S. ARTCC systems that controllers were familiar with. Unlike most projects identified for future installations, we had the resources to accomplish this immediately.

We also ran into another troubling air traffic control problem for which we didn't have any solution. Each ARTCC position had an electric clock and the accuracy was dependent on the frequency of electric power. We used base power and the speed of the generators at the power plant varied constantly as the power load changed. Since the frequency of the power determines the accuracy of electric clocks, they were not accurate enough for air traffic control purposes where a few seconds error is unacceptable and it was impossible to maintain accurate time. I was looking through a magazine one night and saw a clock advertised that used two flashlight batteries. It claimed to have the accuracy we required. The next morning I sent a cable to our Washington support office, requesting they purchase such a clock for us and send it to us as soon as possible. This inexpensive clock did everything the advertisement said it would and the air traffic controllers were fully satisfied with it. This technology, which was new at that time, is now commonly used for wristwatches and wall clocks.

Once we had identified a number of urgent projects and prepared an abbreviated program, we were able to get started on the budget. It was complex because we 50 Americans were paid by our FAA Regional Offices and FAA Washington received 10% in addition to that for administrative and technical support. We also had a contract with the Taiwan Telephone Company for the services of five of their engineers and technicians. In addition to this, we had what they called Direct Hire agreements with about 15 Filipino technicians and a local hire agreement to fund a host of Vietnamese that ranged all the way from typists to translators. It was over a 5 million dollar budget but soon found that was just a number because any time the Colonel decided he wanted to add something like a two million dollar radar, no questions were asked. The military had a big piggy bank with deep pockets and nobody was concerned about money. In fact, there was discussion at budget meeting; regarding the more we spent the more prestigious we were.

The United States was the leader in civil aviation which was in its infancy after WW II and in order to further develop the technology and create a market for our aircraft the USAID program established a Civil Aviation

Assistance Groups (CAAG) in many Third World countries. When the North Vietnamese defeated the French Foreign Legion at Dien Bien Phu in 1954, the French left the country in shambles and most of those with French passports went back to France. USAID sent in a few advisers whose number kept growing as conditions kept deteriorating. Finally, by the time the French abandoned it completely and we got involved militarily, we had become the doers rather than the advisors. By the time President Johnson got approval for his Gulf of Tonkin Resolution, permitting him to send in a half a million military troops CAAG was actually running the entire aviation program, both civil and military.

The 50-member American CAAG group was a very unusual group, coming from all over the U.S. meeting each other for the first time in Vietnam. The group consisted of a GS-16, CAAG Chief, who was a retired Navy Captain that had all the political skills it takes to get promoted to such a position. He played tennis with the Chief of USAID for a few hours every day but usually got back to the office by quitting time. He was assigned a car and driver that picked him up in the morning, drove him anywhere he wanted to go, during the day or evening, waited for him and finally, taking him home at night. We also had an Airport Engineer, Airport Terminal Traffic Control Chief and an Air Route Traffic Control Center Chief. Our terminal control chief only had two American advisors because all airport terminal traffic was actually controlled by Vietnamese controllers. Our air route chief supervised the American controllers that actually controlled all civil and military traffic in Vietnam airspace, which reached out from Saigon to Taiwan, Hong Kong, Manila, Singapore and Bangkok. I was Chief of the Electronic Branch, which usually had about 25 American technicians and the same number of Taiwanese and Filipino technicians.

The electronics branch which was the largest group had two supervisory electronic technicians: One supervised the technicians that actually maintained all the equipment used by American controllers at the Saigon Control Center and trained or assisted Vietnamese technicians that maintained other Tan Son Nhut Airport facilities. The other supervisor was responsible for new installations and made major repairs to facilities outside of the Saigon area. This had been my position when I first arrived before I replaced my supervisor who was Chief of the Electronics Branch, before he left a few months later. We also had one electromechanical technician that tried to keep the country that was powered by engine generators operating. They supplied power to operate practically all the facilities in Vietnam as the Viet Cong had managed to disable most of their commercial power systems. When you consider that all of these men were volunteers, selected by our Washington staff, solely on the basis of their qualifications for jobs in a war zone where they had to be away from their family, they were an outstanding crew. Generally, they were men that had worked in various places, doing different things and could adapt to almost any job they were assigned. None of them were advocates of the Vietnam War but most were military veterans of previous wars and like me were concerned about helping as many of our military people come back home as possible. Also, none of us had much money and it came at a time in our life when we needed more money to support a growing family. Since everyone got a promotion and 25% hazardous duty pay increase, it offered enough of an incentive to justify the risk of living and working under adverse conditions in a war zone. It was surprising how well everyone got along together under such difficult circumstances. We were always under a curfew, which varied from 6 to 10 PM, depending on the security situation at the time, with artillery fire within a few miles almost every night. The night sky was lighted up with flares bright as day for more than a month during the Tet Offensive. In the 3-1/2 years I was there, only 2 of my men left before their 1-1/2 year tour of duty was completed. One left because his wife had emotional problems back home and the other was a Japanese technician from San Francisco who was harassed by the U.S. Military because they thought he was Vietnamese.

Sadly, one of our Filipino technicians was killed when he fell from a 150-foot radio antenna mast. He was installing a new antenna for our Saigon/Bangkok radio telex circuit when a U.S. Army truck ran into one of the guide wires supporting the 150 foot tower that was pulled down. His wife and family lived in the Philippines and his body was transported back home on an U.S. military plane escorted by his American CAAG supervisor.

The Vietnam War started about the same time as the feminist revolution and the abandonment of traditional morals in the U. S. so it was not surprising that most of the Americans were divorced. Housewives sat around the house all day watching soap operas on TV that glorified the working women that were having exciting affairs at the office and belittled those that were home raising their children. They couldn't resist getting a piece of this exciting life, making husbands and sometimes children a burden that got in their way. Divorce was the solution of choice because in addition to freedom, they got child support, alimony and with birth control pills readily available, they were truly liberated. In Vietnam, men not only got away from the feminist movement but also earned the additional money needed to support their former wives who were having a ball at their expense. In many cases, American men took a Vietnamese wife with them when they returned to the U.S.

We also had eight or ten Vietnamese in our office staff, who would probably fall into the typist rather than secretary classification because their English language capability was limited. I was always suspicious that one of the typists was a VC spy but wasn't concerned because we didn't have any secret information or weren't involved in any classified activities. It was kind of like an inefficient typist pool where letters had to be corrected and retyped several times. Our American administrative assistant supervised the Vietnamese clerical staff and our translator. We also had an excellent Vietnamese warehouse man that did a remarkable job of keeping track of what commodities we had in the warehouse. The warehouse man and two engineering draftsmen worked for me. Both the draftsmen (a man and woman) were less than 4 feet tall and the woman probably didn't weigh 80 pounds but they were both very professional. The man could do the most professional 3 color overlay drawings I have ever seen. He was also an artist and I met his artist friends that painted most of the pictures that venders sold in downtown Saigon. The woman was married, past middle age and had a son about 18 years old. The two draftsmen prepared the engineering drawings for all our new installations in Vietnam.

It would also be an understatement to say that we didn't have some problems. Because of the lack of supervision, the technicians that had been there for some time before I arrived had more or less established their own rules and work habits. Although our radar technicians at the control center had little to do except being there in case they were needed, they had refused to do anything else. That is, they would be there in event one of the three radar displays failed, which was very seldom because it was state of the art solid-state equipment and if one did fail they could get by with two for a short period of time. Although only one was scheduled to work at a time, they got into the habit of logging in on duty when they didn't have anything else to do. This not only gave them someone to talk to but also allowed them to collect considerable overtime for what was supposed to be their time off. One of our first orders of business was to put a stop to these abuses and assign them additional duties. This included taking care of the communication equipment, which was located in the same room where their radar equipment was located. There was some complaining at first, but they realized all the time that they were getting away with something they shouldn't.

VN-4 SAIGON TOURIST

We worked eight hours a day, Monday through Friday but days were quite long because we had a two-hour break during the middle of the day. This was the traditional siesta period commonly observed, during the heat of the day in most countries with a hot humid climate. Both sides interrupted even the war during this period. We had air conditioning both in our apartment and office but the Vietnamese people didn't. In fact, they didn't like air conditioning because they caught cold, coming into air-conditioned buildings from the outside. We only worked four hours on Saturday but started an hour later so there wasn't much afternoon left by the time we fought the heavy traffic from the airport to Saigon. With the 10 PM curfew, Saturday afternoon was primarily a time to take a nap and rest up from a stressful week.

Although Ed and I had spent most weekends during the last month working on the CAAG budget, we usually walked downtown to the center of the city to eat at the International House on Saturday night. It was an International Club frequented primarily by Americans because we were most of the foreign civilians in the country. It was a good place to eat and get a drink in the type of environment we were used to. Also, they usually had a band for entertainment.

The tree-lined road went through the park across the street from our apartment to the center of the city. The once elaborate park had obviously fallen on bad times, years ago because what appeared to have been lily ponds had crumbled into disrepair. Some of them still had water trickling through the crumbled ruins as if over the years, no one had bothered to shut off the water. There were always small groups of four or five naked boys about six years old splashing around in the little pools about three inches deep. Sunday morning the park with lush green grass was filled with groups of Boy Scouts or Cub Scouts in small groups of five or six with their scoutmaster. Each group sat in a circle around their troop flagpole with their banner on top that identified their little group. It was heartening to see the pride these children had in belonging to their group and the respect they showed for their scoutmaster. Most of them probably didn't have a father and if they did he was undoubtedly in military service

As we walked down the sidewalk toward the center of the city, older women were squatting on the sidewalks telling fortunes with a deck of cards or ancient fortune telling sticks. If a woman had a headache or perhaps some other medical ailment, another woman used two coins, which she held between her thumb and index finger to continuously pinch a spot on another woman's neck until it became red. When you saw a woman with a red welt on her neck, you knew she recently had a treatment to cure whatever ailed her. When we approached the center of the city, the entire sidewalk was covered by some kind of a cloth or canvas canopy. This protected them or their wares that they were selling from the hot sun or the rain as the case may be, because it seemed like it was always one or the other. You could buy almost anything if you looked long enough but always had to bargain for anything you bought. At first, it was somewhat of a mystery how so many items that were seldom in stock at the Base Exchange (BX) could be so abundant at the sidewalk market. The sidewalk market resembled our flea market, except for the fact that most items were still in their original unopened cartons. Also, when these scarce items were in stock at the Base Exchange they were usually far more expensive.

Never having been exposed to a society that was so openly corrupt, it was hard to comprehend a society where open corruption was the way of life. Ocean going ships docked in the port at Saigon, bringing in all types of electronic goods from Japan were being unloaded from both sides. Most of the material unloaded on the dockside of the ship probably went to the BX. All the material unloaded over the other side of the ship into small boats in the water below, undoubtedly was sold on the black market. Obviously it not only a Vietnamese operation because it was carried out openly in broad daylight, every day of the week under the watchful eyes of American supervisors. Like so many things about the Vietnam War, it was unreal to see so much expensive state of the art equipment still in its original carton, for sale far below cost a block or two off Saigon's main street.

Even in the midst of the war, Saigon, the city the French called the Paris of the Orient was still a beautiful city. The wide streets, interrupted every few blocks by a traffic circle were well maintained with a statue in the center of each circle. The old French hotels had all been taken over by the U.S. military or used as housing for American civilians. High woven wire fence, extending out from above the second floor windows down to the center of the sidewalk protected them so terrorists couldn't drive by and throw a bomb into the building. They also had a sandbag wall on the outside of the fence for further protection. The Caravel Hotel which was perhaps the most luxurious was headquarters for the international press. They all lived there with their Vietnamese girlfriends and spent most of their time in the elaborate open-air lounge that covered the entire top floor which was actually the roof of the building. Potted trees and umbrellas shaded them from the tropical sun and sudden rain showers. Unlike Ernie Pyle, the distinguished WW II reporter, Vietnam era reporters didn't go out to the battlefields in search of war stories. In fact, the primary news story of the Vietnam War was that so little happened. In reality, there wasn't such thing as a WW II or Korean War type battlefield. When editors back home pushed their reporters for a news story, reporters tried to find a deserter who had wandered into off limits Saigon to scare up a cock and bull story. The American Press Corp was one of the many disgraces of the Vietnam War.

Watching people in Saigon was one of my favorite Sunday pastimes. There were few cars but the wide streets were filled with bicycles, 50cc Honda motorcycles and little blue French taxis. Sunday was definitely family's day out and it was common to see the husband, wife and from one to three children on a single bicycle or motorcycle. The women dressed in their bright colored traditional dress, called Ao Dai balanced one or two small children on her lap. She balanced herself and the children on the frame of a bicycle with both legs dangling down on one side without even holding on. Their dress with a high tightly fitting neck, long sleeves and skirt slit from her ankles to her waist on each side was worn over a pair of white satin slacks. They also wore high-heeled shoes, which had the upper part of the shoe missing from her arch back to her heel. The heel of the shoe, which was held on only by her toes just, skimmed the surface of the road, leaving a space between the arch of her foot and the sole of her shoe. This was quite a balancing act with a couple children sitting on her lap.

We walked by the Imperial Palace, which was on our street as we went back to our apartment. The palace with bright red trim was in the center of a block surrounded by a well-kept garden enclosed by a wrought iron fence. The two guards in bright colored uniforms that guarded the entrance were pleased when I took their picture. Across the street from the palace entrance was a small park, which had been occupied by a small group of Buddhist monks for several months. There were perhaps eight monks sitting in a circle in the shade of a grove of trees, where they had been peacefully protesting the Catholic controlled government in this overwhelming Buddhist country. There were perhaps 50 people standing around the perimeter of their circle just watching them sitting there doing nothing. There were also several reporters from the international press, taking pictures of them. I couldn't believe how rude they were, crawling around in the center of the monk's circle, taking pictures with their cameras right in front of their face. It seemed this demonstration started a few months earlier when several monks drenched themselves with gasoline and burned themselves to death in downtown Saigon.

VN-5 HEW HOUSING

There were also minor housing and transportation problems that developed during the first few months we were there. Because of the rapid buildup of American personnel, we had more people than housing. With four or five men sharing an old French villa, where they had to share a cook and maids, there wasn't any privacy and they got in each other's hair. This problem cleared up after about six months when they completed complexes of two room apartments so everyone had their own little apartment. When I arrived in Vietnam in June 1967, I was very fortunate to be able to share one of the best apartments in Saigon with Ed Vie our Airport Engineer. Our apartment was within a block of both USAID buildings where most of the USAID personnel worked before the big military buildup. When President Johnson lied to Congress about an alleged attack on an American ship in the Gulf of Tonkin, they authorized him to expand military forces in Vietnam to half a million men. Thousands of additional American civilians and third country nationals, working under an alleged USAID program, funded by the US Military, also came in to support the expanded war effort. This created an acute housing shortage but fortunately, Ed and the man I replaced were USAID employees that were there before the military buildup and had good housing. Before the military got involved, their family was allowed to reside in places like Manila or Bangkok which were safe haven residences close enough so they could visit their family more often. That was no longer the case when the military took over and paid for the entire operation with military funds. The other 24 members of the group that I arrived with were housed four or five men in villas spread all over Saigon. At best, it was a stressful environment and tempers flared. Our office was at the airport, just outside of the MACV Compound, known as the Pentagon East and traffic was so bad it was almost impossible to get to work. On the other hand, those that worked at either of the USAID buildings near downtown Saigon lived in hotel rooms far from work and had very poor accommodations.

I had only been there for a couple months when I heard about a massive building program, which was intended to alleviate the American civilian housing problem. They were building a couple of walled in American apartment complexes out near the airport and all of us civil aviation personnel would live in these compounds. I watched them build the larger of the two apartment complexes and had the opportunity to select my future apartment long before it was completed. Everyone would have their own apartment and by getting my name in early; I was able to select a corner unit on what they called the sixth floor. Ed decided to move into another complex but I chose this one because most Federal Aviation people worked shifts and living there would simplify the transportation problem. The complex consisted of two identical, end to end mirror image buildings that were quite large by Vietnam standards. It was surrounded by a cement block wall about 8 feet high. You entered the compound from a busy city street through a gate with an adjacent guardhouse where unarmed Vietnamese civilian guards checked passes. There was a parking area between the gate and the end of the first building with a narrow driveway between the wall and side of the first building to a small area near the entrance of the two buildings where you could pick up and drop off people. Except for a small entry area, where the Vietnamese concierge (a French word for one that has charge of the entrance to a building) had a small table and a telephone, the entire ground floor was for parking bicycles, scooters and small motorcycles. The reinforced concrete buildings had 7 floors of about twenty, 2 room apartments, each with a tiny kitchen and bathroom. The entire 9th floor was a large party room and there was a very large concrete water tank on one end of the flat roof to store up water when it was available. I selected a sixth floor, front corner apartment next to the elevator on front of the first building, where I could look down on the entry area and at the end of the other building. There was an outside walkway, like a deck about 4 feet wide from the hall by the elevator that continued around the end and the full length of the front side of the building, on each floor. It was quite a masterpiece for construction workers that had to mix all the cement by hand and pull it up on a rope, one bucket at a time. Commercial power was unreliable and voltage regulation was so poor it burned out electrical appliances in Saigon. Fortunately, they provided a diesel power plant to furnish power for the complex so we had reliable power.

When I returned to Saigon from home leave in November, everyone was all excited about the coming move that they expected would take place about the first of January. One day the concierge at the building where I was living asked me if needed a maid for my new apartment. He said that if I did, the niece of one of the caretakers of our present building was looking for a job. I had never thought about that because I had been more or less sheltered from problems of that type because Ed was an old hand at that sort of thing and we had a well-established smooth operating arrangement where we were. The man and his wife who were our cook and maid left a list of what we should purchase at the commissary each week and we give them some money to make additional local purchases. Meals were always ready, our clothes were washed, the apartment was clean and the beds were made. I had never thought about hiring a maid but after thinking about it for some time, it was obvious that I would need a maid. Since I didn't have any other leads, I told the concierge to have both his building employee and his niece come and see me and we would talk about it. I was disappointed to find that neither of them could speak any English but I soon learned that with the recent influx of Americans, it was extremely unlikely that I could find an English-speaking maid. I told the concierge, who was translating for us that we wouldn't be moving for over a month but I would keep her in mind. The first of the year, just before we moved in, the concierge from our old building was transferred to our new building complex. Not having any other prospects, I told him I would give her a job when I moved in and see how it works out. At least he could translate and if any problems developed he had contact with her uncle who was also an employee of his employer.

Those of us that never lived in the Third World had always thought of maids being a luxury for the affluent and never envisioned needing one.

You soon find out things are different in the Third World, where they don't have washing machines and have to wash clothes in the shower because their isn't even a bath tub. Also, there are lots of clothes to wash because in the hot humid climate you probably have to change clothes 3 times a day and of course it is almost impossible to dry them in the humid air. I planned on making my own breakfast and eating my evening meal at an officer's club. I did like to have a bowl or soup or something light at my apartment for lunch so I could relax a little before I had to fight the traffic back to work. Although, I would have to buy what I could at the commissary, it wasn't very close and I had to go during lunch period at noon rather than eat lunch. No matter what you did, it was necessary to buy many of the necessary things at the local market which was a very time consuming job. It was practically impossible to work under these adverse conditions and also be without a maid. Usually a maid worked for two or even three people in different apartments but at least initially, my new inexperienced maid that couldn't speak any English would only be working for me. If you had to tell her something, you left a message and she would get someone that could speak English to translate it. I suspect being a translator was probably the best paying job in our new apartment complex.

This would be my first Chinese New Year or Tet as they call it in Vietnam and it was interesting to see everyone painting their houses and fences, getting ready for this festive holiday which was like our Christmas and New Year's put together. It is a time to visit family and friends, the first day being reserved only for family and special friends in accordance with an ancient protocol. If a Vietnamese family visits you on the first day of Tet you know they consider you a special friend. We moved in a couple weeks before Tet, at which time I found I had to buy drapes for the three large windows in my new corner apartment. I had to order the drapes and a matching bedspread, paying for them when they were delivered. This meant that I would have to keep $300 to $400 on had that was reserved for that purpose. Since I didn't want to carry it around in my pocket, I put it in an envelope in the bottom of a dresser drawer so it would be available when I needed it. The maid usually arrived in the morning after I left for work but stayed until after 6 PM when I got home. About two weeks after she started working, I came home and she was gone. Immediately, I found the money was missing and went directly down to the concierge's office and told him what happened.

VN-6 VIETNAM JUSTICE SYSTEM

During the next week, I got a close up and personal education in the Vietnamese justice system. Immediately, the concierge called his supervisor and told him what happened. After the conversation with his supervisor, he told me, don't worry because if she doesn't pay the money back her uncle will have to because he recommended her and of course his job is at stake. That night, after the concierge, the maid's uncle and their company boss had a meeting they came by and told me they would pick me up in the morning. The next morning the three of them picked me up in a van with a driver and we drove over to where the maid lived with her family. It was a long distance to what appeared to be a remote rural suburb of Saigon and I couldn't understand how she could get to and from work. Finally, we stopped in front of a building where there were several houses in a row, connected to each other on the end under a common roof with woven wire fencing across the front so you could look into what we would consider the living rooms of all the houses. The living rooms on front of all the houses were separated up above the second floor loft with the same type fence that was across the front of the building. The maid's uncle, who lived next to her house, noted that there wasn't anyone home at her house, unlocked the padlock on his house and went in. He went up in the loft and climbed over the top of the fence between the two houses and went down into her living room where he took a picture of her off a table, climbed back over the top and gave me her picture. I don't understand why he did that but I still have her picture. It was apparent that she hadn't returned home the previous night. I didn't understand what all was happening but they took me back to my apartment and told me they would get back to me later.

A couple of days later, the concierge told me I had to be at a nearby police station the next morning at a specified time. I met the concierge and the maid's uncle at what appeared to be not only a police station but some kind of a jail. They had outside high wire pens where they kept prisoners waiting to have a hearing before what appeared to be a combination lawyer and judge. My maid's uncle had evidently reported her to the police as he was the one held responsible for her theft and they had evidently picked her up and she was being held in one of the high wire pens in the police compound. They called the three of us into a fairly large room with many small round tables like a restaurant and seated the three of us around a table. The judge joined us and soon they brought my maid in and we all sat down around this small round table. It was all in Vietnamese so I could only speculate what was going on but the judge apparently had been well briefed and understood the problem. There seemed to be some type of a confrontation about her identification card as the judge was vigorously questioning her about it, finally reaching across the table and slapping her right across her mouth. He turned to me and said that she has been using her sister's identification card, which he was holding in his hand and keeps lying about it. They took her away and we all departed. As I was leaving the police station, her sister who spoke some English approached me and asked me if I would drop charges against her so she could be released. I told her, I would if she gave back what money she hadn't spent. Her older sister and brother, a military man, was also there and both seemed to be real nice people that were concerned about their little sister. That was the last time I ever saw any of them because it was just before the Chinese New Year and the Tet Offensive intervened leaving the country in complete chaos. My Vietnamese friends had an interesting reaction to the picture her uncle gave me. Every one of them told me you could tell by the look in her eyes that she is no good. Since that time, I have taken special notice of people's eyes and have learned they have a special perception that I am just starting to learn.

VN-7 TET OFFENSIVE

We were all looking forward to the Tet that we had heard so much about and were looking forward to the festivities. It is a gala event that consolidates most of our customs for both Christmas and New Year's into one major event with a massive fireworks display. That evening we went up on the roof of our apartment building where we would be able to better observe the massive fireworks display over the entire city. The sky was continuously lit up, with every conceivable type of fireworks until long after midnight when we give up and went to bed. After all, tomorrow was another workday for us.

The next morning when I got ready to go to work and went down to the parking area, I found that the Viet Cong or VC as they were called had started a major offensive the night before under the cover of the usual Tet fireworks. We wouldn't be going to work for some time because the streets were still littered with dead bodies, there were plumes of smoke coming up from burning buildings all over the city and flights of helicopters were everywhere. Some were individual gunships firing rockets at ground targets but most were flights of several helicopters bringing in American infantry from our big US infantry base at Long Bien to hot spots around the city. The attack was a complete surprise that caught the military as well as the rest of us completely off guard. Armed Forces Radio at Tan Son Nhut Airport was still on the air but they didn't know much more about what was going on than we did. We did learn that the VC had occupied half the airport runway and fighter planes were taking off from one end of the runway while the VC occupied the other end. We had immediate concern because we had American air traffic controllers and at least one electronic technician stranded at the airport that didn't have anything to eat and didn't know how or when they could be rescued. In the meantime, we still had electric power and were living comfortably so like most of the others, I went up on the roof of our building and used up all the film I had taking pictures of the plumes of smoke rising up from buildings all over the city. I also took pictures of the helicopter gunships that were both close and clear enough so you could see the rockets, leaving their rocket launchers as well as where they hit. With military help, the following day we were able to relieve our people at the airport. We hadn't been able to communicate with them because the single telephone in our apartment complex disappeared when the Vietnamese concierge left for home the previous night. We probably couldn't have gotten through to them anyway, because there were several different telephone systems in Saigon and it was almost impossible to call from one to another.

With the exception of the second night, it was a wait and see rather than a stressful period. The second night about the time I went to sleep there was a knock on my door. It was the building warden that had the apartment next to mine wanting to know if I had a weapon. I told him, I didn't but why did he ask. He told me he had been notified that there was intelligence information that there may be a raid on our building complex that night. There wasn't any raid but it was hard to go back to sleep after that. The next night they brought in a few military guards but our building complex was never attacked. We were not able to leave the compound for over a week except in convoy to escort our shift workers to and from the airport about once a day. About the third day, the electric power plant for our complex ran out of diesel and shut down. All our refrigerators defrosted and we had to eat everything in them or it would spoil overnight. Air conditioners, water heaters and the water pump that filled the big tank on the roof were also inoperative. The military provided C-Rations for the next couple weeks until security improved enough so we could get out and purchase some food at the commissary and they could deliver diesel for our power plant.

Information started to trickle in from the Armed Forces Radio and military groups that occasionally stopped by. Someone had observed that there had been a huge number of funerals, during the last month. Investigating, they found the coffins had been filled with arms and ammunition rather than dead bodies, which had been buried in very shallow graves in cemeteries, located in key areas so they were readily accessible for the Tet Offensive. Also, at midnight one night, I heard a loud explosion not far from the front of our building. I jumped out of bed just in time to see some mortar explosion that lighted up the area. It came from the second floor balcony of a school building about 200 yards away. They shot 12 mortars in the direction of Tan Son Nhut Airport. The two-story school building was built without an interior stairway to conserve classroom space but had an outdoor stairway on each side leading up to a deck like structure where the doors leading to the classrooms were located. They actually fired the rockets from the second floor deck. The next morning when I got up the police had all the people in the tangled neighborhood lined up in the small schoolyard, which didn't have any road or street wide enough for a car. In reality, someone from outside the area probably brought the in the mortars, fired them and left. It is practically impossible to determine which side of the war anyone was on because those that picked up the guns left at the cemetery were likely someone's good neighbors during the day. People weren't unhappy with their neighbors but rather the Catholic government forced on them against their will after they defeated the French forces in 1954. At dusk the military started dropping flares from high altitude, keeping the entire area lit up, bright as day. The city of Saigon was lit up like the battlefields of Europe during WW II where it was daylight 24 hrs a day. There was a 24-hour a day curfew for the first week and from 6PM to 6AM for months.

Finally, the airport was opened up to more than limited military traffic and we were able to get to work repairing damage to our airport facilities. The instrument landing system located in what was the middle of the airport battlefield had been damaged extensively but fortunately most of it was from small arms fire that did more damage to the buildings than the equipment and it was operational in a short period of time. It seemed that this was only the beginning of the problems because frequent mortar attacks on the airport continued to do extensive damage. One night, a mortar made a direct hit on the Airport Managers office and the technician's workshop, which was at the base of the air traffic control tower. The demolished building included the classroom used by one of our technicians that was teaching classes to Vietnamese technicians. Fortunately, there was little damage to the attached control tower. The military had built large bunkers along the flight line near the control tower so a direct mortar hit that destroyed an aircraft in one bunker would protect the aircraft in the adjacent bunkers. Every aircraft in the many protective bunkers had been rendered totally useless by explosives detonated in the cockpit area of every aircraft. These explosives had obviously been placed in this position and detonated by the VC Troops that overran the airport during the first night of the Tet Offensive. I had free access to the flight line and was able to take pictures of all the aircraft destroyed in the bunkers along the flight line. The U.S. Air Force never admitted the tremendous number of aircraft destroyed on the ground, during the Tet Offensive.

The Tet Offensive was a real wake up call for the U.S. military. Before the offensive they had been giving the news media optimistic assessments of their progress in pacifying the countryside and militarily control of the conduct of the war. The offensive was not just a concentrated effort in the Saigon area but a major offensive throughout the country. Perhaps, Hue located north of Da Nang near the North Vietnamese border, was devastated more than any other city in South Vietnam. The V.C. went from house to house taking all men women and children out to the countryside where they were forced to dig trenches. They were shot so their bodies fell into the long trenches, covering up the bodies of their massacred neighbors who were shot before them. Col Fender requested that I send a team of FAA technicians to Hue as soon as the as the massacre was discovered. We had to access the damages and determine what material was required to restore air traffic control facilities because they were essential for emergency relief activities. There wasn't any shortage of volunteers and I sent two of my most competent Americans and a Filipino technician by special military plane with the necessary equipment to take care of what we thought would meet their most urgent emergency requirements. Some months later the Vietnam issue of 'Stars and Stripes' had a lengthy story with pictures on the recovery and identification of the thousands of decomposed bodies that had been buried in the trenches.

The Tet Offensive was a major turning point in our operations. Artillery and mortar shells exploded day and night, keeping us as well as the GIs that we were there to support under considerable pressure. Every day, mortars detonated all around the airport and at night, I could see the flashes from the muzzle blast of the artillery in the distance. Calculating the time between the flash when the shell was fired and when we could hear the noise from the muzzle blast told us how far away it was. Initially, it was hard to go to sleep at night listening to the shells detonating in the distance but eventually we got used to it and it had little impact on our work habits. Likewise, we got used to working in our office at the airport with shells detonating all over the airport. We were fortunate that we accomplished as much as we did before Tet because after that all we could do was to respond to the most urgent emergencies.

VN-8 EXTENDED RANGE COMMUNICATIOM

We located many things in the CAAG warehouse and found all sorts of interesting things that we not only could use but urgently needed right now. This included everything from high power radio transmitters to 150-foot towers used as antenna masts. We urgently needed to build two remote controlled, extended range air traffic control facilities (RCAG) to bridge the communication gap across the South China Sea between Saigon and Taiwan. This was a dangerous bottleneck in the ARTCC system because neither Saigon nor Taipei could communicate with aircraft over much of the South China Sea. One of my predecessors obviously had sorted all this out or we wouldn't have the equipment, but hadn't left any records, making it necessary for us to determine where to install it.

I had an excellent relationship with the two Air Force officers assigned to our office and we worked as a team. We worked so close together in our cramped quarters that the back of Lt Col Gray's chair and mine touched each other when we were both sitting at our desk. Col Fender, who had just been promoted, sat across the desk facing Lt Col Gray. He had been head of a communication detachment at Oklahoma City and thought of himself as technical expert in that area. Initially, he treated us FAA people like a bunch or recruits but he soon found out that wasn't the case and before long, he looked to us for guidance. Lt Col Gray, his assistant was still in flying status and occasionally delivered the latest security photos to bases throughout Vietnam. Often, I went with him so I could visit some of our remote facilities and the technicians that were maintaining them. We had to be in a position where we could support the Vietnamese technicians when they ran into problems they could not solve. On other occasions when he didn't have his own plane, we would simply go to base operations at an airbase and he would bum a ride on a plane going to another airbase. It wasn't much of a problem because there always seemed to be someone going in the direction of where we wanted to go. I couldn't have done that sort of thing without his assistance. It was a civil/military operation that worked well.

With the assistance of our CAAG air traffic controllers, Qui Nhon, Da Nang and Saigon were selected as the preferred locations for our new communication facilities that would be controlled from our Saigon ARTCC. Lt Col Gray and I took a trip to Qui Nhon on Air America, an unscheduled CIA airline to look for a suitable site to locate this new facility. Planes had to fly above 5000-feet over the mountains for the entire 250-mile trip because of ground fire in this insecure area. As we approached Qui Nhon, the blue coral reefs and tiny offshore islands appeared, like jewels in the water just beyond the miles of white sand beach. With the mountains in the background, this was a beautiful site, resembling a peaceful world-class resort. There was a single ship anchored in the bay that generated electric power for the little city that extended from the seashore to the mountains a couple miles back. Although it appeared to be a tourist resort, while we were circling for a landing we saw a huge ammunition dump in a valley, just on the other side of the ridge of mountains. The airstrip was parallel to the beach on the north end of town near where we stayed at an American officers' quarters on the beach.

When we got off the airplane near base operations, Lt Col Gray didn't waste any time getting a car and driver. The driver took us up a road on a narrow ridge that separated the city from a leper colony, to the U.S. military complex on top of a mountain. The mountain peak was perhaps 3000 feet above sea level and two or three miles back from the ocean but the circular flat area on top was less than 1000-feet across. The fenced in complex was the site of the massive telephone TROPO system, installed and maintained by the military, to provide telephone circuits to Saigon. It was a state of the art system, using uninterrupted power from an onsite military power plant that furnished power to all facilities in the crowded complex. Immediately, I knew this was the ideal site where we wanted to locate our new facility but there really wasn't any unused space. Finally, Lt Col Gray and I found a bedrock area on the ocean side of the peak that extended out to the parameter fence, large enough for a small building. We hitched a ride back to Saigon and didn't have any trouble selling Col Fender on our proposed site. Keeping with military protocol, it took the power of our Bird Colonel to convince the General, we need this space in their compound. The General also had a building and antenna masts constructed for us with both uninterrupted power and telephone circuits that were required to operate our remote facility from Saigon. The next phase of the project was up to the military but we wanted to be prepared to proceed with the installation as soon as the building was completed.

Every facility of this type is unique; tailor made to fit the environment, using different types of equipment to accommodate special requirements. I ordered a basic set of FAA engineering drawings that I was familiar with, from the office where I previously worked before I came to Vietnam. Modifying these drawings significantly reduced the time required to complete the finished drawings. Our engineering draftsmen did a professional job, making finished drawings from my rough draft drawings. In two months, the building was completed ready for us to install the equipment. After moving the equipment into the building, placing it at the correct location, I turned it over to my most experienced technician to complete the project. This had been a hectic four months and I was ready for my first home leave.

After three weeks home leave, I went to Qui Nhon to check out our new facility, which I understood was installed but for some reason was not yet in operation. Much to my dissatisfaction, the installation technician didn't like my engineering drawings and made his own. He was an excellent installation technician but if he got off on the wrong tract, he could do as much harm as he could good. On the positive side, all the heavy equipment had been moved into the building and the massive antennas were on their masts. On the negative side, all the new wiring had to be removed, equipment racks had to be relocated back to their correct location and it had to be completely rewired.

I went back to Saigon to get the necessary material together, returning with two Taiwanese technicians. Both the Filipino and Taiwanese technicians were good but they didn't work well together. In fact, one of the best

Filipino technicians was of Chinese decent and for some reason wasn't well accepted by the rest of his group. Also, most American technicians worked quite well with the Filipino technicians but not with the Taiwanese. By the end of the week, we had the station rewired and ready for tune up. Our test equipment was quite limited but I was able to borrow what we needed from the U.S. military personnel that maintained the nearby TROPO site. Working through the weekend, we got all the newly installed equipment checked out, adjusted and it appeared to be operating normal.

I contacted Col Fender who requested the U.S. Air Force flight check aircraft, stationed in the Philippines to check out our new facility. They checked both the maximum distance and altitude coverage of our high gain, directional antenna system on the Saigon/Taipei Airway. Coverage exceeded all expectations and Saigon control center now had direct communication with aircraft about 2/3 the distance to Taipei. A similar facility installed by the U.S. military in Taiwan didn't reach half the distance but nevertheless, provided the necessary overlap in coverage so aircraft could be handed off from one control center to the other, always having voice communication with one or both centers.

Col Fender, who was at first overly skeptical of us CAAG civilians, lost no time in soliciting credit from the Air Force for his achievement. This eliminated long delays on this critical airway due to significant traffic backups. He arranged for me to stop at Pacific Air Force (PACAF) headquarters in Hawaii on my next trip to the U.S. This was to explain to them how we built a better facility than they did, making sure they were aware of his accomplishments. Even so, he never saw fit to congratulate those of us that actually built the facility.

Col Fender was so pleased with his accomplishment that he got General Johnson, Chief, U.S. Air Force communication in Vietnam to host a commissioning ceremony at the site. The general picked up top Vietnamese Civil Aviation and CAAG officials in Saigon in his private aircraft that he named the "Blue Whale". It was a C-126 that had been converted to a luxury command plane. We flew directly to the Qui Nhon Airport and up to the mountain top site in several helicopters that his staff had arranged. The Vietnamese had never been there and didn't know what it was all about but it was a very impressive ceremony that would enhance the career of our new Bird Colonel.

While we at the mountain site, I pointed out a sister mountain peak. It was exactly 1-mile away and would make an excellent location for a mountaintop VORTAC. This type of navigation facility provides both azimuth and distance information for both civil and military aircraft. They are used internationally to establish instrument flight airways, which are in effect highways in the sky. Unfortunately, the area could not be secured and enemy troops fired rockets from there at night. He could see an opportunity to replace the still shiny bird on his shoulder with a star and couldn't wait to check it out. He had Lt Col Gray set up a project to provide transportation to take me over to the other mountain to make a site survey. It turned out to be more involved than he anticipated, because the Army wouldn't even take me over in a helicopter gunship without first sending in infantry, because they were afraid their gunship would be shot down. They did send in infantry and I made the site survey from the gunship because they were afraid the area was mined and refused to land. It was an excellent site from a navigation standpoint but they didn't have any confidence in being able to secure the area so we didn't hear any more about the project.

The U.S. Army had a key communications facility on Monkey Mountain, an island about half a mile off shore, connected to the mainland by a bridge. The communications compound was located in the small mountain top compound surrounded by a high chain link fence that overlooked the city of Da Nang to the west and the South China Sea to the northeast. A minefield, consisting of a random mixture of French, Vietnamese and U.S. land mines was located around the outside parameter of the security fence.

When the ultrahigh priority extended range communication project at Qui Nhon was started, we were also doing preliminary work on a similar project at Da Nang and installation of two 150-foot antenna masts with high gain directional antennas in Saigon. Although the Da Nang airport was fairly secure, an approach navigation facility located approximately 3-miles off the approach end of the runway had been abandoned several years earlier because they were unable to secure the area. It was not a desirable place for military personnel to be assigned because the city was off limits to Americans and our troops frequently had race riots at China Beach, a beautiful area along the ocean where U.S. troops were stationed.

Although we used identical equipment for both facilities, the Da Nang facility was located in a large communication building with obsolete WW II military communication equipment. Our transmitting equipment performed as well as our Qui Nhon facility, but we had to reduce the sensitivity of our receivers because of spurious radiation from the old military equipment it was collocated with. This resulted in a significant reduction in coverage for the Da Nang Facility.

VN-9 SUPORTINMG THE VN DCA

After completion of the extended range communication project, which was most critical to our mission in Vietnam, I had to get involved in other projects and programs that were also part of our mission. We were reminded of the importance of our mission every time we drove by the military hospital, located about a half a mile from our office, every time we drove to and from work. There was usually a helicopter, landing or taking off at the heliport in front of the hospital. This was the principal hospital in Vietnam and all the seriously wounded were treated there. As a permanently disabled infantryman that had been hospitalized for 1-1/2 years, I understood better than most what they were going through. My mission was to assist in getting this war over as soon as possible with minimum American casualties.

This was a strange civil war that didn't make sense because we were, protecting the country from their countrymen in the north while at the same time, improving their living standards so they would be interested in defending themselves. We were carrying out a massive U.S. Aid program and fighting a war at the same time in the same place. The primary problem was the overwhelming majority of the population was Buddhist and didn't support the Catholic government. The French colonists forced their government on them when the country was divided in 1954. We were in effect taking sides in a religious civil war, protecting the Catholic minority in the south from the Buddhists, invading from the north to reunite their country. It was an impossible situation and I saw my job as, trying to help as many American boys survive with minimum causalities. Those of us that have been there know that once our leaders have committed men that are too young to vote it is a matter of kill or be killed. In the Vietnam War, it was our President lying to Congress further justifying an unwise decision made by former President, John F. Kennedy.

I had neglected my role as technical advisor to Vietnamese Civil Aviation because of more urgent military priorities. Regardless of that, we all had to work together to get the job done so I went to see my Vietnamese counterparts. They were having some problems at the Dalot Airport and asked me if I could go up there with them. I told them that I would and they made arrangements for us to fly up there on Air Vietnam, their national airline. USAID had loaned South Vietnam money to purchase two B-727 passenger planes some years ago to establish their own airline.

Dalot had been kind of a French resort city in the mountains, about 140-miles northeast of Saigon. For whatever reason, it was off limits to American military personnel and only American civilians like me were allowed to go there. Mr. Quang, my real counterpart was still preoccupied, running his pharmacy so his assistant, Mr. Lang and Tu, another technician went with me. When we arrived at the small airport, I got a brief tour of the facilities and Mr. Lang took the Land Rover assigned to the airport manager and we drove 20-miles through the mountains to the city of Dalat. I ask Lang why every electric line pole had been cut of about 3-feet above the ground. He told me USAID had brought the poles and other equipment for the 20-mile electric transmission line from the U.S. One night after they had set all the poles in place, the Viet Cong cut off every pole about 3-feet above the ground. The power line was being installed to furnish power for the airport, which was using several engine-generators to provide power to operate the airport communication and navigation facilities.

I had heard so much about Dalat and had thought it was at least a minimum sized city but it was in fact a relatively small village. They dropped me off at a very large hotel in the middle of a several acre piece of land on the shore of a fairly large lake. I was assigned an enormous luxury room on the first floor which had two double beds draped with mosquito netting, hanging from the canapé around the top of the beds to the floor. It was a lonely eerie place with an elaborate dining room but not a single person was in sight. That night, when I sat down at a table in the empty dining room, a waiter came from nowhere and gave me a French menu that I couldn't read. He did speak a few words of English so I finally ordered something that was quite good. That evening, I walked around the edge of the property and down to the lake but never saw a single person. This obviously was a super deluxe French resort hotel and it was difficult to understand why it still operating in the middle of the war without any customers. The next day when they came to pick me up, I asked them if there wasn't another hotel in Dalat because this one is just too spooky to suit me. They took me to a hotel near the center of town, across from the market where I could look down on the intersection in the center of the village. It wasn't very classy but I felt more comfortable and secure, mainly because there were more people around.

I soon discovered my Vietnamese counterparts were more interested in tourism than their problems at the Dalot Airport. As we drove around the lake, they showed me an area by the lake, which was across from a cemetery where young couples whose family had not allowed them to marry went to drink poison together. It was very romantic because they were buried together in the cemetery across the road. Young Vietnamese couples, especially from good families are not allowed to marry without the approval of both their families. I asked them why there was a large mound of dirt, like a small hill in the middle of the cemetery. They told me a year or more ago, Viet Cong soldiers came into the city and massacred something in the order of 400 men, women and children at the marketplace just across from the hotel where I was now staying. The market consisted of rows of level terraces about 10-feet wide, extending from the road around the hill, like seating in an amphitheater. There were several aisles or stairways in the center, going from the top to the bottom of the hillside market, providing access to all the terraces where venders sold all types of merchandise. The huge mound of earth in the center of the cemetery was the mass grave where they buried the mutilated bodies of those killed in the massacre.

Our next tourist attraction was a waterfall, more than 10-miles from Dalat over a narrow dirt road. Mr. Lang who was driving the Land Rover hit a similar vehicle, damaging its back fender. Lang was a great talker who intimidated the driver of the other government vehicle, making him believe that all he needed to do was bend the fender out so the tire wouldn't rub against it and we continued on our way. It was a nice little waterfall probably not more than 20-feet high but waterfalls were rare in Vietnam. It was a very hot day even in the mountains and we went into a lone concession building near the falls to get a cold drink. It was a fairly large building for a place like this and the three of us, who were the only customers, sat at a table in the rear, near the entrance. There was an elderly man who appeared to be the owner and three girls that were apparently waitresses.

One of the girls waited on us. I was apprehensive, being out in the middle of what seemed like no man's land and was relieved when three uniformed South Vietnamese Army men came in. Relief soon became apprehension when the three-armed military men attacked the owner with the butts of their rifles, causing us to leave immediately. None of us were armed and couldn't have done anything to help the man even if we had been. We were several miles down the road before I actually found out what had really happened. My two Vietnamese associates were sitting in the front seat, excitedly talking very fast to each other, and ignoring the fact that I was there. Finally, they calmed down enough to explain to me what it was all about. The three men apparently wanted the three girls who were daughters of the owner and he wasn't about to let them have the girls. We don't know whether they killed him or not or what happened to the girls. They told me when you get out of the cities and village's military men are the law and they do whatever they want. After that, when I flew over the waterfall on the way to Quin Nhon or Da Nang, I always looked down on the waterfall wondering what actually happened that day.

The next stop on our little tour was a little park just outside of Dalat near a fork in a couple narrow dirt roads where we sat in this pretty wooded area for a long time watching people walking on the road. They had been out in the forest collecting wood, carrying bundles of wood on their head down the hill to Dalot. I also saw families of little dark skinned people, consisting of a man, a woman and perhaps three or four children walking down the road. These little people, less than 4-feet tall were carrying everything the family owned, moving from one place to another. They told me they are the mountain people and lived on wild roots and animals they could kill much like the Bushmen in southern Africa.

That night we all had dinner together with the airport manager, technicians and air traffic controllers in a second floor room of an obscure cafe off the main street in Dalot. Besides our bowl of rice, we used our chopsticks to help ourselves to the various types of meats and vegetables served family style. It was a good tasty meal but I was somewhat concerned when Mr. Lang swallowed one of the pills he carried in his pocket. He told me he always took antibiotics when he left Saigon so he didn't get some kind of an infection. Perhaps, I was fortunate because I never took any antibiotics and never got sick. The primary topic of the conversation was about two technicians that were detained for two days by the Viet Cong near the airport. Apparently, it was a brainwashing or what they called a reeducation session where they tried to convince the technicians to assist them in their fight to free their country from colonial powers. Both of them returned unharmed so we didn't have any way of knowing whether they had been reeducated or were Viet Cong themselves, passing along bits and pieces of information to their Viet Cong comrades. In either case, there probably wasn't anything of strategic importance in Dalat that could disrupt the war effort. The next morning they picked me up at the hotel and we drove up the mountain past the 20-miles of cut off electric poles to the airport. I examined the control tower and the few facilities associated with it at the obscure airport. We caught the once daily Air Vietnam flight back to Saigon. Obviously, the primary reason they ask me to accompany them on this trip was to justify the trip, which was in effect a vacation they wanted to take

BAM ME THUET VOR.

I thought I was familiar with the details of our operation, when a military officer from one of the seaports where they bring in heavy equipment contacted me. He asked me what they were supposed to do with the large truck and van that had been in storage there for several months. He told me this was the large van that the engine was damaged when it was offloaded from a ship about a year ago. The oil pan had been punctured and the engine froze up because all the oil leaked out, making it necessary to get a new engine from the U. S. They had received and installed the new engine and he wanted to know what we wanted them to do with it. I told him, I didn't know but would get back to him and let him know in the next few days. Fortunately, Mr. Dao our warehouse man had some recollection of the CAAG ordering a mobile visual Omni-directional range (VOR), some years ago to be used for site tests to determine whether or not a facility of that type would operate at a particular site.

It couldn't have happened at a better time because after the Tet Offensive our Army had established a helicopter base at Bam Me Thuet in the mountainous highlands approximately 400 miles north of Saigon. This portable VOR would be an ideal facility to serve as a navigation aid so the helicopters would always know their location in reference to their home base. It wasn't possible to drive the trucks from the seaport to Bam Me Thut because of security problems, so the Colonel arranged to have both vehicles shipped to Nha Trang by ship. From there both vehicles could be driven in a military convey to Bam Me Thuet about 80 miles to the northwest. Considerable time passed and Lt. Col. Gray finally located the vehicles at Nha Trang. When they off loaded the VOR van from the ship they had again punched a hole in the oil pan and drove it until the engine froze up because all the oil leaked out. By this time the need for a VOR at Bam Me Thuet was critical. Military command considered airlifting the VOR van to Bam Me Thuet with one of our giant helicopters commonly referred to as a flying crane but it was so heavy they would have had to land to refuel every 20 miles and it wasn't practical. Finally, they decided to load it on a flatbed truck and haul it up in a military convoy. Again, we lost track of it when it left Nha Trang and was unable to locate it.

We had been unduly delayed, getting an operational VOR in service to satisfy urgent military requirements, waiting for what was supposed to be an operational facility. We couldn't further delay the installation of the new facility we had originally planned to install at that airport. It was a major project even though some years ago, someone had ordered all the prefabricated building parts, including the steel beams, 10-foot side panels for the 36-foot square building. The 50-foot circular deck had to be assembled and all electronic equipment had to be installed and wired in place to make an operational facility. Also, all this had to be transported by ship and military convoy like the VOR van that was lost. Initially, we had to select a site to locate this facility because we didn't want to install such a large complex facility in a location where it wouldn't function properly. The real purpose of the portable test VOR was to locate a permanent site where we could be confident the new facility would function properly, rather than be used as a temporarily emergency VOR.

I went to Bam Me Thuet with two of my Vietnamese counterparts to select a site for the new VOR. It is preferable to locate facilities of this type off the approach end of the main runway so in addition to being a long-range navigation aid it could also be used for a straight in approach to the airport. We borrowed a WW II jeep from the airport manager and drove about a mile past a Montagnard village near the airport, through a herd of water buffalo to an open area that overlooked some rice patties. It was apparent we weren't going to get where we wanted to go in a jeep and would have to use some other type transportation. I went to see the helicopter base commander, telling him we were looking for a site for a new VOR and asked him if they could take us two or three miles beyond the approach end of the runway so we could look over the terrain. He said, no way, that is where the V.C. fires mortars at the airport from every night. We finally selected a location near the center of the airport, which would be more secure and still perform its most urgent function.

That was an interesting trip because that night my Vietnamese counterparts dropped me off in the village at what they called a hotel and they never told me where they were going to stay. I speculated that it was probably at the house of one of the technicians that lived there. The village of Bam Me Thuet consisted of a few little shops of some type along a short piece of dirt road, with the so called hotel being the main building in the center of the village. The room was one of a number of three sided shelters, around the parameter of what we would call a yard or garden with trees and other smaller bushes. The bed had wood slats about two inches wide and perhaps a quarter of an inch thick with a small space between them, rather than a mattress. I slept on the wood slat bed without any type bedding which seemed unusual in this mountainous area where it was supposedly much cooler. There wasn't any electricity in the village and even if there had been they probably couldn't have had lights because you could tell by the time between, seeing and hearing the artillery mussel blast, the artillery was less than four miles away. It was also a dark night and it was impossible to find the outdoor toilet in the dark. I was relieved when my Vietnamese counterparts picked me up the next morning.

Several months later, a U.S. Green Beret that had been assigned to live and work in the Montagnard village came to the airport. He told them about this van full of radio equipment that had been given to the village by the U.S. military because no one had claimed it. The Montagnard tribesmen were fierce enemies of both the North and South Vietnamese but they were very friendly to Americans and provided considerable support to the U.S. Military. Perhaps, centuries ago the Vietnamese had driven them back from the seacoast into the mountains. The Montagnard people were tall, fairly dark skinned people that except for being a little darker resembled the American Sioux or Chippewa Indians. They lived in long narrow thatched roof, multifamily buildings, having a floor about three feet above the ground and a stairway to an entrance on each end of the long narrow buildings. This mountainous area was also semi-tropical where plants and roots were plentiful and they lived by collecting roots and killing small game. They had planned on removing the radio equipment from the disabled van and use it like a storage building. The van was towed back to the airport but by that time, we were in the process of building a new VOR building and installing new equipment at the airport. I left Vietnam more than 2 years after we first learned this VOR van existed and we were just finishing the new facility at the time I left. That was one of the many very expensive problems, resulting from too many Americans, too little communication and practically no coordination of American efforts in the Vietnamese civil war. We had our program laid out and had already accomplished some of the most urgent projects before the Tet Offensive. The extended range communication system and the air traffic control telephone key system were two of our most urgent projects. We had modernized the Saigon air traffic control tower, which at that time was the busiest airport in the world. It was operated exclusively by Vietnamese controllers, as were all civil airports in Vietnam. This was particularly difficult as well as frustrating because we had to keep the facility fully operational during the process. It was even more frustrating when our colonel decided to embark on a two-year project to build a new modern control tower after this job was completed.

DCA ORGANIZATION

About two months before I completed my second tour in Vietnam, the CAAG Chief called me into his office and told me he wanted to talk about developing a formal organizational plan for the Vietnamese Department of Civil Aviation (DCA). He reminded me that in accordance with our civil (not military) mission we need to develop a formal organization for the entire Government of Vietnam, Department of Civil Aviation. After having previous management experience and working directly with engineering and other technical aspects of the organization for 3-1/2 years, I was probably better qualified than anyone else to develop such a plan for this portion of the overall organization. This plan would not be something that could be implemented at this time but would identify training and staffing requirements to meet their ultimate future requirements. I told him that I could develop such an organization that would parallel the FAA, downsized for a small country that would include those functions that would include international civil aviation requirements. I pointed out to him that Vietnam was still very much in a state of flux because of the future development of the countries communication and transportation capabilities. Also, the availability of commercial power would practically cut staffing requirements in half. As an example, terrorists or Viet Cong sabotage like cutting down every pole on 20 miles of power line that was being constructed from Dalot to the airport had to stop. The basic problem is that we are trying to develop a country, which is in a state of war and a few terrorists can destroy millions of dollars' worth of development overnight.

He said he would relieve me of my duties as electronics branch chief and let my assistant take over my job so I could devote all my time to this project. This would give my assistant who was going to replace me an opportunity to get fully involved while I was there to help out if necessary. I told him that I would do the best I can and try to do it is such a way that the basic organization would remain intact when positions have to be eliminated because of future development. This approach has serious shortcomings because I know Third World countries would much rather add unneeded positions than eliminate them from the public payroll. The more positions you add, the less money is available to pay trained competent technicians. The down side is they are more likely to quit and get a higher paying job with industry in a developing country. Then you have the added cost of training and developing new technicians.

This assignment didn't come as a complete surprise and I had already requested and received position descriptions from FAA for all the positions that might be involved. I didn't need staffing charts because I was well aware of FAA staffing requirements for all types of facilities. We had also trained a number of electronic and electromechanical technicians that we had immediate need for in the U.S.A. under USAID and ICAO sponsorship. Although this gave me a head start, I don't think the Lord himself could venture a reliable guess on what future requirements may be. There were just too many unknowns involved.

I started out with an organizational chart with a staffing chart that would satisfy all the requirements for an ideal Vietnam Civil Aviation Organization, considering that after the war was over, they had commercial power and telephone communication service. Then I added positions that would be required until these qualifications were satisfied at each facility throughout the country, marking them as a temporary requirement. A separate package was prepared, complete with position descriptions and grade level for every location or office from the Chief Electronic Engineers Office down to the smallest remote location where technicians are assigned. Lines of supervision, field offices and others offices providing special services were all identified in the master chart. With the help of the DCA technicians and those that were supposed to be their current supervisors, we actually placed the names of the technicians that were trained and others that were currently filling those positions on the charts.

An organizational chart and position descriptions, which outlined the skill level and duties of each position along with their pay grade level was a new concept to them. I took some time and went over this concept individually with those technicians that had enough experience and background to understand. They all approved of the new concept and saw it as an opportunity to progress from one grade level to the next with a corresponding pay increase. The position description, duties and pay level also outlined training requirement for each position so they knew what was required of them and what pay they could expect. I stayed clear of how much it would pay in dollars and reference it to pay level from one on up depending of the overall complexity of the job and whether or not it was a supervisory position. I did make some minor changes based on their recommendations regarding, which facilities would fall under the jurisdiction of a particular field office.

I also went over the organization/staffing /position descriptions/training requirement plan with the CAAG Chief, explaining my rational for presenting it in such a way that it clearly indicated which positions would no longer be required when the national inter-structure was further developed or restored. He was well satisfied with the overall package.

VN-10 CORRUPTION CAPITAL OF THE WORLD

During my last 6 months in Vietnam, corruption was rampant and some of our CAAG group got at least somewhat involved. We were not allowed to have U.S. currency commonly known as green dollars in Vietnam because you could sell it for 2 to 4 times its value in Vietnamese money. Since we had to buy things on the local economy, we needed local currency for such things as paying our maid and for all local purchases. We also had a third type of currency, which was called MPC or red dollars. This was the type money we received when we cashed a U.S. dollar check at a U.S. Military bank and was the only acceptable currency at the military Base Exchanges or at the commissary where we purchased most of our groceries.

This currency was worth about half as much as green dollars on the black market. China was selling everything they could at the expense of their own people to get U.S. green dollars so they could buy much needed products on the world market so China was a lucrative black market for U.S. green dollars. Some of our air traffic controllers got involved in this illegal activity by endorsing their pay check over to a scam artist who gives them about twice its value in MPC or perhaps 4 times its value in Vietnamese currency. I understand a couple of my technicians also got involved in this illegal activity. This wasn't something they could get involved in overnight because paychecks were usually deposited directly in a State side bank and it took some manipulating to get it changed so it was sent directly to them. I understand that about the time I left, someone got wise to what was going on and shut it down.

I ran into corruption that was more serious, about the time I left Vietnam in December 1970. Sunday morning was always a bad time for me because the restaurants were closed and I didn't enjoy sitting around my little apartment by myself, trying to make breakfast especially when I usually didn't have anything to fix.

One day, I met the maid that had worked where one of our Philippine technicians lived on the street near my apartment. He lived on the other side of Saigon with a teenaged girl whose mother owned the house. She was a pretty slick chick herself and was one of the favorite mistresses of the local Catholic priest who lived with her part of the time. On three or four occasions, I sit around the kitchen table in this big house with our technician, Ernie Pernobie, his girlfriend, her mother and the maid talking about everything in general. The maid, who was Cambodian, knew me well enough to stop and talk to me on the street. She told me she now worked at a restaurant near my apartment complex. It was located in a villa somewhere out in the middle of about a square mile area of adobe type houses patched together like a crazy quilt with narrow paths around the small buildings. She told me it was a really good restaurant near where I lived operated by black American GIs. One Sunday morning, I went exploring and found this restaurant and this lady was working there. I undoubtedly was rather conspicuous because I was the only one in civilian clothes and there was only one other white man in the place. They served an excellent meal and the price was unbelievably cheap. I thought a great deal about it during the following week but didn't mention it to anyone.

I knew there must be something shady about it but I was real curious and went back the following Sunday. Nobody paid much attention to me or asked any questions but I knew there was something wrong, when I saw quite a number of black GIs coming up to a back window and getting what appeared to be a hamburger. The following Sunday, I went back and when this same woman waited on me she inconspicuously whispered to me, "You don't come back any more". I knew it was a serious warning that they were suspicious of me and I never went near the place again.

A few weeks later there was a major front-page news story in the "Stars and Stripes "about this restaurant and other related activities. The GIs involved were AWOL (absent without leave) from our Army in Vietnam, living out in the jungle of little adobe houses. It was in fact a large sophisticated operation that cooperated with other GIs that delivered meat and other perishable foodstuffs to officers' messes throughout the area. Their associates threw bundles of the finest meats and other supplies off the military delivery trucks at various places and they had someone there to pick them up. The AWOL GIs not only ate better than the officers but had enough left over to run a large restaurant. In addition to the many AWOL GIs, our military police picked up many others that were involved, but unfortunately the ringleader escaped to Thailand. I am sure the AWOL GIs have no doubt that I was the spy that turned them in.

Theft and corruption was perhaps the only thing that was both stable and predictable during the Vietnam War. Ships loaded with liquor, soft drinks, expensive Japanese TVs and other electronic equipment came up the river from Vung Tau, and were unloaded at the docks in the Saigon port. I am sure everyone that had been in Saigon for any length of time had watched those unloading commodities off both sides of the ships. Commodities unloaded on the dock side were obviously intended for sale exclusively to Americans at military Base Exchanges and Commissaries but many items often didn't make it to their intended destination. Commodities unloaded on the other side that was lowered down from the deck with ropes into small boats waiting alongside the ship were obviously destined to go directly to the black market. Items such as small Japanese refrigerators that could be used in hotel rooms where many American civilians had already lived for more than a year were very much in demand. The first indication that a shipment came in was when they showed up in large numbers on the black market. If you were looking for one, you could expect they would start to show up at the Base Exchange in the next few days. Even then, you had to be vigilant because there was also a black market in the ration coupons required to buy such hard to get items. GIs or American civilians that didn't want these hard to get items bought them to sell at a premium price on the black market, further depriving those that they were intended for.

Theft was uncontrollable, one night someone pulled over a mile of large communications cable out of the ground at Tan Son Nhut airport and sold it for the salvaged copper. This was one of our operating communication cables that went right through an area where an American military group was temporarily camping out. This was in the same area where one of our Filipino technicians was killed when a U.S. military truck hit a guy wire pulling down the radio antenna tower.

Some American civilians were also involved in selling an automobile on the black market. American civilians were authorized to import a car duty free with the U. S. government paying shipping charges. Vietnamese government taxes on a new vehicle were several times the cost of a car, making them very expensive. Americans were not allowed to sell a car that they brought tax free to Vietnamese until they had complete their tour of duty and then they were not allowed to sell it for more than they paid for it. If they sold it for more than that, the profit had to go to a charity. One scam was to buy a car and lease it to a wealthy Vietnamese for some outrages price until their tour was completed and then sell it to this same individual when they completed their tour. During the lease period they also had tax free diplomatic license plates.

VN-11 PEOPLE OF VIETNAM

When I arrived in Vietnam on July 12th 1967, it was a cultural shock for a farm boy from mid-America. I was dead tired from about a 24-hour flight in the center seat of a cramped airplane only to be dropped off on the hot tarmac at Saigon's Tan Son Nhut airport. As I rode into Saigon (where I would share an apartment with Ed Vie) in his open WW II jeep, everything was so strange to me. The strange buildings all seemed to look alike and the pungent smell of decaying garbage in the hot humid climate was overpowering. I was grateful to Ed who was a 1-1/2 year veteran of this area, for helping me to overcome the cultural shock. In about a week's time, I started to recognize buildings along the road as we went to and from work and I could tell men from women but couldn't identify one person from another. I was also overwhelmed by the job as I previously explained and was slow in getting acquainted with the office staff on an individual basis. Also, the Vietnamese people, like most foreigners are shy and reserved when you first meet them. They show little emotion and take plenty of time, looking you over, seeing if you know what you are doing before they are ready to accept you. Once they accept you, they are your true friends and you better believe what they tell you, because they don't lie.

A couple months after I arrived in Vietnam, I was sitting in the park across the street from our apartment when I noticed this man riding around the park on his 50 cc Honda motorcycle, the vehicle of choice in Vietnam. He looked me over as he slowly rode by where I was sitting and even watched me from a distance. I was a little concerned because I didn't know if he was casing me to see if I would be a good robbery victim or what. After while he rode off but the next week he was back and when he drove by real slowly, I said hello to him and he stopped. It was apparent that he just wanted to talk to an American and practice his English. He was taking English classes at USAID where he worked but wasn't very proficient. He also wanted to learn more about these Americans that had showed up in great numbers during the last few months. I didn't know any Vietnamese and after observing so many Americans that had been taking Vietnamese language classes for over a year and still couldn't say even a few words that a Vietnamese could understand, I decided I could put my time to better use. When you consider Chinese, which is only a 3 tone language is extremely difficult to learn, it would be a waste of time for me, a tone-deaf person to try to learn Vietnamese, which is a 5 tone language. The Vietnamese are an ambitious, intelligent people that know it is essential for them to learn English to get ahead in the world and don't miss an opportunity to learn our language. Tung became a close friend and I saw him often during my 3-1/2 years in Vietnam.

I visited his home, which was near our apartment often and learned more about Vietnamese family life. My first observation was there were very few men in their homes and second many of those like Tung were not blood relation to the woman that raised them, that they called mother. So many of those that would have been the man of the house were in military service on one side or the other in this civil war or had been killed in the war that had been going on for generations. Previously, girls were raised under a much disciplined code of ethics that assured that they would still be virgins when they got married. The family arranged marriages and those that strayed were invalidated, gifts or dowry were returned and the families disowned their daughter, which in many cases had to turn to prostitution to survive. Everyone loved children and even babies born to those girls who were forced into prostitution were welcomed in most homes, where like Tung they were raised as their own children. On the other hand, mixed race children who obviously had French or a black American father seemed to always end up in an orphanage rather than being raised by a Vietnamese family. There were very few people in Vietnam with either French or black blood even though the French assisted by black Africans had ruled Vietnam for more than a century. They could be easily identified because they didn't have the straight shiny black hair that is a defining trait of all Vietnamese. Also, in contrast to the French, children with white American fathers were sought after by most Vietnamese families, which in an overwhelming majority of the cases consisted of only an adult woman. These children were passed around from one family to another every few months so more families could share Vietnamese/American babies. Raising children in Vietnam was more or less a community project where everyone looked after their welfare and disciplined them. As soon as they were old enough to walk the children played together in the bicycle paths between the houses wearing only a T-shirt covering the upper part of their body. Children didn't wear diapers, which was convenient because they didn't have adequate facilities to wash them. During the rainy season the daily downpour flushed the streets and bicycle trails, keeping them fairly clean. It was an informal arrangement but even though every woman worked, there was always someone around to care for the children. The black Africans were undoubtedly brought in by the French from their African colonies to serve in the French Foreign Legion that controlled their French Indo China colony with an iron hand. Although, it wasn't clear whether or not they were actually a uniformed part of the French Foreign Legion, all stories that had been handed down for generations agreed that these black men raped the women and killed the men, answering to no one. Discrimination against the blacks was an obvious resulted of handed down legends.

My friend Tung was drafted into the South Vietnamese Army and when he came home months later, he told me they had sent him to Cambodia. I asked him what the Cambodian people were like. He said," Very bad, very black". Along this same line, Cam Van, one of the secretaries in our office stopped by my apartment one Sunday with her 3 children and speaking of her daughter who was about 7 years old, said to me, "Isn't she pretty, she is almost as white as you are." It wasn't that I was very white after spending a couple years in the tropical sun but rather a mother's perception that one of her two daughters' was prettier because of her lighter colored skin. Prejudice based on skin color is a world rather than an American problem.

After returning from Cambodia, Tung decided to get married and built a small room about 10 feet square, utilizing one outside wall of his foster mother's home. He built it out of adobe blocks with a single door that opened in the narrow alley or walkway between houses near the side door of his family home. The small empty room with one small window looked so desolate; I walked up a street near his house with him where a man was selling homemade furniture. I told him to select a piece of furniture that he would like to have in his new house and I would buy it for him. After, carefully examining every piece of furniture very carefully, he selected a dresser with a mirror that had six drawers. The vendor carried it on his back down the street and through the narrow alley to his new house. I paid him the equivalent of $50 he was asking and Tung was very proud of the first piece of furniture he ever owned even though his little room was still dark and almost empty. He still hadn't found the woman he wanted to marry by the time he was called back into military service and I never saw him again.

I met another Vietnamese man in much the same way as I met Tung in the park. Like Tung, I met him in the park and he had a 50cc Honda motorcycle. He insisted on taking me to his house on his Honda so I could meet his family. He obviously was more prosperous than Tung because his house was much larger and was located on a real street rather than a bicycle trail that wound around between the crude adobe houses. He introduced me to his wife and 12 girls that ranged from about 12 years to a tiny baby. It was evident his family was happy, not only to meet an American but have one in their own home. I visited them a number of times but I always had to follow him with my car to his house or he took me on his Honda because I never could find his house. One Sunday, I invited the entire family to my apartment and had some coke and ice cream. His wife had to stay home with the two smallest children but we loaded all we could in my car, which was a new 1968 Chevrolet Nova, and he took the rest of them on his Honda. They were all dressed alike in identical dresses that their mother had made for them from the same material. He was very proud of them and lined all 10 of them up in a row by age so I could take some pictures of them. I am sure it is a day they will remember all their life. I continued to see the family over the remaining years that I was in Vietnam.

Cam Van's, husband and his family originally came from the Mekong Delta area where her husband's family had owned a considerable amount of rice land. As a result of a previous USAID initiated land reform program, their rice land was divided up into smaller plots and redistributed to the peasants that didn't own any land. In return, they were paid a small amount for the land, which would be paid over a period of years. That was some years ago and the value of the Vietnamese currency had depreciated so much due to inflation that they only received what was now equivalent to a few pennies a month. Her husband was a military officer who had been trained as an aircraft mechanic in the U.S. and could speak fluent English. I learned a great deal from him because he was a very knowledgeable person and we could communicate very well. He had two brothers, one of whom was the commander of the crucial DaNang Airbase and the other was a Congressman. I visited their home in a Saigon suburb and got to know their three children, a boy about eight, and two younger girls who couldn't speak any English. Her husband was involved in the baby lift where hundreds of orphan babies were being flown out of Vietnam to the U.S.A when Vietnam fell to the Communists in 1975. Their family came to the U.S. at that time and after living in several refugee camps, finally settled in Fairfax, Virginia, across the river from Washington D.C. Although he had a U.S. Aircraft Airframe and Engine (A& E) mechanic's license and had even gone back to school to update it, he was unable to find a job in his specialty. Finally, he got a job maintaining and collecting money from the coin boxes on washers and dryers at laundries in the Fairfax, Virginia area. Their son who had lost a year in school because he had polio had the highest math score in the Fairfax, Virginia School system when he graduated from eighth grade. His sister, who was a year younger but in the same class, had the second highest math score in the same school system.

Perhaps the maids that worked in our large American apartment complex were our primary source of Vietnamese cultural education. Initially, very few of them could speak any English and there was one in particular called

Ba Hoa, meaning Mrs. Hoa that made things work. She was what we would call an entrepreneur, getting jobs for maids; translating and interpreting notes of instruction left by their American Employer and training new maids regarding what was expected of them in this foreign culture. For example, a toilet was something on top of the hole in the ground that most affluent had in their house was to sit on, rather than squat on with both feet on the seat. Although we never heard about it, it was apparent that the maids paid Ba Hoa for her services because she had to support a family. She was an interesting person that had five children, four girls and one boy. Her 21-year-old daughter lived with what were apparently relatives in Da Nang and her boy and three 3 younger daughters lived with her and some relatives near Saigon. Her oldest daughter was born before she went to work in France as a maid for a private family. It was some kind of an indentured servant program where she got a ticket to and from France and had to work for a certain amount of time for a certain amount of money. Ba Hoa and two other maids in our large complex had worked in France; having much in common they were often seen together. Ba Hoa had also been a cook in France, which made her the Queen Bee.

They talked openly of their French experience and since I never knew any of them to lie about anything, I accepted what they told me without reservation. Ba Hoa, having been both a cook and maid was kind of one up on the others because they were just maids. Although they had very little time they could call their own while they were in France, they had occasionally been able to get together and discussed what was going on in the French families where they worked. If you think maids don't know everything that is going on in a household you never had a maid.

My apartment near the elevator on the front corner of the building was a convenient place for people passing by or waiting for the elevator to congregate. One Sunday afternoon a group consisting of several CAAG people and the three maids had a lively discussion in my apartment. They talked openly in some detail about the sexual activities of the families where they worked. Although we had always heard that the French were both the most sexually permissive and professional lovers on earth, we generally considered it was just something else that they bragged about. The maids who were previously employed by the French agreed that if this were true it was not coincidental but a matter of training and experience. They unanimously agreed that when a boy became old enough to be sexually active, his mother or her best friend taught him the intimate skills of lovemaking. Likewise, when a girl became old enough her father would be her tutor. We told them there must have been some pregnancies that resulted from these activities and ask them what happened to the babies? None of them were aware of any pregnancies or any babies that resulted from this activity. We were embarrassed by their frank forthright conversations and changed the conversation to something that we Americans were more comfortable with.

I had several maids during the three years that I had an apartment of my own. The first one that stole money ended up in jail before the Tet offensive intervened. My second maid was the wife of a Vietnamese technician that worked for me for a short period to help out. The third was a young woman that didn't speak any English that Ba Hoa got for me worked about a year. Unknown to me, Ba Hoa knew she was going to get married to a Vietnamese policeman and wouldn't be working anymore so she made arrangements for another girl to work in her place. The girl that was helping out turned out to be a cousin of my previous maid and had previously worked for two American ladies that shared an apartment in the other building in our complex. She was an excellent maid that learned good English in the short period of time that she worked for me for more than a year before I left Vietnam. She was raised on a farm in the delta and told me about her life on the small rice farm. Her mother died and life was unbearable after her father remarried so she moved to Saigon where her mother's sister worked. When I was getting ready to leave, I asked her to check the price of a pair of ceramic temple dogs at the Saigon shops. I wanted to purchase them to take home with me and she would be able to buy them much cheaper than I could. The next night when I came back to my apartment, there was a pair of black ceramic elephants sitting on the living room floor. She had already gone home but the next time I saw her, she told me, "The temple dogs, too expensive but I buy these elephants for you". They were a gift from her and she wouldn't take any money for them. Before I left, I had some things that I wanted to give her because I wasn't going to take them home with me. We loaded them in my car and I took them as far as I could go with my car and we carried them the rest of the way through the adobe jungle to her room. It was a small room with only a bed in it, located just off a catwalk over the river. The community toilet was on the end of an extension of the catwalk above the river. She obviously didn't have either running water or cooking facilities.

By the time I was able to take my first family visitation leave, most of our Vietnamese office staff came to my apartment bringing me gifts to take home with me. They consisted of things that were unique to Vietnam such as ceramic vases and black lacquer pictures with mother of pearl inserts. Although it was a total surprise to me, it obviously meant that they expected me to bring them a gift from America when I returned. This became a reoccurring ritual and every time I went home, I brought back something that was uniquely American for each of them. As I got to know them better, I learned my chief draftsman was also a professional artist. He had many artist friends and about every other Sunday they stopped by apartment to visit for about an hour. One of them was the best-known artist in Saigon that painted most of the pictures that were for sale on the streets of Saigon. He painted some pictures for me and I brought him some artist's paint from the U.S. because it was difficult to get in Saigon. Practically every Sunday, some of the people from our office and their family stopped by my apartment briefly for a social call.

Mr. Dao, our warehouse man's daughter got married and I was the only American invited to the reception. It was a large private reception held in a very large dining room where there were many round tables, each seating 10 people. All the Vietnamese from our office attended and I sat at a table with Cam Van and her husband. The reception, which followed the Buddhist wedding, was much like what we would expect here in the U.S.A. but it was impressive to see all the Vietnamese dressed up in their finest native clothes.

Back in the U.S.A., Americans had a much distorted impression of the role of Asian women and Vietnamese women in particular. Perhaps it was a result of the feminist revolution in the U.S., where Americans women felt it was necessary to degrade the Asian women in their effort to justify their feminist takeover of U.S. society. They abandoned all family responsibility and wanted to be free to just go out and play at their former husband's expense. Many men in my group were victims of the American feminist revolution and came to the Vietnam War zone to get away from it all but I don't know anyone that went to Vietnam in search of a new wife. As we learned more about the Vietnamese culture, it was apparent that what we had been taught about the subservient Vietnamese women was based on old wives tales rather than fact. The Vietnamese culture had survived centuries of wars, French colonization, onslaught by the Catholic Church and was now involved in the Kennedy-Johnson war which cost, perhaps a couple million more men's lives. Their culture had suffered centuries of wars and there were few men left in their overall population which meant that most babies were born to unwed mothers who were head of the household. Unlike what we consider a traditional 2 parent family, the Vietnamese mother is head of the household, making all family decisions regarding raising, disciplining and educating her children and she also controls the family purse strings. If she enjoys the luxury of having a husband, when he is not fighting in a war, he will probably have two low paying jobs and turn all the money he earns over to his wife to manage. If he is in the military, it pays so little she will probably have two jobs outside of the home in addition to raising her family. In Vietnam, having two jobs isn't so a family can have two cars and a boat but is necessity to keep a grass roof over the family house so it doesn't leak too much and put enough food on the table to keep the family from starving. Like other Third World countries, they don't have welfare in Vietnam.

All the men in my electronic group worked directly with the Vietnamese technicians and got along well with the Vietnamese people. The air traffic controllers didn't either work with or socialize much with the Vietnamese. There is considerable difference between the type of personality required to be an electronic technicians and an air traffic controllers. Their jobs are diametrically different and each one requires both different skills and personality. Controllers are extroverts that talk a lot, think and make decisions fast but prefer to socialize with those that are part of their group. On the other hand, electronic technicians are introverts that aren't inclined to brag but have to make difficult complex decisions, which often involve considering a number of options. All the electronic CAAG staff worked and socialized well with the Vietnamese rather than confine their socializing to their own group. For example, one technician who was a devout Catholic spent much of his off duty time working at a Catholic orphanage, doing such things as repairing washing machines or other appliances. Many of them reached out to families to do things that they were grateful for. After I left Vietnam, many of the technicians in my group married Vietnamese girls and brought them back the U.S. when they returned. I have never heard of one of these marriages that failed.

There were so many American military men in Saigon it was hard to believe it was off limits to all American military personnel that didn't actually live and work there. Practically all-military activities were carried out at MACV, known as the Pentagon East located at Tan Son Nhut Airport where most of them lived. American civilians all over Vietnam were well liked and highly respected by the Vietnamese people. I had the rare opportunity of meeting and visiting the homes of both what you would call the peasants and those holding prestigious positions all over Vietnam. I felt that I really got to know an overall cross section of the Vietnamese people from all parts of South Vietnam. The Buddhists are a pacifist non-violent people that were exploited for generations by both the French colonial and the 12-year Kennedy-Johnson American war that followed. Obviously their culture has been suppressed to the point much of it has been destroyed but let us hope there is still enough left so they can put some of it back together. Now that they have achieved their independence from colonial rule as we did in our revolutionary war, we can expect these brilliant industrious people to make major contributions to world society. The Vietnam War has also destroyed much of the U.S. feeling of honesty, integrity and wellbeing, leaving us with a sense of guilt towards the 58,000 American and over 2,000000 Vietnamese boys that were killed. All this was a direct result of our drug addicted president's decision to get into the war and another presidents lying to congress so he could send 500,000 troops to that narrow strip of land on the South China Sea.

VN-12 HOME LEAVES

It had been a long hard 4-months and I was pretty stressed out when my work schedule provided the best opportunity for my first 3-weeks home leave. By the time I returned to Vietnam, installation of the Qui Nhon facility should be completed. Busy as I was, I still missed my family a lot and tired as I was, I couldn't wait to get home.

Joy, my oldest daughter, who was now a flight attendant with American Airlines, planned a family vacation at an Acapulco, Mexico resort. She got airline passes for her mother and sister and used her airline discount to get reservations at a deluxe resort, located on the mountain overlooking the bay. For a small fee, I was able to get my routing changed so I flew from Saigon to Acapulco and on to Minneapolis from there. It was a real upscale resort with two attached apartments, a common patio overlooking the village and a private swimming pool. They also served meals in a common dining room as a part of the package. We enjoyed watching the fishermen, bringing in their morning catch and hanging up their nets to dry, swam in the ocean, explored the beach in a rented jeep and went for a short cruise on what looked like an authentic pirate ship. After a memorable vacation, all of us except Joy flew back home to Minneapolis. Joy flew directly to New York where she was based.

It was nice to get home again but I was so stressed out from 4 difficult months in Vietnam and the jet lag that I wanted to sleep all the time. It was so nice to see my family, friends, relatives and the people I had previously worked with in the Minneapolis Area Office. All this was a firm reminder of what I had given up to take this job.

Perhaps, I would have been able to schedule this trip so I could have been home for Christmas but this was uncertain and I probably would have lost one of my three home leaves if I waited that long. This trip was specifically scheduled around my youngest daughter's last football game at Richfield High School. She was the only majorette for the high school band. It was a great honor to be the only majorette in the marching band for this upscale school, with 1200 students in the graduating class. I was proud to watch her lead this very professional band down the football field. Unfortunately, she was in her last year of high school and this was my only opportunity to see her perform.

Unfortunately, my home leave ended much too soon and I continued to question whether or not I had given up too much for too little. Soon I was back on a narrow body Pan American jet with the seats so close together there wasn't room for my knees. After about an 18-hour flight, I arrived back in Saigon, confused from the jet lag with insurmountable problems waiting for me. It was afternoon when I arrived and went right to work at our office near the airport terminal.

The next two family visitations were after the Tet Offensive and I flew directly back to Minneapolis because I was really stressed out. It had been an extremely difficult period trying to repair the damage done by the Viet Cong, during the offensive and the continuing terrorist attacks all over the country that followed. These family visitations were strictly rest and recuperation leave to spend a few days with my family to alleviate some of the stress and get my head screwed on straight after all the madness. Although I never got rested up, I was better prepared to go back and hit it again.

During these family visitations, we decided that I would go back for a second tour after my first tour was completed in 2 years. Although tours were only 1-1/2 years, it was necessary to stay 2 years if you were going to stay for a second tour. If I be stayed 2 tours, I would be rewarded with a 30 day home leave between tours and in my case a promotion to a higher grade level which would enhance my future career. I also had college expenses and two daughters' weddings to pay for.

We started planning early for an exciting home leave. My wife took some tours out of Tokyo, went to Taipei where the families of the 5 Taiwanese engineers that worked for me in Vietnam lived. They showed her the part of Taipei that tourists never see and she went to Hong Kong where the sister of one of our Taiwanese Engineers sister had her own business. She also took her on tours of Hong Kong to see what few outsiders never see. From there she came to Saigon and stayed with me for a week at my apartment. I was able to show her around the Saigon area and introduce her to some of my Vietnamese and American friends. This gave her a better understanding of what life in Saigon was all about. I knew pretty much what was secure and what wasn't and the continuous roar of artillery fire in the distance didn't bother her too much. She had an around the world, airline ticket and we came back via way of Singapore, Kuala Lumpur, Bangkok, New Delhi, Tehran, Beirut and Ankara. We especially enjoyed the botanical gardens in Singapore, which were located in a semi-tropical park in the center of the very modern city. At that time Kuala Lumpur was in the early stages of modernization and we took some tours through the rubber plantations in the countryside. Bangkok was a very interesting place with its many beautiful Buddhist temples, floating markets and the Thai dancers. We few on to Ankara where we saw so many unusual things as we toured their huge market and the Red Fort in New Delhi, the Taj Mahal in Agra and the abandoned fort south of Agra. This is where one of their ancient rulers built a fort on a hill in a desert area where he maintained separate houses and servants for his Christian, Hindu and Moslem wives.

India was the poorest country we visited where people lived in buffalo dung houses and the women had to carry water from wells miles from her house. It was a country where the ruling class had many luxuries and the peasants had so little. It was also a country where peasant women rented sick or dying babies to get charitable contributions at the open-air markets. We were both shocked and disappointed in Tehran where the city resembled one of our western cow towns. We perked up our ears when we heard Americans talking at the adjacent table when we were sitting in a hotel restaurant in downtown Beirut. They were FAA pilots that worked out of Beirut, flight checking navigation aids in this part of the world. They told us there was absolutely nothing to do in Beirut unless you want to stick around until Wednesday, when you can see the crown jewels at the imperial palace. We took their recommendation and went to Beirut where there was much to see and do and we also went on a tour of the ancient ruins of Balabakk, which was an important market on the camel caravan route. We had planned on stopping in Rome and Madrid but it was Easter weekend in Rome and there was so much air traffic that we had to circle 2 hours before we could land. By that time we were totally exhausted and just wanted to go home so we took the same plane out of Rome and came directly back to the United States. We saw so many things we will never forget in so many interesting places but in the end, home was the best place of all.

During my end of tour physical, they found I had lost all sight in by right eye, which previously had 20/20 vision. Extensive tests at the University of Minnesota showed I had previously had a hemorrhage that probably resulted from stress that I wasn't aware of but regardless of cause the damage was permanent and could not be corrected.

We started planning for the end of my second and final tour, which was still 1-1/2 years away. It was a foregone conclusion that I would be coming back to the Minneapolis Area Office that I left from and all planning was based on that assumption. Since my daughter was employed by American Airlines, my wife could get a free pass to Australia, which was on an American Airlines route. We would meet in Sidney and spend a few days there before we stopped at a resort in the Fiji Islands for a few days on the way home.

Jackie, my youngest daughter transferred from the Mankato to the Minneapolis campus of the University of Minnesota so she would be company for her mother who was living alone. Just before I came home on my next visitation leave, my wife advised me that we were going out for dinner with our daughter and her boyfriend. This troubled me because I had never even heard that she had a boyfriend. She was a consciences student and her mother picked her up from college in Mankato every Friday and took her back on Sunday so she didn't have time to socialize and never even dated at college. Also, it sounded like it was more than just a casual dinner on a night out. I couldn't understand how she could get so involved in such a short time. Although, he was in her high school graduating class, I hadn't heard of him. It was apparent that for some reason they didn't want me to know what was going on but it apparently had got to the point where they had to let me in on it.

It reminded me of the time I was invited for a formal dinner at the home of a girl I was dating many years ago in Chicago, who was interested in marriage. I'm sure everyone in her family knew everything about me except her father who didn't know I wasn't Catholic. When we sat down to the table and she said the blessing, her father stared holes through me when he observed that I didn't cross myself. It was a very Irish family and to make conversation, I said my grandparents emigrated from Northern Ireland. That was the wrong thing to say because her father was obviously a big contributor to the Irish Republic Army whose mission was to kill as many Protestants as possible. There was considerable tension and it turned out to be a very quiet evening. Although I wasn't in a position to get married at that time, she would have made a good wife but I was not about to raise my children in the Catholic Church and wouldn't consider having a father-in-law whose mission in life was to kill Protestants. She understood my objections and we parted the best of friends when I was drafted into the Army.

Even though I was unhappy with the situation I had been forced into, my former experience made me aware of how important this meeting was and I exercised considerable restraint trying to be on my best behavior. He was not at ease and couldn't look me in the eye, giving me the impression that he felt that I could look right through him and didn't like what I saw. The bottom line was that that I was not impressed but hoped it didn't show. I was uncomfortable with the situation but not having any other option; I yielded to my wife's judgment since she was a full time mother that was in the best position to make that judgment. I had confidence in her judgment and concluded she wouldn't approve of anything that wasn't in the best interest of our family. I had further concern about her not coming to see me in Vietnam when her sister came because her future husband didn't approve. Obviously there was some reason she didn't want to talk to me.

Before my last home visitation my wife advised me that they were going to be married in our home church when I got home. They had a nice wedding and my only contribution was to keep the cash register full. We wished them well and they moved to a military base in Texas where he was assigned but for some reason didn't go to Vietnam. This put me in awkward situation because my primary reason for going to Vietnam was to get enough money to send her to college. Since I had already made a commitment and felt that I was doing what had to be done well, I decided to stick it out.

When I completed my tour of duty in Vietnam I met my wife in Sidney where we toured the city, which is more American than America and went on a day's tour to the Outback which covers most of the continent from Perth in the west to Sidney. We flew on to the Fiji Islands where we had reservations at an upscale resort for a few days. Joy had enough seniority with American Airlines so she could move to Los Angeles a couple of years ago. She planned her wedding to take place when we stopped in Los Angeles on our way home. It was a nice wedding with a few guests that was held in a little wedding chapel. We met our new son-in-law's parents, his only brother and his wife at the wedding.

Before I left Vietnam, I was informed that the Area Office where I previously worked in Minneapolis was being closed and I was being assigned to a similar office in Chicago that was going to become a new Regional Office. My airline ticket was written from Saigon directly to Chicago rather than Minneapolis so we had to stop there and I checked in at my new office. I was both physically and emotionally exhausted so I appreciated getting a couple weeks leave in Minneapolis so I could rest up and sort things out. This new development would make it necessary for me to move from Minneapolis to Chicago and neither my wife nor I welcomed the move.

VN-13 VIETNAM WAR VS. WW II

PRELUDE TO WW II

As a WW II combat infantryman, I had the opportunity to view both wars from an up front and personal vantage point. Having personally observed both wars in some depth, I am in position to point out their similarities as well as how they differ. In WW-II, I saw it primarily from a kill or be killed front line combat infantryman's standpoint while, during my three and a half years in Vietnam, I not only had an overview but also was actively involved in the entire war in all parts of the country. Every morning when the Colonel returned from his early morning briefing at MACV, he briefed me on what had taken place during the last 24 hours. When I was away from Saigon, I always attended the early morning briefing of whatever command was responsible to in that particular area. It was essential for my own safety as well as accomplishing my assigned mission. In general, I was always pretty well informed on what was happening throughout the country and who was involved. I was also a member of a military inspection team that made one inspection a month to various military bases that ranged from infantry compounds in the highlands to air bases in the delta. It was generally a high military command operation but as a civilian with a combat infantryman's background, I could talk freely with the infantrymen that carried a gun. I got to see how they lived and could talk openly with mutual understanding about missions they had participated in.

Since wars result from failure of international diplomacy we have to start with the political situations that could not be resolved. WW II was a direct result of failure of the armistice to resolve the various issues WW I was fought for. Germany was unable or unwilling to pay the penalty imposed on them for the cost of the damage resulting from WW-I, which they initiated. German and other European Jews, getting control of the national wealth and enslaving the rest of the population further aggravated it. These events lead to extreme poverty that in turn was the catalyst, which lead to the rise of Nazism. The Nazi Party rapidly developed into not only a German but also a European anti-Jewish movement. Rather than disarming as required by the WW I armistice, Germany designed and built new armament at such a rapid pace that by 1930, Germany was again ready to threaten the world. Although Hitler became the leader in the rise of Nazism it was a very strong movement well supported by the general population. The nations of the world sit by and watched Germany rearm in violation of the WW-I armistice but no one did anything to stop them. Finally, the countries of Europe kept appeasing Germany as they captured one country after another, until they had captured all the countries in continental Europe and were in the process of taking England when we got in. Some of the British Royal Family and Joseph Kennedy our ambassador to England, who was the father of our future president, John F. Kennedy, were some of the appeasers that advocated giving Germany a free hand.

The United States was struggling through the Great Depression when Roosevelt became President of our isolationist country in 1932 when we were also in the midst of our worst drought in history. With all the problems at home with the Mafia type labor unions on strike the Depression didn't end until we were actually attacked by Japan at Pearl Harbor on December 7th, 1941. Roosevelt had campaigned for his 3rd term using the slogan "Keep American Boys out of Foreign Wars". This was the beginning of our national welfare program, which persists to this day and since he had campaigned against getting us into the war he couldn't start a military reediness program and maintain his popularity. Instead of preparing for war he resorted to socialist programs like WPA rather than a military readiness program to provide employment. Finally when we were attacked he sent men into battle totally unprepared in WW I uniforms and little obsolete military equipment.

During these difficult years, the war was raging and we were openly sending war materials to Europe in American ships German submarines didn't sink our ships because they didn't want the US to formally enter the war. Roosevelt, the great orator was the first president to have access to national radio and his periodic Fireside Chats were listened to by everyone that had access to a radio. The country was isolationist and he refused to expend any of his popularity preparing the country for the inevitable war. During the time Roosevelt was campaigning for his third presidential term, he refused to meet Japanese diplomats at a Hawaii summit. At the same time, his campaign slogan was, "Keep American Boys out of Foreign Wars". Unprovoked, Japan attacked the U. S. Naval Fleet at Pearl Harbor on December 7, 1941, about a month after Roosevelt was reelected to his 3rd term. Japan's fleet had been unaccounted for over a month before the surprise attack that destroyed our entire pacific fleet, which was bottled up totally unprepared in Pearl Harbor. What little military equipment we had was obsolete and we were totally unprepared for WW-II without any trained military personnel. Roosevelt had concentrating on useless make work welfare jobs like WPA rather than preparing the U.S. for the coming war, which was inevitable. We didn't start recovering from the great depression until we actually got in involved in WW-II after the Japanese unprovoked attack on Pearl Harbor.

PRELUDE TO THE VIETNAM WAR

Generations ago, in the 1860s, the French colonized territory which included the countries of Vietnam, Cambodia, Thailand, Burma and

Laos, which together were known as French Indo China. The French were taskmasters that took control of every faucet of the colonist's life degrading them to slaves, whose lives were strictly controlled by their French masters. Over a period of many years all countries except Vietnam gained their independence from France. Saigon that the French called Paris of the Orient, Dalot their summer resort in the mountains, Mekong Delta with its rich farm land and over 1500 miles of beautiful white sand beaches together was unquestionable the prize of the Orient. It was also a source of very intelligent, hardworking indentured servants that they could take back to France for maids and other servants. The Vietnamese were Buddhist, which are probably the most peaceful religious group in the world but they deeply resented the Catholic religion being forced on them. Only those that the French could coerce into, making believe they were Catholic, could be the Headman, which we would call mayor of a remote village or hold a job of any importance. The French brought in foreigners they called, "The French Foreign Legion" from their African colonies to maintain order. They were feared by the Vietnamese people because they were the law and raped and killed as they saw fit. The French had to educate some of the Vietnamese so they would have the necessary technological skills to build and support a modern city like Saigon and resorts like Dalat. Again, the most important education was done in France where they had to speak French. If a student had claimed his allegiance to the Catholic religion, he would get 4 years of college and become an engineer. If not, he would get 2 years of college and become a technician. In the French system the individual with the most degrees is always boss regardless of whether or not he has the skill or initiative to even do the job. The Vietnamese people were very dissatisfied with their life under French rule.

After WW II, Ho Chi Minh's forces, which had been trying to drive the French colonists out of Vietnam, became active in northern Vietnam. They had acquired American artillery and other war material abandoned by Chang Kai Sheik, when they were forced out of Mainland China. Ho Chi Minh requested a summit with President Truman who ignored his request. Understandably, Truman was so preoccupied with the restoration of Europe under the Marshall Plan that he may not have even been aware that the U. S. was still supporting France's Foreign Legion. In 1954 Ho Chi Minh's communist army defeated the French Foreign Legion at Dien Bien Phu. The long narrow country was divided in two parts; North Vietnam controlled by the communists and South Vietnam controlled by the French. The people of Vietnam had one year to determine whether they wanted to live in the north or the south before the border was sealed.

The Catholics made a mass exodus from Hanoi the capital of North Vietnam to Saigon the capital of South Vietnam before the border was permanently closed a year later. The Catholics that came down from the north filled the overwhelming majority of the key South Vietnamese government positions. Under the French system they had the most academic degrees and since there was no longer any contact between the north and the south, it was not possible to verify educational claims. In many cases they resorted to individuals making a claim, certifying their education by simply, doing what we would call having it notarized. This resulted in having a Catholic Government rule an overwhelmingly Buddhist population. Finally, the French abandoned Vietnam, destroying everything of importance, including the drawings of the Saigon power system, which no rational engineer could figure out. South Vietnam was in total chaos and the U.S. initially sent in a few advisors to try to help them out.

When John F. Kennedy, an Irish Catholic was elected President of the US he denied promised air support at the last minute to an army of Cubans who were trying to reclaim their homeland from Castro. Those that weren't killed when they hit the beach spent most of the remainder of their life in Cuban jails. This resulted in a major confrontation where Cuba allowed the Soviet Union to station nuclear missile in Cuba, less than 100 miles from the U. S. It was a major showdown that almost resulted in a nuclear war with the Soviet Union. Although the all-out nuclear war was avoided, we had to make major concessions to the Soviet Union and the U. S. public was never reassured.

In order to try to get the American public's mind off his near catastrophic blunders, he expanded the number of U. S. advisers in Vietnam and without seeking Congressional approval started the shooting war and had their president assassinated. The U. S. didn't have any strategic interest in Vietnam so after the French departed it was no longer a French Catholic colonial war but rather an American Vatican war. It was a gross injustice to the Vietnamese people, costing millions of them their life.

HOW THE FIGHTING MANS ROLE DIFFERED

Both wars started from distinctly different political backgrounds but from the standpoint of the young men that fought them, there were both similarities and differences. In both cases, they were drafted off the streets of America but there was considerable difference in how that was done. In WW-II every youth that graduated from high school could expect to be drafted into military service for the duration of the war plus six months. Like all such programs everyone was not treated equally. For example, if the head of the local lumberyard happened to be on the draft board and your father happened to be a carpenter, you could arrange to get a farm deferment even if you had never farmed. In the Vietnam War, they used the same lottery system but fewer recruits were required and they were only drafted for a period of two years and they would only have to serve one in Vietnam. It soon became known as the poor man's war because those that had money enough to attend college were deferred. As a result primarily minorities and men from poor families fought the war because wealthier families could send their sons to college.

The WW-II recruit, drafted for the duration of the war plus six months couldn't visualize any future to look forward to. The entire world was engrossed in an all-out war that we were not prepared for either from an equipment or training standpoint and we entered on the losing side. Our Pacific Fleet had been destroyed at Pearl Harbor; our troops in the Philippines had been killed or captured by the Japanese, the tank battles in North Africa were not going well, Germany had full control of all of continental Europe and it appeared to be inevitable that England could not hold out much longer. When we left home, it was hard to visualize that we would ever return but we saw it as our only hope for survival. The Vietnam War recruits left home knowing they would only have to spend one year in Vietnam but it would also be a year of their life wasted because the war didn't have any clear purpose. Although we had complete control of the air and didn't expect to encounter any mechanized armor in this narrow strip of seacoast about 50 miles wide and 1500 miles long, it was like a guerilla war with land mines and surprise mortar attacks. Perhaps their greatest hardship was the lack of support from the American people. The draft dodgers that spent the war in American colleges that burned their draft cards or demonstrated against the war and those that went to places like Canada or Sweden to avoid the draft had a devastating effect on their moral. Jane

Fonda's trip to Hanoi representing the American entertainment industry's antiwar protesters was a low blow to the moral of the men that were getting their legs blown off in the minefields of Vietnam. Also Dan Ratner's biased and often-untrue media coverage was instrumental in placing blame on the fighting men for the Kennedy/Johnson war. In an effort to get congressional approval to expand the war, President Johnson deliberately lied to Congress, alleging the North Vietnamese had attack an American ship on the open sea in the Gulf of Tonkin. As a result of his deliberate lie, Congress approved the Gulf of Tonkin Resolution, which authorized him to deploy a half a million men on the narrow strip of land called South Vietnam. American servicemen's moral plummeted when they witnessed all the corruption and it became apparent they were not fighting for a just cause but rather as a result of politician's lies. The American public and the news media in particular were outraged and antiwar demonstrations broke out all over the U.S.A. The news media focused the blame on the American servicemen drafted off the streets of America that were forced to fight the war, rather on Presidents Kennedy and Johnson. Overnight the servicemen being killed or maimed and all of us that were there to support them became baby killers. Congress did not initiate any action to impeach President Johnson for his deliberate lie that resulted in the death of the majority of the 58,000 Americans service men that were killed in the war.

Those of us in WW II had full support of the American people and even the wartime farmers kept a low profile to hide their guilt. Those of us that came home from WW II held our heads high with pride while the Vietnam Veterans took off their uniform and got lost in the crowd so people wouldn't accuse them of being baby killers. Although, I was not a uniformed veteran, I know firsthand what it was like to suffer the scorn of the American public, who had been brain washed by the news media, the entertainment industry and the draft dodgers being educated at our colleges and universities to become our new American leaders or teachers to brainwash our children. It is difficult to rationalize that these youth whose life had been interrupted were responsible for the war they were forced to fight.

WW II flight crews had a dangerous job with a high causality rate during the initial phases of the war in Europe when they were trying to destroy the factories in Germany, where they were making additional armament to prolong the war. Fighter-Bombers also played a very significant role in the

Pacific war where P-38 pilot Richard Bong alone shot down 40 Japanese aircraft. There was a significant difference between the dangerous missions of our WW-II bomber and fighter aircraft crews and those in Vietnam because we had complete control of the air. Military rank or pay grade was the most obvious difference in the two wars. Although the Air Force's mission was very limited in the Vietnam War, there were undoubtedly more Colonels than there were 2nd Lieutenants in WW II. In both wars, flight and ground crews undoubtedly had had better food and living conditions than any other group in our military service. With that exception, the introduction of the helicopters in Vietnam was the principal difference.

The Navy played a significant role in WW II after being almost annihilated in Pearl Harbor. The Pacific Fleet and the aircraft on their aircraft carriers took the blunt of the Pacific war. Their major victory in the battle of Midway was the turning point in the Pacific war. They also provided cover firepower for the Army and Marines as they captured one island after another from the savage Japanese in the bloodiest battles of the war. In the Atlantic their mission was to provide primary support to protect our troop and supply ships from the German submarines. The Navy was a minor player in the Vietnam primarily, providing support assistance like the ship that provided power for Qui Nhon.

The Army and the Marines both served similar functions, often fighting side by side on the front line, under the most adverse conditions. In WW II most of their joint operations were in the Pacific theater where they fought their way across the pacific, capturing one island after another in the bloodiest battles of the war. The army got the blunt of the fighting in Europe where the infantry literally climbed up the cliffs overlooking the English Channel and fought their way across France into Germany one step at a time. They fought hedgerow to hedgerow all the way to Paris but were held up waiting for France's General De Gaulle to come up from the rear and formally capture Paris from the escaping Germans. This political decision give the retreating German army time to establish a new line of defense at the Rhine River but as in the past he French were not there to help. The battles of the Rhineland and the Arden Forest, better known as the Battle of the Bulge were undoubtedly the most difficult battles of the war because of the deep snow and extreme cold. During more than two months on the front line, we continuously advanced under continuous artillery fire, without any shelter with nothing to eat except frozen stew

"C" Rations. There was only one occasion when I could remove my shoes from my frozen feet and change my stockings. The wounded died and their bodies were frozen in the snow because it wasn't possible to rescue them. It was a time when death was welcome because men who had been drafted for the duration plus 6 month would never leave the front line until they were either killed or wounded. If they survived and weren't wounded to bad, they would return to the front line after minimal treatment. The causality rate was extremely high and to the best of knowledge there were only 3 of us in the Infantry Company that I went overseas with that survived and we were all seriously wounded. One of us was also shell shocked and I never was able to find out if he recovered. To sum it up, we lived in the snow, slept in fox holes or slit trenches, ate nothing but frozen stew and practically all of us were killed in about a two-month period.

As I traveled throughout Vietnam, I was particularly interested in how a Vietnam era combat infantryman lived and what type of combat they engaged in. I found living conditions were generally pretty good but some places were better than others. I was most impressed by an infantry camp up in the northwest highlands near the village of Pleiku. My first impression was that it was a resort in the mountains. The principle activity for the GIs stationed there seemed to be watering the lush green grass. In front of each living quarters building or barracks there were large windows that could be opened up for ventilation and there were row after row of freshly shined shoes. When I first saw this at a barracks in another camp, I was dumbfounded and couldn't believe that they actually had maid service. I was only in a couple of the barracks but was fascinated to see what Vietnam era living quarters was like. The single story buildings were quite long and about the width of the old 2 story barracks we had in infantry basic training camps. There was an extended hall extending down the center of the building with rooms for 2 men on each side of the hall. One side of each army cot was against the walls that separated the rooms. On the outside wall below the long ventilation window was a countertop with drawers and a wardrobe on each end. Each man had perhaps a thousand dollars' worth of the highest quality Japanese electronic equipment sitting on his half of the countertop.

I had lunch in their mess hall with the enlisted men, which was about the same as any mess hall in a stateside camp as well as other camps in Vietnam. This gave me the opportunity to talk to them about their combat missions, which I was anxious to hear about. Unfortunately, none of the men at my table had ever been on a combat mission but some of them knew someone that had and told me best they could what it was like. They were picked up by one or more helicopters and dropped off in an open area, near the location, where they would conduct a reconnaissance mission. I understood what they were trying to tell me, because one time I run into an infantry outfit when I was out in no man's land in a radio direction finder truck. I was trying to locate the source of radio signals that was interfering with our airport instrument landing system, making it unusable. I was parked out in an open area, when I looked up and saw an approaching line of infantrymen walking about 10 feet apart as far as I could see in either direction coming toward me. I just said, "Hi" to them as they passed. None of men knew anyone that had been away from camp overnight but I was sure that wasn't always the case. You can hardly compare that to WW II combat infantrymen living and fighting under constant artillery fire in a foxhole in subzero weather for months at a time, knowing they will be there until they were either killed or wounded. The one thing they all had in common was a calendar where they checked off every day, telling them how many days until their one-year was up and they could return to the U. S. This of course was one of the major differences between Vietnam and WW II where there was nothing to look forward to as you were going to be there for the duration of the war and 6 months.

Perhaps, medical care for the wounded on the battlefield was another major difference between the two wars. According to the U.S. Army; "The Illustrated History of WW-II, "John Ray: Department of Defense statistics, 37.6% of the mortally wounded service men died in WW II and only 27.5% in Vietnam. In WW II there were probably many more wounded that died of neglect or froze to death on the battlefield than survived. At best they had to be transported long distances to evacuation hospitals, which were little more than an Aid Station. In Vietnam the wounded were picked up on the battlefield by helicopter and if their injuries were serious, they would be dropped off at the helipad at the entrance to a general hospital where they received state of the art treatment.

With the exception of the GI Bill which provided college benefits', veterans of neither war realized few, if any benefits for their sacrifices. According to the above source, WW II took the lives of an estimated 405,400 men and Vietnam 58,200 men. Perhaps some would argue, being able to continue speaking English rather than German and the right of antiwar demonstrators to demonstrate in the streets as being positive. On the negative side, President Roosevelt's selling us out at the peace table was an overwhelming catastrophe. His failure resulted in the Korean War only five years later, the Cold war and the Vietnam wars that followed. Our ailing president who was no longer competent to make important decisions and Alger Hiss, his chief advisor, who was later convicted of being a Russian spy, negotiated the peace treaty with Russia. These two post WW II shooting wars added approximately another 95,000 men to the WW II death toll.

At the end of WW II, twelve of the sixteen million service men were discharged and didn't have either a job or a place to live. About 2,000,000 of us were disabled and with all the unemployed able-bodied service men that had just been discharged, no potential employer would consider a disabled veteran. This was a crucial time for those of us that were discharged because we had not only been deprived of our youth but were longing to get married, raise a family and try to get on with our life. Many of the WW II veterans signed up for the National Guard or Reserve so they would get a few dollars pocket money each month and in five years' time were called back into service to fight the Korean War. Who would have even thought that there could possibly be another war after the Great War to end all wars?

Twenty years later the sons of the WW II veterans were called on to fight President Kennedy's war in Vietnam, which in no way was in America's interest. It was simply a war to distract attention from Kennedy's major blunders and to maintain a foothold in Vietnam for the unwelcome Catholic Church, which was instrumental in getting him elected. Fortunately, there were jobs for the returning Vietnam veterans after they discarded their uniforms and got lost in the crowd. The draft dodgers that President Carter welcomed home and those with college deferments were now qualified to teach the veterans' children. These pedigreed teachers with their ultra-radical liberal ideas were now well established to brainwash the veterans' children and grandchildren.

VN-14 POST VIETNAM CHICAGO

I rested at home for a couple weeks before I started my new job in Chicago but I really didn't know what I would be doing there. My wife was reluctant to even consider moving to Chicago but she rejected the idea of me taking an early retirement which of course meant that we wouldn't have enough money to live on without me getting another job. I took our eight-year-old car, leaving her with our newer car and got a room in a cheap motel for a week. I had been getting 25% extra hazardous duty pay and free housing in Vietnam and now we would to have to pinch pennies if I had to live in a motel very long. Hopefully, this was very temporary situation, and once I got established we would find an apartment and sell our house in Minneapolis.

I wasn't overly welcome when I reported in to my new office on Monday morning because they were obligated to give me a job when I returned from Foreign Service and everyone hoped that it wouldn't be theirs. Everyone was also aware that that all three Area Offices, including Chicago were being replaced by what would be called the Great Lakes Region, which would be located in that vary building. I had read the newspapers and watched TV enough that I was fully aware that the word Vietnam was a nasty word associated with baby killers. Dan Rather type media moguls had made saints out of the draft dodgers and murderers out of those men that were drafted off the streets of America and somehow they became responsible for the war. Although I was well known and highly respected in the Minneapolis Area Office, I only knew a few people in Chicago and they were only casual acquaintances

With all the changes taking place the office was in turmoil as well as a state of flux. As it turned out, I had one important supporter that I had never even met that turned out to be my supervisor. He was a former District Supervisor that had supervised a group of sectors in the Detroit area who was personally aware of some of the significant engineering problems that that I had solved. As a temporary expedient, he divided the Navigation/ Communication Section of his Engineering Branch, into two parts, keeping the present supervisor in charge of one section and putting me in charge of the other. The existing staff was divided between our two sections. It turned out that the state of Michigan where my supervisor came from was in my area. Splitting the section was kind of a hard pill for my competitive supervisor to swallow because we would be in direct competition for a similar position at a higher grade when the new region was established.

From a job standpoint, this turned out to be a good week and I also rented a cheap furnished apartment on a monthly basis near our office. I couldn't afford to live in even a cheap motel for very long and I had to have some resemblance, of a home base even if I was traveling much of the time. I went back to Minneapolis, an 800-mile round trip that weekend as I planned to do on most future weekends. After a couple weeks my wife came back with me to spend a week looking for an apartment and we looked around but it was kind of a halfhearted effort and she didn't seem to be enthused with any of them. It was obvious that she disliked the temporary apartment that I was renting by the month as much as I did. I did a considerable amount of traveling throughout the portion of the area where I was assigned and didn't get back to Minneapolis every weekend. I was amazed how much technology had advanced in the 3-1/2 years that I had been in Vietnam and I would have a lot of catch-up work to do. One weekend I told my wife we couldn't live this way indefinitely and she said, "Let's just put our house up for sale and do what we have to do."

The Friday after we listed our house for sale, I got a call from her at the office saying there was a family emergency and she wanted me to come home immediately. She was very upset and hung up the phone before telling me what the emergency was. Her strange behavior suggested it might be a suicide so I immediately called my younger daughter Jackie who lived nearby and asked her to go over to our house immediately. I told her I would catch the first flight back to Minneapolis and would call her at our house to pick me up at the airport. When she got to our house a few minutes after I called, her mother and her dog were both gone but she had left a sealed letter for me. When I got home, I read the letter saying she didn't love me anymore, wanted a divorce and wouldn't be back until I left. Jackie called her sister Joy in Los Angeles who came in the next morning but obviously, neither one of them knew what was taking place. That night the door bell rang and it was a law enforcement officer serving me a divorce warrant, which included a court order forbidding me from writing a check on our only checking account. My paychecks had always been sent to my wife and she deposited them in this account so either of us could write a check to get cash. There was also a letter in the next morning's mail from our bank verifying that our bank account had also been closed. This left me almost destitute because all I had was a few dollars in my pocket and I wouldn't even have enough money to go back to work in Chicago. The court order also outlined her terms for divorce, which I couldn't possibly meet. The family emergency was obviously a scheme concocted by her shyster attorney to get me back in Minnesota so they could serve divorce papers on me. Also, I couldn't even talk to her because she said she wouldn't be back from wherever she went until after I left. Her proposed divorce settlement made it clear for the first time that there was another man involved because she was asking for considerable financial support for the first year and very little after that. Obviously, she intended to get married as soon as our divorce was final and couldn't get maintenance support after that. It also cleared much of the mystery about my youngest daughter's hurry up marriage that she would never talk to me about. It was obvious that when she came back to Minneapolis for her second year of college and saw what was going on, she could see that a divorce was inevitable and wanted to get out before her family crumbled around her. Before, I couldn't understand why a girl who went to the prom with a classmate who became the chief council to a multinational corporation would consider marrying a classmate that took 5 years to finish a 4-year high school.

My ex-wife's romance didn't work out as she expected because her Romeo was no longer interested in her if he had to support her. Playboys and gigolos will tell gullible women anything that will pacify them in order to get a cheap date that somebody else is paying for. Also, women that are supported by someone else are cheap and plentiful so why would anyone buy a cow when you can get milk for nothing.

This hit me at a time when I was physically and mentally exhausted, trying to recover from 3-1/2 very stressful years in Vietnam, followed by further pressure from starting a new job in Chicago. My first thought was to just give up and check into a hospital but after thinking it through, I realized this would be the end of my career that I had worked so hard to develop. Once you have been treated for emotional problems your career is at best stalemated, as they can never depend on anyone that has ever had emotional problems. No one in my family was ever divorced and I always thought of it, as a failure in life, just as bankruptcy is a financial failure. My daughter from Los Angles stayed with me until her mother called a couple days later and both daughters insisted that she had to come home and straighten out the mess she had created. I told her that I had my whole life invested in her and my family and wouldn't consider a divorce until she saw a psychiatrist to make sure she was fully aware of what she was doing. He said she did so there was no alternative but to proceed with the divorce. After 26 years, I ended up with an 8-year-old car, which was stolen a few months later, and half of what we paid for our house 10 years earlier minus the realtor's fees.

At 48 years of age, I would not have been able to recover without the full support from my daughters.

The strange thing about a divorce is that everybody knows what is going on except you. My friends were also my wife's friends and even though they knew a divorce was eminent they distanced themselves from it and me as well, because they didn't want to be involved. About a year later they were comfortable telling about my wife's affairs while I was in Vietnam. Hindsight also indicates, when my youngest daughter moved back home from college, she too could see what was obviously a pending divorce and got herself involved in what turned out to be a failed marriage so she could escape before it blew up in her face. Our failed marriage was one of the millions that could be attributed directly to the feminist movement that plagued American families and expedited the moral decay of our society.

These were not happy days living in Chicago where I was an outcast just because I had been in Vietnam. I didn't have anyone there that I could really call a friend and you couldn't say life was good. It was kind of like when I lived there about 30 years ago before I was drafted into military service. Poverty stricken, I shared a sleeping room with another young man about my age. One night he took me to a dancing class with him at the YMCA and an aggressive little redheaded girl met me. We had an excellent relationship and she even talked about marriage but I was about to be drafted and wasn't about to get that involved. Also it was apparent that it wouldn't work out because her father was a radical Catholic that supported the IRA to kill Protestants and I wasn't about to raise my children in the Catholic Church. We parted best of friends when I was drafted as we both understood why a girl educated in a Catholic school with a father who was an IRA supporter and a Protestant that didn't believe in such things could have a happy marriage.

I knew through mutual friends that she graduated from Marquette University in Milwaukee and married someone who attended a Catholic boys' school. During this lonely period, I couldn't help but wonder what happened to her. I expected that after her marriage made in the Vatican, she would be happily married with a whole bunch of kids. Nevertheless, I would have liked to call her even if she was married because after all we parted as good friends; not lovers but I didn't even know her married name. One day when I was looking through the greater Chicago phone book, I locate what could be her father's name and phone number. There wasn't anyone I would rather not talk to but I finally got enough nerve to call and ask if he had a daughter named Mary Jane. Fortunately, he obviously hadn't recognized me when I asked about Mary Jane and gave me her phone number suggesting that I call her. When I called her, she sounded real excited when I told her who it was and we had a lively conversation, talking about the yesteryears. She told me she graduated from Marquette University and was a Doctor of Veterinary Medicine. When I told her that I was divorced and had two daughters the mood changed abruptly and there was a very long pause. Finally, she told me in a slow tortured voice that she was married for a brief period but it didn't work out and she now lived by herself in her own condominium in the same building as her aging parents on the far west side of Chicago. It was apparent from our conversation that her ex-husband had graduated from a Catholic boy's school and liked boys rather than girls. Finally, I said we should have dinner together one of these days. Enthusiastically, she said Oh, I think that would be fun but after a long pause she said in a depressed voice, I don't think that would be a good idea because I am no longer the girl you once knew. It was evident that her brief frustrating marriage had a major impact on her life and she was probably chairwoman of the hate men committee of the Women's Liberation Movement. Although I never called her again, I felt sorry for her because she certainly didn't hate men when I knew her. Her frustrating divorce with the help of the Women's Liberation Movement had obviously made her a bitter unhappy woman.

My daughter, Joy from California came to Chicago often, helping me find an apartment and getting my life back on track. When they started closing the Minneapolis office, more and more people that I knew moved to Chicago and I felt more comfortable there. I spent considerable time in travel status; working on facilities that I had previously identified that needed major improvements and was making good progress. In a few months, truckloads of all types of files and records started arriving from the two Area Offices that were closing. I was designated as the one to sort them out and help with the establishment of a new filing system for the new Great Lakes Region, Engineering Division. This was a big job because there were thousands of files for various types of facilities in the new region that extended from Ohio in the east through Montana in the west. I had previously helped set up the filing system for the Minneapolis Area Office when three large Districts were consolidated into an Area Office several years ago. Marie, the lady I worked with both on this and the previous project had been promoted and was now the Administrative Officer for the Engineering Division for our new Great Lakes Region.

I first met Marie at the La Crosse, Wisconsin airport office where she worked for the FAA for half a day and for the airport manager the rest of the day. I was there on a routine inspection out of our Minneapolis District Office, when one of our District Office relief technicians was relieving the field office chief who was going to a specialized school in Oklahoma City. Our relief technician had apparently established a special relationship with this brilliant, petite little woman who was not only as cute as a bug's ear but was also a human dynamo. When the three of us had dinner together that night, she gave me a kind of a resume of her extremely unusual background. She was a USO Girl in Korea, kind of skipped over getting married and having three sons and was Secretary for Kennedy for the State of Wisconsin when he was running for president. She was particularly excited about Bobby Kennedy and recalled that she couldn't wait for him to come around to motivate her every month. Apparently this is what resulted in her Catholic divorce, which they call a separation. Her youngest son grew up to look like Bobby Kennedy was quite small at that time and she had now latched on to our relief technician who had been assigned there for a couple months. A few months later, she got a job in our District Office and moved to Minneapolis where she ended up in the program office. By this time she had a well-established-relationship with our relief technician who also worked out of our office and by this time his marriage was also on the rocks. Her supervisor discovered she had assigned our relief technician, who was now her live-in lover to a special school in Oklahoma City without his knowledge or approval. Because of their relationship it was considered the same as nepotism and the District Supervisor was going to reassign both of them to different locations. It turned out to be a major battle between her union and not just the District Supervisor but the Division Chief in the Kansas City Region. The decision was made to transfer both of them and she called on her old friend Senator Proxmire who squelched the move at the Washington level and the whole thing was dropped. Because of her involvement in the Kennedy Presidential Campaign, the FAA considered Proxmire's intervention was a political payback by the Democratic Party. Some years later when my wife and I were in La Crosse visiting one of her Foreign Service coworkers that lived in the close knit community where Marie was raised, we learned the rest of the story. It turned out that she was also Senator Proxmire's mistress before she got involved in the Kennedy campaign. In fact he was responsible for her becoming Secretary for Kennedy in the State of Wisconsin. Their intimate relationship was documented on home movies at the nearby American Legion Club which they often frequented.

I was aware of all these incidents but had not been involved, making it possible for me to have an excellent working relationship with her. I always enjoyed working with talented, can do people who were willing to work hard so everyone could take pride in a job well done. It was a pleasure to work with her when we established a completely new file system in both the area and the regional office.

During this period of time they were also in the process of filling the positions that would be required to staff the new Regional Office. I was selected for the Navigation/Communication Chief position where both the establishment of new facilities and maintenance of existing facilities were under my jurisdiction. Previously the component parts of new facilities came as separate units and had to be installed in equipment racks and wiring the individual components together was a slow time consuming task. Most new equipment was now being purchased as a unit that could be set in place and it was only necessary to do the external wiring. The maintenance inspection program for all this category facility was also the responsibility of this section.

About a year later, I got a call from our International FAA Office in Washington asking me if I would consider taking a two-year foreign assignment to Bolivia, S. America. USAID had made an aviation loan to Bolivia more than 20 years earlier which included two Boeing 727 planes, airport construction work and air navigation/communication equipment. The final stage of the contract had been delayed twice by two communist coups. Equipment shipped by airfreight many years ago, had been off loaded at numerous destinations along the way and was probably still in warehouses or freight depots. Bolivia was a landlocked country in the high Andes Mountains that didn't have either railroads or highways to transport people or equipment. La Paz the Capital City, where I would be living was at 12,500 ft and the airport runway elevation where I would be working was 13,200 ft. I would receive a 20% pay differential because of altitude and isolation. Much of the equipment had become obsolete sitting in original packing crates and they thought my current experience, working with old vintage equipment in Vietnam would be helpful. They told me they couldn't locate an engineer in FAA that has the necessary experience that could speak Spanish and if I took the job I would have to learn Spanish because most of the people that I would work with couldn't speak English. They would send me to language school at the Foreign Service Institute in Washington D.C. where Ambassadors and other Foreign Service personnel learned foreign languages. I told them that this was a big order and I would have to give it some serious thought before I could make a decision. They said they would like to have an answer in a week and I told them that I would get back to them by then.

Although my job was going well, I wasn't happy living alone in the Chicago Area. My divorce and having my car stolen at my apartment give me a feeling of insecurity which didn't leave any good memories to fall back on. I didn't like fighting traffic on the toll roads and perhaps most of all; I didn't like eating alone. On the other hand it was certainly a challenging job, starting by searching for equipment in all the warehouses and depots between Miami and Bolivia. I never lived and worked at an altitude of 13,000 ft but I remembered as an aviation cadet that you get light headed at 10 to 15 thousand feet in the altitude pressure chamber. On the other hand, if other people could do it, why can't I? Perhaps my biggest challenge would be learning a new language and directing a major project in that language at 50 years of age.

After thinking about it for a few days, I talked to my Division Chief who would have to release me and assure me that I would have a job when I returned two years later. It is like being loaned to the Agency of International Development for two years with them paying my salary and all other costs. This disrupts the region's program, requiring them to fill my position and making arrangements to have a position for me when I return. He said, he considered it a worthy project that he thought we should support and he would release me just as they did when I went to Vietnam.

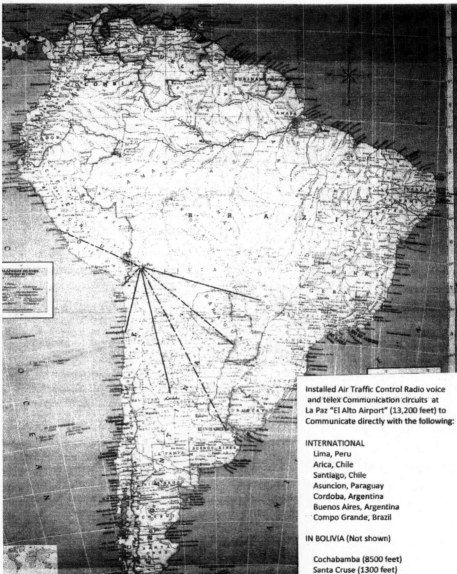

Installed Air Traffic Control Radio voice
and telex Communication circuits at
La Paz "El Alto Airport" (13,200 feet) to
Communicate directly with the following:

INTERNATIONAL
  Lima, Peru
  Arica, Chile
  Santiago, Chile
  Asuncion, Paraguay
  Cordoba, Argentina
  Buenos Aires, Argentina
  Compo Grande, Brazil

IN BOLIVIA (Not shown)

  Cochabamba (8500 feet)
  Santa Cruse (1300 feet)
  Trinidad (400 feet)

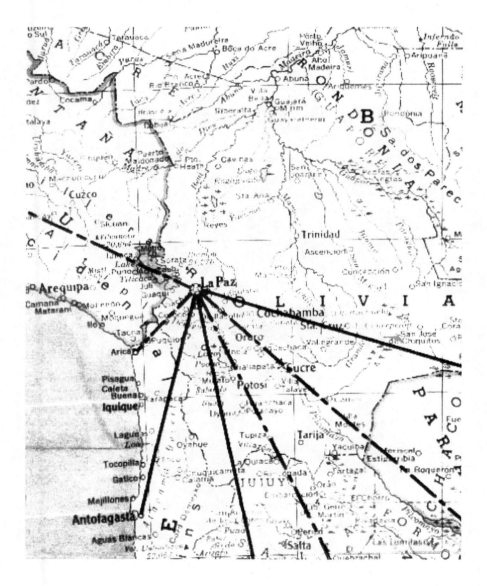

Indian take embasy staff for Reed Boad ride on Lake Titiaca

Going to work at La Paz's El Alto Airport

V

LIFE IN THE ANDES

LP-1 PREPARING FOR NEW JOB

After considering my new job opportunity, I decided that it was an opportunity that I couldn't refuse. The Chicago Regional Office, which I helped establish, had been good to me and it was a good place to work but after Vietnam and a surprise divorce there was too many unpleasant memories there. The post Vietnam atmosphere where returning military service men took off their uniform before returning home also affected civilians like me. Anti-American people like Jane Fonda, John Kerry and Dan Rather that should have been convicted of treason, lied to the public and somehow made us responsible for the stupid Kennedy/Johnson war, even accusing us of being baby killers. It was time for a new environment that would give me time to heal.

I would be going to Spanish language school at the Foreign Service Institute in January 1973 and once I left I wouldn't be returning to Chicago before I left for Bolivia. My division chief asked me to think about whom would be a good man to replace me as navigation/communications chief when I left. I already had someone in mind and he agreed with my choice. I had to terminate the lease on my apartment, put my furniture in storage and dispose of the car I bought when mine was stolen in front of my apartment. Regardless, whether I shipped my present car to Bolivia or purchased a new one after I arrived, the U.S. Government would pay to ship it. It was an advantage for me to buy a new car after I got there, because I would be exempt from paying customs duty, which was several times the cost of the car. Also, when I completed my tour, I could sell it for far more than I paid for it. The U.S. Government requires that you give any amount in excess of what you paid to charity so you don't make any money on it but have a new car all the time you are there.

My Spanish language class started in the middle of January at the Foreign Service Institute in Washington and would last for 6 weeks. There were many classes in session in every conceivable language for ambassadors and other government employees that were assigned to U.S. missions all over the world. There were only three of us in my class and the teacher was from Bolivia where I was being assigned. They kept the classes small so we could get more individual help to accelerate the program. I was 50 years old and it wasn't easy to learn a new language. We listened to cassette tapes for hours at a time in one of a multitude of booths they had for that purpose. We also had a 2-hour class in the morning and afternoon and took tapes home at night to study nights and on weekends. Each of us also had a portable cassette recorder that we took back to our motel at night so we could study several hours every night and weekends. I would liked to have had more than 6 weeks of classes because I was going to have to direct a major project using Spanish because very few of the people that I would be working with could speak any English. FAA said that would not be possible because I had to get over to FAA Headquarters and review the project files before I left and they couldn't delay my departure any longer.

FAA Headquarters was on the other side of the Potomac, across the Washington Mall from the Smithsonian Museum. I would be working in the International Office, reviewing the files on this project in an effort to learn more about what the project consisted of and how much had actually been completed so I could determine where I had to start. The project, which started about 20 years ago, was for the purpose of developing an aviation program in this landlocked country. It was financed by a USAID loan that included building or upgrading four airports (two of which were international), the purchase of two Boeing 727 aircraft to start a new national airline and a communication/navigation project. The later project provided domestic and international communication and navigation facilities to support this and other international air carriers that would land or over-fly Bolivia. The radio communication network distributes weather information, flight plans and other aircraft movement and control information throughout South

America, which would be printed out, automatically on what we would now call a mechanical telex machine. The other sideband on that same transmitter would provide direct voice communication between air traffic controllers in two different countries that were the anchors cities for all South American Air Traffic Control. High-powered transmitters were required at La Paz because it was the intermediate relay point between Lima and Buenos Aires. The first two phases of the overall loan project were almost completed before the project was interrupted by two separate communist coups that left the project in limbo. I would be replacing a FAA flight standards pilot who managed the development of the new airline. My job was to complete unfinished details of both these projects as well as being project engineer to manage and actually install the communication-navigation equipment.

Bolivia was a landlocked country with neither highways nor railroads, making it necessary to ship all equipment by air. During the delay resulting from the coups, electronic equipment which had since become obsolete was offloaded in warehouses all the way from Miami to Bolivia and there wasn't any way to determine what had been delivered, what was in warehouses along the way or what was lost and never would be recovered. Recently, FAA had written the specifications and contracted to purchase two ten-kilowatt and 20 one-kilowatt transmitters with the necessary receivers and ancillary equipment. This should have recently been delivered to Bolivia. Unfortunately, we hadn't been able to determine if any of that equipment had actually been delivered. Bolivia was pretty well isolated from the world and didn't have telephone communication, as we know it. British Cable and Wireless, using radio links, which were neither reliable nor readily accessible, provided what telephone service they had with the outside world. After I learned what I could about the status of the project, I was ready to leave but for some reason there was some unknown delay.

I later learned the delay had to do with the FAA/USAID agreement regarding my salary and benefits. I was considered a participating agency employee where FAA actually paid my salary and benefits and would be reimbursed by USAID, who could not pay any employee more than the ambassador's salary at that post. Without even knowing that was a problem, I sat around the International Office doing nothing for a couple weeks. Finally, the problem was cleared up and I departed for Bolivia on May first.

LP-2 ARRIVED IN LA PAZ

Braniff was the only, US air carrier that went to Bolivia. It left Miami about 2AM and stopped in Lima en route to La Paz, Bolivia. As we approached the La Paz airport called El Alto meaning the, high in Spanish, we started letting down after we went through the mountain pass, which was 15,000 feet above sea level. As we let down to land at the airport, which was 13,200 feet above sea level, the pilot started depressurizing the cabin down to runway pressure. By the time we landed we were light headed because under normal conditions, the gas masks drop down when the cabin pressure drops below 10,000 feet. I felt kind of woozy, taking my carry on baggage from the airplane to the terminal building where I would go through customs. FAA sends your picture to your new post to make it easier for the person meeting you to find you. I had never met the man that I was replacing. He met me and helped me clear customs. I had been up all night, and was tired as well as being light headed at this high altitude and it was difficult to even think so I appreciated his help, getting me through customs. This was also the acid test to determine whether or not I would be able to communicate in this Spanish speaking world where anyone that could speak English wouldn't admit it. Unknown to me, May 1st is a holiday in most countries of the world and the local people that I would be working with were off that day.

By the time I got my luggage, it was the middle of the afternoon and the man that I was replacing took me down the narrow winding road with switchbacks to the apartment that had been reserved for me in La Paz. This was about 1000 feet below the airport where he left me so I could get some rest and would be ready to report for work the next morning. The airport is right on the edge of the Alto Plano which is a high flat plain about 200 miles long and 50 miles wide that was referred to in the book, "Garden of the Gods" as the place where spaceships from outer space landed. On the south end of the Alto Plano there was a 21,190 foot snow covered mountain called Illimani that was the prominent landmark in the crisp clear air that vas clearly visible for hundreds of miles. Illimani usually had a circle of clouds that looked like a halo just above its snow-covered peak. The city of La Paz was like a huge stadium cut into the edge of the Alto Plano, like half of a bowl that opened into a valley thousands of feet below. After you go down below the Alto Plano, the terrain drops off sharply and no matter which way you go it is either up or down. Even the only main street in the city is a fairly steep grade down toward the valley.

The building where my 6th floor apartment was located had an elevator which was essential at this high altitude where you had to stop and rest between floors when you walked up. Each floor had two fairly large apartments with a kitchen, dining room, living room, three bedrooms and two baths. Each apartment was completely furnished with dishes, bedding and everything you would need with exception of a washing machine but even though we were only 17 degrees below the equator it was always cold, particularly at night at this high altitude. Everyone had to have a cook/maid because you would be eating at least your evening meal at home and it took a considerable amount of time to shop in the market where it was necessary to go to a different merchant to purchase each item. Washing clothes was also a time consuming task without a washing machine, because the maid had to wash them in the bathtub or shower. It reminded me that one of my first jobs would be to hire a maid but for the time being what I really needed was sleep.

The next morning, I woke up early and found there that there was nothing to eat in the house so I had to go out and look for a restaurant before I tried to find the American Embassy where my office would be located. I went down the elevator and was standing in front of my apartment when a large station wagon went by and stopped in front of an apartment across the street when some women, who appeared to be Americans, were getting in. I went over there before they closed the door and asked them if they were going to the American Embassy and they said, "Yes, get in if that is where you want to go." Our embassy was on a side street several blocks up the main city street in a bank building. The bank was on the ground floor and our embassy had all floors from the second floor where the marine guard post was located and on up. After the marine guard checked my credentials, one of the ladies from the van, whose name was Edna Gutierrez, asked me if I had had breakfast and I told her that I hadn't. She said they had a small cafeteria downstairs and I asked her if they took American money because I hadn't had a chance to change money yet. She said "No, but I will treat you to breakfast," so we went to the cafeteria and had breakfast. She told me that she was the record supervisor for USAID and was aware that I was coming because she received and distributed all the cable traffic. Also, she said the man that I was relieving usually didn't get in very early but after I saw him, I needed to come to her office and she would brief me on such things as security and use of the Army Post Office (APO). She took me up to the third floor where the man that I was replacing had his office. He was there and introduced me to the people in the program office where my office would be. About all I got done that day was to meet some people, change some money and find out where the restroom was. When it was time to go home, the elevator door opened and there was the lady that took me to breakfast. She said she usually walked home at night because it was downhill and asks me if I wanted to walk with her, which I did.

The following morning Harry Tabor, the FAA man that I was replacing took me up to the airport and introduced me to the people that I would be working with for the next two years. Ele Melgraho was Chief of Electronics for ASANA, the government organization that provided all aviation services. We hit it off well from the start and I was pleased that he could speak some English. With his poor English and my poor Spanish we could communicate surprisingly well.

LP-3 URGENT PROBLEMS WAITING

The next morning Ele picked me up in his personal car and took me up to the airport. A bus picked up his technical staff at 7AM in downtown La Paz each morning and left the airport to bring them back at 1:00 PM. This was a relatively short day but considering the high altitude you were as tired as if you had worked a 10-hour day. This was the first time that I had actually been able to talk to Ele about the project we were about to start together. He told me that the communication equipment had arrived some time ago and they had been waiting for my arrival. He shocked me when he told me they had just received notice that the code circuits they were presently using with Lima would be discontinue in less than a week because Lima was retiring all their code operators. They had been using a code circuit and obviously would not be able to communicate with Bolivia unless we got our new independent sideband transmitter and receiver in operation before that. Also, all airline flights to La Paz would have to be cancelled.

The equipment was still in the factory crates and I hadn't even seen an instruction book. They didn't have a receiver station so we temporarily installed an equipment rack in Ele's office. After locating the ISB receiver that was on the correct frequency, we installed it in the equipment rack and sat the teletype console beside it. It was also necessary to fabricate an antenna that was suitable for this frequency and install it on the roof of the terminal building. The Lima transmitter was already in operation and they had a strong enough signal so we could adjust our equipment so we could copy their messages well. For the time being, Ele's office would be the receiving communications station for Lima. They did have an elaborate log periodic antenna system installed for both Lima and Buenos Aires on the other side of the airport for a receiver station. However, they didn't have a building, power or control cable installed yet, so it wasn't much help at this time.

In order to have a circuit we also had to have a transmitter, which posed more of a problem. They had a nice transmitter station building, plenty of power and the same type antenna system as they had for a receiver station. The only problem was we didn't have any buried control cable between the airport terminal and the transmitter station. We needed about 3000 feet of 50 pair cable and it had to be buried in a trench between the two buildings. Ele got on the telephone and somehow managed to get two reels of 50 pair cable and a splice kit from British Cable Wireless. They didn't have such a thing as a power trencher but the next morning when we got to the airport they had almost half of the trench dug and there were about 25 labors out there digging like mad. By the time Ele and I got one of the 1000 watt transmitters uncrated, and connected to power and an antenna they had the trench dug and the cable in it. We still had to install the ISB tone equipment in the rack in Ele's office, splice and terminate the cable on both ends but with luck we would get a system in operation before the code circuit was terminated. I had never spliced a 50 pair cable but I had seen it done and knew how to do it. The next day we finished the temporary installation and got the transmitting system in operation. We used a 1 KW transmitter rather than the 10 KW transmitter in our temporary installation because it would have taken considerably more time to properly install the huge10 KW transmitter which will be used on this circuit.

We were pleased with our accomplishment, which would give us the opportunity to methodically plan how we were going to proceed not only at La Paz but also at 3 additional domestic airports and several international circuits. Although we had some problems with the Lima transmitter we had just installed, we didn't consider it unusual for a new installation where we had to take several shortcuts that we knew would have to be done over later. In the meantime, we quit at noon like everyone else and I spent the afternoon at my office in the Embassy. This got to be a normal routine because of transportation problems and I needed time to outline the scope of the project, make plans and prepare engineering drawings for the completion of the overall project. This was the first afternoon that I had got back to the office and as I was going home, Edna was again there to walk home with me. She told me that she was having a dinner party for some Embassy people the next day and one of her guests just called said he or she would not be able to come. She asked me if I could come and since I obviously didn't have any other plans; I told her I would be happy to come. There were about a dozen people at her formal sit down dinner and it gave me the opportunity to meet some of the Embassy people. I was in an unusual position where I didn't interact very much with the Embassy staff because I worked primarily with the local people at the airport and just had a part time office at the Embassy.

LP-4 TRANSMITTER PROBLEMS

We didn't sit back and crow about our accomplishments very long because it soon became apparent that the transmitter problem that we had been experiencing was not just a temporary problem but something far more serious. Specifications for the communication equipment prepared by FAA engineers at Washington headquarters included a statement that the equipment must operate at an altitude of 13,500 feet but I found myself in the position of, having to prove why it didn't meet that specification. Little was known about operating high power radio transmitting equipment at such high altitude because this was the only place on earth that it was ever tried. I spent many days and nights at the airport, trying to determine exactly why the equipment would not function as required in the specifications. Obviously, the contractor would take the position that I didn't know how to operate the transmitters. After much research, I determined the problem was caused by several inter-related causes, none of which could be corrected without major engineering modifications. The cooling fans, which were an internal part of the transmitter cabinet, did not cool the high wattage radio tubes. They operated at a slower speed on 50-cycle power and the lower volume of air at this high altitude was not adequate to cool the high wattage radio tubes. There was also an arcing problem that resulted from low-density air at high altitude not being as good an insulator as air at low elevation. When transmitters were operated above half their rated power, radio frequency energy arced across insulators to grounded parts of the compartment where the radio tubes were installed. Reliable operation of the transmitters was limited to about a quarter of the transmitter's rated power.

It was practically impossible to call my Washington office because of the antique telephone service in this isolated area and I could not go into enough detail in an embassy cable so I decided to write a complete engineering report. Since we had an APO, they should receive it in a few days and would have the full story. Every night for the next month I typed out a letter to keep my office informed but didn't get any reply. Finally, I sent a letter to the offices that supervised my Washington office explaining my communication problem. I got immediate response from my Washington office and my new supervisor that I didn't know I had showed up in a couple days. He updated me on the turmoil in my Washington office. The Iran Hostage Crisis had just developed and we had a quite a large technical staff there at the time which they had to bring back to the US. This resulted in a reduction in force in our Washington Office and the Chief of our Iran CAAG Group was now my supervisor. When he returned to the US he went on leave and had not reported for work in his new job. In the meantime, all the correspondence I sent was thrown in the drawer of what would be his desk. When the new Chief of the FAA International Office was alerted by my letter, he was called in immediately and found a drawer in his desk full of my urgent communication and came to La Paz the next day. The general that was the former head of the office and the engineer that had given me such outstanding support in Vietnam no longer worked there. My new supervisor sent a copy of my engineering report to the factory design engineer before he departed and he also arrived in La Paz a few days later. He verified my findings agreed with my diagnosis and designed modifications that would require the installation of modification kits, which had to be made up at the factory. A few months later, they shipped modification kits for all the transmitters and sent a factory technician to install them as soon as they arrived. The modification were somewhat successful but still didn't do the job and the chief design engineer came back to reassess the situation. His conclusion was that all 22 transmitters had to be returned to the factory in New York to be redesigned and returned. We couldn't send all the transmitters at once because we already had some circuits in limited operation. The project was delayed to the point that I wouldn't be able to get the project completed because so much of my time had to be consumed keeping the equipment in operation so air carriers could continue to land at the airport. Things don't happen very fast in the Third World but in spite of that, we did get some things done and many other things started.

LP-5 GETTING SETTLED

By the end of my second week, the crises had somewhat stabilized and I had to get my life organized so I could get on with my work. I had so many problems facing me when I arrived that hadn't had time to take care of personal survival things that had to be done as this was going to be my home for 2 years. I tried to work them in but still I had to hire a maid and order a car because it was obvious that had to have transportation to do my job. Initially, the USAID loan included a station wagon which would be available only to the project manager but that was long ago and the vehicle was not only wore out but there weren't any parts available.

In addition to all the problems I encountered my first week in Bolivia, I had a headache like most people get when they first arrive at a high altitude post. In addition to having a headache in back of your head and neck, your mind doesn't work very well either. This is caused by the thin oxygen deficient air but goes away in about a week when you system generates another pint of blood to carry the limited number of red blood cells throughout your body.

I had seen Edna on the days that I got back to the embassy in the afternoon and she had offered to look for a maid for me. Everyone at the embassy had a maid who knew other maids that were looking for a job so there wasn't much of problem finding one. With my limited Spanish, it would be difficult to negotiate an agreement with even an experienced maid and feel that we both understood the ground rules. Edna probably had as much experience as anyone did because she had hired maids in countries all over the world. Spanish was her first language or mother tongue as they call it, so that qualified her as being truly bilingual by international standards. Once we agreed on the rules, my Spanish was good enough we could communicate with the maid well enough for everyday activities. The maid did the washing, house cleaning, purchased the groceries and prepared dinner at night. It was a relief to get that problem taken care of.

There was a Chevrolet dealership just down the street from my apartment and I stopped in to see about buying a new car. All their cars were made at San Palo, Brazil and they had to order them from there. I ordered a Chevrolet Opala, which they recommended for high altitude use in the mountains, where you have to climb steep grades. It would have a gear ratio that was necessary for use in the mountains and the same large engine that was used in US Chevrolet Impalas. This was a standard engine manufactured in Brazil that was used in American cars. After WW II, the rich iron mines in northern Minnesota were depleted and they had to import iron ore from Brazil, which made iron and steel very expensive. Initially, they started building steel mills in San Palo and exported the iron and steel to the US to reduce costs. It had now progressed to the point where they had automated engine-manufacturing factories and exported the finished engine to the US. I was anxious to get my new car because it was apparent that I couldn't do the job I came down here for without the necessary transportation. My car would be shipped from San Palo, Brazil to Santa Cruz, Bolivia that was the end of the railroad. They told me the car should be delivered to Santa Cruz in about 2 months where it would have to go through Bolivian customs. Santa Cruz was on the edge of the foothills on the east side of the Andes Mountains, which was a 2-day drive over the mountains to La Paz.

I kept checking with the auto dealer in La Paz but it was about 2 months later that they received notice that my car had arrived in Santa Cruz. They didn't have telephone communication with their dealership in Santa Cruz but they assured me that I would be able to pick it up anytime. Bolivian Airline provided passenger service to Santa Cruz, which was one of the 4 airports in Bolivia that I was associated with. I was extremely disappointed to find that my car had not cleared customs and I had to fly back without it. A couple weeks later, the La Paz dealership received the customs documents confirming that my car had cleared customs. I accepted Edna's offer to fly down with me to pick up my car. She bought her car in the US and after clearing customs in Santa Cruz it was hauled to La Paz by truck.

It was a nice shiny 4-door sedan and still smelled like it just had come off the assembly line in San Palo and was ready to start the 2-day trip to La Paz. We had to go from Santa Cruz, which was at 1,300 feet above sea level through the mountain pass, which was above 15,000 feet down to La Paz at 12,500 feet. The first day we made it to Cochabamba, a small city in a valley 8,500 feet above sea level, which had been isolated for so long that the people all looked alike. It was during the rainy season and the water was so deep in one of the city streets that I had to shut off the engine and negotiate with a group of boys to push us through the high water so it didn't drown out the engine. Water came in around all 4 doors as they pushed us through and we stopped on the other side of the flooded area to make sure the oil pan hadn't filled up with water. There was a bridge over a flooded river as we left the city and on the other side of the bridge there appeared to be a fork in the road except what appeared to be the main road was blocked. There aren't any road or trail signs in the Third World and if you come to a fork in the road, the rule is to take the most traveled road. Regardless of the rule, there was only one way to go and we proceeded down this road for about a half a mile until we came directly to the river that went under the bridge we just crossed. The road obviously went across the river but we didn't have any idea where the roadbed was in this flooded river. We sat there about 10 minutes and to our surprise a large bus came down off the shallow bank and entered the river on the other side. In the middle of the river, the bus made a sharp turn to the right and continued across the river, coming up the shallow bank beside us. Trying to remember where the roadbed was, we crossed the river without difficulty. About another half mile up the road, busses were backed up, parked on both side of the narrow road for as far as we could see. I walked down between the two rows of busses until I came to a washed out bridge where a bus had fallen into the river, completely blocking the road. As I walked back to the car, I looked at the names on the busses and none of them were going where we thought we were going. We turned around, crossed the river again and proceeded to the main bridge where the road was completely blocked by mountains of dirt. It was then apparent that there had been a major landslide and a bulldozer was opening up the section of the landslide that had obscured the road. We waited until the road was passable and proceeded on our way. We had filled up with 20 cents per gal gasoline in Cochabamba and should have enough to get back to La Paz because there wouldn't be any place to get gas along the way.

This also meant that there wouldn't be any place to eat but Edna was an experienced Third World traveler and always had a picnic lunch. The scenery was beautiful with snow-covered mountains and green valleys but we probably didn't meet more than a couple vehicles all day. We stopped by a small mountain stream where llamas and alpacas were grazing to eat our picnic lunch. We could see a girl dressed in red that was watching over the animals that she was herding, peaking over the crest of a hill. Baby llamas and alpacas that apparently hadn't seen many people came right up to the small stream to drink where we were eating. We were starting to get up in the higher altitude where road was very steep and ruts were very deep from truck traffic in this wet weather. The road is one single lane, just wide enough for a single car and there was a place for the cars coming down the mountain to pull over to let those going up the mountain pass about every half a mile. You could see cars coming up or going down the mountain for several miles and it was an established rule of the road that traffic coming up the mountain had the right of way. Traffic coming down the mountain would have to pull off at a turn-off to allow them to pass without stopping. There wasn't anything that resembled a guardrail and you were close enough to the edge, you could look down for thousands of feet. After we went through the pass at about 15,500 feet, the road let down gradually to about 13,000 feet and there was over 100 miles of straight blacktop road to La Paz.

When we got back to La Paz, the floorboards in the back seat of my new car had been bent up about 4 inches from running over stones between the deep ruts and I had to take a heavy sledge hammer to pound them down where they should be. When you are coming up the steep mountain roads with deep ruts your car will get hung up on the big stones between the ruts if you aren't going fast enough so you slide over some stones to more solid ground. The stones were probably put in the ruts by some trucker that got stuck in the deep muddy ruts.

The embassy had rented a garage for Edna's car near her apartment which was just across the street from mine because in the Third World, any car that is left on the street will be stolen. There was only one car in the two-car garage where Edna kept hers and they rented the other half for my car. Once I received my car, I could drive to and from work and my schedule would not be subject to the limitations of the local staff and I could work on into the night if necessary. This was often necessary to identify and correct the problems that resulted from the new equipment not meeting specifications and consumed much of what should have been my free time.

LP-6 OFFICIAL TRAVEL

During my first months in Bolivia, Ele and I visited Cochabamba, Santa Cruz and Trinidad, the 3 other cities that were involved in our project. Although we traveled by air, it was interesting to travel with Ele who was a native of Cochabamba and knew every nick and cranny of the entire country. I learned much about their culture and he took me places where I saw things that I didn't know existed. It was a country of stark beauty with numerous mountains peaks from permanently snow capped 21,190 foot Illimani down to Trinidad where tributaries of Amazon River started about 400 feet above sea level almost 2000 miles from the Atlantic Ocean. This explained why the Amazon River is such a wide slow moving river. Trinidad is a very small village located in cattle ranch country that was accessible only by air. U.S ranchers from the Dakotas and Montana had homesteaded in this area and had large productive ranches. In accordance with homestead requirements, all beef produced in this area had to be consumed in Bolivia and since there wasn't any roads all meat had to be shipped by air. Building the airport was part of the USAID aviation loan agreement that I was involved with. The primary purpose of, this airport was to provide a means to ship the meat out over the high mountains to the cities in Bolivia which were not accessible by road. It turned out to be an almost insurmountable task because this was lowland country, which was probably once a riverbed, and there wasn't any aggregate or gravel in the entire area to construct a runway. It took several years to bring in enough gravel by barge from a couple hundred miles upstream because the small river that skirted Trinidad was only navigable for a short period during the rainy season. A good runway had been constructed that would accommodate the old WW II cargo planes they used to haul the meat to the other cities of Bolivia. Many of these old planes crashed in the mountains because were either overloaded or poorly maintained and could not clear the mountain peaks. The slaughter house where they butchered the beef was located right on the airport and since they didn't have refrigeration, halves of the beef were hung up overnight, loaded on planes and hauled out the next day. This was one of the three airports in Bolivia where we were installing telex/voice communication with La Paz.

The so-called hotel was a room full of cots just off the short main street. There was one restaurant in Trinidad, which seemed to be quite busy but after a short wait Ele found a table. A newspaperman from the US asked if he could join us and we told him he could. He was employed by an Eastern US newspaper but had come to Bolivia because he was writing a book on Bolivia. Ele could have told him just about anything he wanted to know about Bolivia but he had read someone's book and even though he thought he knew all about it, his brief physical presence was necessary to establish him as an authority. The restaurant closed early because the diesel power plant that provided electricity for the village was shut down early at night because all the fuel had to come in by air. It was also interesting to note that a foreign student from the US Midwest, who couldn't speak any Spanish, was staying with the station chief's family who couldn't speak any English. Their daughter in turn was staying with his family in the U.S. They said he was a foreign student, going to school there but he told me that he and another American student, who was also there just sat in back of the small class room and didn't have the foggiest idea what was going on. Fortunately, the two Americans could talk to each other. This was supposed to be a student exchange program where the station chief's daughter was staying with a family in the U.S. and their son was staying with her family in Trinidad. I later made several other visits to Trinidad in connection with this project but after my first visit I was not astonished by anything.

I made several trips to Cochabamba with Ele and I always saw something different because it was his hometown and he enjoyed visiting places he frequented before he moved to La Paz many years ago. Ele had previously been Chief of the Airport Station in Cochabamba and was still highly respected by the present staff. Cochabamba was in a valley on the edge of steep mountains peaks between La Paz and Santa Cruz and the people had evidently been isolated in that valley for centuries because they all looked very much alike and didn't resemble any other people that I saw in Bolivia. According to statistics over 80% of the people in Bolivia were Indians and most of the rest were mixed race. Although Spanish was the official language, the two Indian languages, Aymara and Quechua were probably more common outside of the primary cities and villages. We made tentative plans regarding where we would install the new equipment in the existing building and determined what was required for that purpose.

We later brought the equipment and required installation material from La Paz in a large station wagon or truck. It was very hot and Ele took me down to the river that was used to transport aggregate material to Trinidad, which was perhaps 25 miles out of Cochabamba. Along the route, we stopped at one of Ele's old swimming holes which were little more than wading pools where we took off our shoes and soaked our feet while we sit in the shade of the surrounding trees. As we proceeded down toward the river, I saw some very small black people that resembled what they called mountain people in the Dalat area of Vietnam. In Vietnam they were nomadic families of 4 or 5 people that you often saw moving from one place to another on the narrow roads carrying everything they owned. They lived on roots from plants that they dug up in the wooded area along the way. I asked Ele about them but he didn't know who they were or where they came from.

One evening Ele asked me if I would like to join then in the morning on a trip to a nearby mountain peak to make some communication coverage tests. Apparently it was something requested by ICAO for some new system they were exploring. Although it had nothing to do with my program, I am interested in that sort of thing and told him that I would like to go along. Basically the test was to determine whether or not line of site radio coverage was possible from the mountain peak near Cochabamba to Santa Cruz. Early in the morning about six of us started out in what I would call a large commercial version of a station wagon. We drove for about an hour up mountain roads that corkscrewed around the mountain peak. We stopped to pickup four Indians that were waiting for us by the road that had obviously been prearranged because we couldn't see any Indian village from the road. We drove another half hour and stopped along the road where they unloaded some radio equipment and a little gasoline powered electric generator. The Indians who had lived at this high altitude all their life had barrel shaped chests. They put this equipment on their back and pranced right up the steep mountain which was right in front of us. All I carried was my camera which seemed like it weighed a ton and I couldn't walk very well so I was far behind the rest of the group. When I finally reached the icy crest of what I thought was the tallest peak, the polished ice crest was so slippery you had to punch a hole in the ice in order to get a foothold. From the crest, I could see the group had set up their equipment on another crest about 50 feet away and were in the process of making their planned tests. It was a beautiful place with snow covered mountain peaks all around us. I took a roll of film and promised everyone a copy of the pictures. It didn't help my reputation any when the film got lost in the mail and I didn't get a single picture. While we were up there, we had lunch which consisted of a pocket full of raw lima beans. Apparently they are rich in protein and you just keep chewing on them all the time. They also carried a case of bottled soft drinks up the mountain so we had something to drink. Their experiment was a failure but we sure slept well that night.

Before we left Cochabamba where we stayed overnight, Ele turned off the narrow road on to a trail that went back about a half a mile through the woods to a banana plantation. This plantation had evidently been there for quite some time as there were some empty places through the mature trees. It appeared that after they planted the bananas but didn't have a local market and it probably wasn't economically feasible so ship them somewhere else. I didn't know much about bananas but I never dreamed that there were so many types of bananas. Ele purchased enough stocks of various types at ten cents a stock to fill up the back of the station wagon to take back to La Paz. We drove back to La Paz over the same mountain road as Edna and I did. It was the only road so there wasn't any choice but it was now the dry season so we didn't encounter any problems like Edna and I did when we drove my new car back from Santa Cruz.

We went to Santa Cruz on another trip to get that part of the project lined up like we had the others because we hadn't been there yet. I had been there twice when I picked up my car but didn't get a chance to see much of it. I was more impressed with it than any of the other Bolivian city that I had seen so far. It was a rather flat area with an elevation of about 1350 feet in the south eastern part of Bolivia toward the Brazil/Paraguay/Argentina border. There were few Indians there because they liked the high country and people from Argentina, who were primarily of German and Spanish decent, had migrated to this area. This was the home of Bolivian President Banzer, who undoubtedly was responsible for building a new airport terminal which was now under construction. It seemed like there was little resemblance between any two towns in Bolivia and every one of them had people that didn't resemble each other or share a common culture. If you like steak, Santa Cruz was the place to eat because they have an outdoor restaurant with a huge grill where you can get all the steak you wanted for a small price. They keep coming around with a plate of hot grilled steaks as long as you wanted to eat. I previously explained that there was an abundance of beef because all the beef from ranches in Trinidad had to be consumed in Bolivia. There were also oil fields south of Santa Cruz near the Argentine border but I never got down there because Argentina didn't like Americans at that time and had been making good on their promise to kill one American a week.

They had all the necessary facilities to install the new equipment at Santa Cruz except there would be a communication station in the new terminal building which wasn't completed enough for that yet. This was a brief overnight stop so Ele found a place we could stay for almost nothing and we took the only flight back to La Paz the next day. Santa Cruz wouldn't be a location that would delay our project.

We had been planning the La Paz installation since I arrived, because it was the major control facility for the entire project. Also Ele was responsible for all the aviation communication and navigation facilities for the entire country and couldn't spend all his time working with me on the project. Unfortunately, there didn't seem to be anyone else that that could fill in for him. Having been a supervisor myself, I realized he couldn't spend all his time on one thing, neglecting everything else. Early on, we had laid out the requirements for both an equipment operations room in the terminal and a receiver station building with electric power and buried communications cable. These things had to be built by others and so far we hadn't been able to motivate anyone. We had a pretty good idea of what we wanted to do but we also knew that things don't happen very fast in the Third World. We took a trip to Lima, Peru which was one of the two principal international stations that we had the most radio traffic with. There we met with their electronic staff, visited some of their facilities and met face to face with the people we worked with every day.

While we were there I also visited the International the Civil Aviation Organization's (ICAO), South American Office, whose chief was formerly the head of Bolivia's aviation program. ICAO was one of the many United Nations organizations with technical assistance groups in about every specialty you can think of throughout the world. I had some things that I wanted to call his attention to, regarding members of his staff interfering with the job I was trying to do in Bolivia. They had a man that claimed to be a technician that had been in Bolivia for some time before I arrived that apparently didn't have anything to do but find fault with my project even before I arrived. First, he constantly expressed his dissatisfaction because the equipment was obsolete even before it was installed and tried to convince the Bolivian government that we were dumping some obsolete junk on them. He didn't realize that most of the equipment had been purchased and the project had been on hold for about 20 years because the country had two Communist coups during that time. Even though the company that manufactured the transmitters made good on their guarantee, he tried to convince the Bolivian government that they were more American junk. He did have a point there because the transmitters did not operate at 13,500 feet as specified and the project was significantly delayed because they had to be shipped back to the factory for major modifications. In the manufacturer's defense, they designed high powered transmitters at a higher altitude than that type equipment ever operated. Since he was probably the Bolivian aviation chief that was involved in negotiating the loan some 20 years ago, he was fully aware of the problems involved.

Also, I called his attention to the fact that Bolivian technicians had taken the position that they were not going to assist in the installation of new equipment unless they got a pay raise. They were using this as a lever to get more money and although I had neither influence nor authority over such things it would certainly delay the project and all the funds would be used up by the end of my 2-year contract. Also, this was their only opportunity to learn how this new type equipment operated and they will not be able to maintain it once it is installed. Also from ICAO's standpoint this was the relay station that connected Lima and Buenos Aires, the two anchor stations for all of the South American air traffic control system.

All senior officers in Bolivia aviation were military men headed up by a general who had little or no interest in aviation. Now that all radio code circuits had been discontinued, every radio operator took the position that it was now his job to sit and watch the telex machine automatically print out the messages that he previously copied in code. They considered the telex printer a labor savings device to make their job easier rather, than automation that made it possible for one man to take care of all the circuits with less work. I succeeded in getting his attention and since he was still highly respected in his own country he made a trip to Bolivia and got their attention. Although the Bolivian electronic technicians would not reconsider, ASANA hired 5 telephone technicians to help with the installation. They weren't skilled enough to be of much value but his trip to Bolivia pointed out to top officials that their failure to support this project was harming all aviation in South America.

After his visit, General de la Vega, who was Chief of Civil Aviation in Bolivia, came to see me at the airport and we had a very interesting conversation. He brought along an interpreter but the conversation started out in Spanish. Since this was an important meeting, I spoke through the interpreter to make sure there wasn't any misunderstanding on some key points. After I made a few comments, I could tell from his eyes following every word that he understood English as well as I did. I looked him in the eye and said, "Oh I see you speak English". Looking embarrassed, he said, "A little". I found out later that he graduated from Harvard. In South America, people that speak English are looked down on and they don't want anyone to know. When you are flying someplace in South America, as soon as you get airborne you can expect the persons that is in the seat next to you to lean over and say "I speak a little English." Since there isn't any one he knows that can hear him, he wants to practice speaking English because people that speak English are looked down on.

One day Ele told me they were going up to look at another site on top of a mountain peak that was less than an hour's drive from the airport and asked me to go along. Again this wasn't part of my project but I did need to understand the big picture so I knew what was going on. Several of us went in a vehicle like we used at Cochabamba to go up the road that went to the Chacaltaya Observatory and the so called clubhouse for the ski slopes. This world class observatory located at 17,000 feet was measuring cosmic radiation from outer space. They had some type of collectors sitting out about 100 yards, which were connected to the building by some type of cables. I don't know how it worked, but the cables in the building were connected to round steel tanks which were probably 5 feet in diameter and perhaps 15 feet long. The tanks were laying on their side with these cables connected to them. Electric power from a power line that came up the mountain provided power for both the observatory and the nearby ski lodge. The road coming up the mountain was a typical Bolivian mountain road that had been carved out of the side of the steep mountain slope with turnoffs for passing about every half mile. The road was so narrow you could look out the car window and see vehicles that didn't make it, thousands of feet below as there weren't any guardrails to obstruct your view.

We went up to look at a proposed new communications site which was on a mountain peak 500 feet above the observatory. A bulldozer had made a crude road up this last 500 feet and I understood they had leveled off the top for a small building. Unfortunately, our vehicle would not operate above 17,000 feet and although some of our group walked up the last 500 feet, I was not able to do that. This was part of the same ICAO communication test that they made at Cochabamba. At 17,000 feet you are pretty light headed and should be using oxygen but we didn't have any.

LP-7 OUR EMBASSY IN BOLIVIA

I had worked in Vietnam for 3-1/2 years under a somewhat similar relationship with USAID and the American Embassy where I still got my pay check from the FAA. There were thousands of Americans between me and the Ambassador and there were few if any social gatherings because of curfews and other wartime restrictions so there was little interaction of Americans outside their own little group like our CAAG group. For example, the woman that later became my wife was in Saigon the same time as I was there, but I never had occasion to meet her. My Vietnam experience gave me little insight into the interrelationships between the various groups that made up an embassy. When I arrived in Bolivia, I was assigned an office in the USAID portion of the embassy and Edna, who I soon became well acquainted with, was the records supervisor for USAID in Bolivia as she had worked in USAID missions around the world. Over a period of time, she explained what each group was responsible for and the pecking order within the group. The ambassador who is appointed by our president may not be a diplomatic genius but he is like a dictator and can have any American removed from the country on short notice, for any reason that he sees fit. There are two types of ambassadors: (1) the political type that probably has little knowledge of foreign affairs that was usually a big donor to the president's campaign. (2) A career diplomat, who undoubtedly had been deputy chief of mission at a number of foreign posts. The first type was generally a reward to a donor that had made major contributions to the president's election and the second was for a sensitive post where diplomatic skills were required. Although few outside of the diplomatic service knew it, the Deputy Chief of Mission was always a career diplomat that actually ran the embassy.

Although, even a small embassy had a councilor service that issued passports to Americans that were in the country and visa's to foreigners that wanted to visit the United States, they also made sure Americans that got in trouble with the law were fairly treated. They also had a commercial section to assist in arranging foreign trade between the host country and the USA. Also even though USAID, US Information Service and other groups like military aid, which we had in Bolivia, were not directly supervised and managed by the embassy, they fell under the overall jurisdiction of the Ambassador. All of this was above board and pretty well understood by everyone but every embassy also has a political section which is kind of a gray area. The political section was actually two independent sections known in the embassy as POL-1 and POL-2. POL-2 was actually the CIA referred to in general conversation as the Company and had little to do with the embassies political section known as POL-1.

POL-2 submitted a daily message to Washington, using the embassy communications center in the building which had the required encrypting equipment and a high powered radio with antennas on the roof of the building. Edna's best friend Anne, and Norm, her live in boyfriend, who we often went out with were both in the intelligence service but we never talked about that. Anne and Norm, a retired Navy Captain, who had been in Naval Intelligence had previously worked together in both Paris and Vietnam. That was the extent of our knowledge about their intelligence activities. Later we learned that the Company had an isolated getaway in Cochabamba where their employees could spend a weekend or a few days where they could let their hair down and relax.

We received 20% premium pay for living in this high altitude environment where there was hardly enough air to breath and the daytime sun was penetrating but it never really got warm. As soon as the sun went down it was cold and houses didn't have any central heating. There was an abundance of electricity generated by the huge hydroelectric power plant that used water from Lake Titicaca located on the Alto Plano near the airport. Even with abundant electricity it was impossible to heat our large apartments which were not insulated, with space heaters. There was nothing to do in La Paz and you were so isolated from the rest of the world that it was practically impossible to even make a telephone call. It was perhaps the world's most beautiful country but it was necessary for the embassy staff to do things together in order to keep from going stark raving mad. Edna and the other women in the mission had a lot of fairly small formal dinner parties and we made a lot of weekend trips to points of interest outside the city. The embassy made a car and driver available to groups that wanted to get out of the city for the weekend provided they pay the driver's salary and expenses.

LP-8 WEEKEND/HOLIDAY SIGHTSEEING

URMIRI

My first excursion was to Urmiri where they have hot baths. We left La Paz for the three hour trip on the on the Oruro highway which was the only flat straight road in Bolivia. The road went straight toward Illimani, the 21,190 ft snow covered mountain that was the landmark for the Andes Mountains and only the driver knew where we went from there. Norm had to go back to Washington on personal business so I went with Ann and Edna. It was good we had a driver because there wasn't any sign where you turn off the main road on to what appeared to be a trail. A few miles down the road, the trail entered a short tunnel through a small hill into a compound that is surrounded by steep hills so the sun drops out of sight early. There were two large swimming pools that were empty except for a man and two nice looking young ladies in one of them. Although he appeared to be in his thirties, he told us he was the 100 years old manager. He told us that he appeared to be younger but this hot spring water had such magic qualities that it made him look like a young man. They also had rooms for rent and served meals. He asked Edna in his Castilian Spanish if we wanted rooms with a Roman bath. Not knowing just what to expect, she said we would take one of each and another for our driver. We went into one of the two large swimming pools where the water was about as hot as we could stand and they also had a sauna which was also heated by the water from the hot springs. There were small branches from eucalyptus trees that give off a fragrant aroma in that hot steaming spring water. With the exception of the three people that were in the swimming pool when we arrived, we were the only ones there. After the evening meal, it got dark because the sun went down early over the hills that surrounded the pools. They had a small power plant that provided enough electricity to operate the meager lighting system until they shut it down about 10 PM.

Ann and Edna had the room with the Roman bath and since we still had our bathing suits on we would try out the bath. The bath was located on one end of the room which had twin beds that you accessed through a large opening in the wall that didn't have a door on it. There was a strong pipe railing around the two sides of the cement bath that weren't against the outside wall and stairs where you walked down in the bath which was about 4 feet deep. The temperature of the water was controlled by a large valve or gate that determined how much of the water from the hot springs was allowed to enter. It was a novel, one of a kind arrangement that was possible only because of the hot springs. We drove back to La Paz the next morning across the barren like Altiplano where you occasionally saw a woman or young girl herding a few sheep or goats and perhaps a llama or two. They made cheese out of goat and sheep milk but we didn't stop and buy any on that trip.

THE YUNGAS

After I got my car which was essential to do my job, I was in position to go places and do things that I couldn't have done otherwise. It was a Brazilian Chevrolet Opala which was a 4 door sedan with a large engine and mountain rear end that was specially equipped for mountain driving. A high horsepower engine is necessary because a gasoline engine without a supercharger will not operate above 17,000 Feet. By that time Edna and I had gotten to know each other quite well and she was my chief guide. I could comfortably haul four people in my car and we explored many remote places in this beautiful land with such unforgiving terrain.

The Yungas was about a 3 hour drive from La Paz, up over 15000 feet through the mountain pass and down to the semitropical area on the other side of the mountain. Herds of llamas and alpacas grazed along the road and it was sometimes snow covered so the road was impassable. From the summit, the road down the other side was a series of sharp switchbacks that extended for miles as you dropped down thousands of feet. This was considered somewhat of a deluxe mountain road because it had two narrow lanes for traffic. Even though one was so close to the edge that from the passenger side windows, you could look down in the valley thousands of feet below. Perhaps the road would have been just too narrow for two cars to pass if they had a guardrail. There just wouldn't have been enough room between the vertical cliff on the mountain side and the sharp drop-off on the valley side. Having two lanes of traffic made it possible to meet a vehicle coming up the mountain without having to pull off at places about a mile apart and waiting for heavily loaded trucks to grind their way up the mountain. There were many trucks coming up the mountain with their large open box filled with loose oranges that they were hauling to La Paz from the orange groves in the valley. It was not unusual to see a truck down in the distant valley that went over the edge with a load of oranges. Once you got down the steep slope there was what you might call a small village and the road forked to the North Youngas or to the South Youngas. We took the road to the South Youngas, not because there was a sign but because someone in our group had been there before and knew the way.

We stayed at a motel which was in a very small village several miles down from the junction in the road. There wasn't any restaurant there so you had to bring your food with you but there was a place overlooking the valley where you could buy soft drinks or a beer. The motel had an outside swimming pool which wasn't crowded because we were the only ones staying at the motel. It was a semitropical area and the weather was nice, which is something we missed in La Paz where there was hardly enough air to breath.

About once a month, they had an open air market on Sunday morning in the street of the little village where Indians living in the extended area brought things to sell or barter. This included everything from handiwork the women made to sheep, goats and llamas that they had raised. When they had their Sunday market, someone with a truck load of cheap pots and pans as well as other items the Indians needed came to the village and parked on the main street. It was kind of like a country store that sold about everything the Indians couldn't make themselves.

I was there quite a number of times and often took guests from the US there because it was such a contrast from La Paz. Also, it gave them the overall prospective of this unique country with all its scenic beauty and harsh environment, where you saw stick crosses along the road where someone died and was buried along the road. It wasn't always possible to get to the Yungas because one time when my daughter and her husband came to visit me, there was so much snow in the mountain pass that we couldn't get through. The llamas and alpacas were digging down through the snow to get a few bites of grass to survive until the snow melted in a few days.

CHACALTAYA OBSERVATORY

I previously discussed the observatory which is actually located on the edge of the Chacaltaya Glacier and is adjacent to the ski lodge. From the ski lodge which actually hangs over the edge of the ski slopes, you can sit in a booth by a window and see the steep slopes and the associated ski lift in the thin 17,000 foot air. This was not a place for amateurs and there wasn't any skier on the slopes that day because this was not the skiing season and there wasn't any powered snow. The glacial slopes were actually wind polished ice so it would not have been possible to ski at that time. They did serve alcoholic drinks in the clubhouse which was hardly appropriate at this high altitude where people were already light headed. One of their favorite drinks that they were pushing at that time was pesco sour. This was a drink made from fermented grape seeds that were left over after the juice was extracted from grapes used to make wine.

Both Edna and I had been here and had been through the observatory but I wanted to see if my car could go up the newly bulldozed road to the top of the adjacent 17,500 foot peak. Like the civil aviation vehicle that I previously came up here in, it would not operate above 17,000 feet and even though it would have been a beautiful view for over 100 miles in the crisp cool air, we couldn't walk up to the top. It was a beautiful view, overlooking the city of La Paz and the vast countryside as we carefully drove down the one lane road toward La Paz. If we went over the edge from this narrow one lane road, we would probably end up in the valley about a mile below. When you had company from the US, it was an interesting place to take them because they were scared to death. The trucks that had gone over the edge that you could just see in the valley below and the crossed sticks, marking graves where someone died along the road also called their attention to the fact that that they were not on a US Interstate highway.

THANKSGIVING IN COCHABAMBA

Special American holidays like Thanksgiving, Christmas, New Year's and July 4th are a particularly lonely time to be far from home and family. Ann, Edna and the ambassador's secretary planned a trip to Cochabamba over the Thanksgiving holiday. Ann had the connections to reserve the CIA getaway in Cochabamba for the long weekend. They had ordered some turkeys through our embassy and each one of them had their maid cook a turkey, make the dressing and prepare the other things that goes along with it. It happened that my daughter, Joy was visiting at the time and she joined the group. We all made reservations on what they called the ferrobus, which is like a streetcar powered with a conventional gasoline engine that runs on steel tracks like a streetcar through the mountains. It is about 275 miles and takes 8 or 9 hours which is about the same time required to drive a car through the mountains. It was an interesting trip through the rugged mountains with roasters and boxes of other goodies sitting in the aisle. The house with a large rose garden and swimming pool was previously the home of a mistress of one of Bolivia's many previous presidents. The property even had a swimming pool for horses, which was made with an incline so the horses could walk down the incline into about 6 feet of water. They employed a permanent maid and gardener to keep the place shipshape and acted as keepers when someone was not using it. When a group was using the place, they took up a collection to pay the maid and gardener for local purchases they made because you had to either bring your own food or eat out. There are several good restaurants in this 2nd largest city of Bolivia which has a population of about 150,000. Cochabamba is located at about 8,500 feet in a flat isolated valley, surrounded by mountains, which makes it a welcome change from the colder climate at high altitude La Paz. Although there are some interesting ruins outside of the city, we didn't have any transportation and limited our sightseeing to the Saturday market in the city where they sold handicraft. Edna bought paintings of a Cochabamba man and a woman. I bought a home knit alpaca sweater that was both very warm as well as heavy and something that resembled a stocking cap that covered most of your face that had a chin strap to hold it on. I give that to my brother because I thought it would be suitable for Wisconsin winters.

This was a nice getaway from the harsh La Paz climate and an opportunity to socialize with embassy employees on this very American weekend where we all missed being home with our families. When we took the ferrobus back to La Paz, the aisles were no longer filled with roast turkey and all the nice things the girls brought along to make the holiday so enjoyable.

LAKE TITICACA

The south end of Lake Titicaca is about an hour's drive northwest of El Alto, the La Paz airport over a narrow unmarked road on the flat Alto Plano. All of a sudden, the south end of the giant dark blue lake surrounded with snow capped mountains came into view. With the exception of an occasional reed boat with a small white sale there wasn't much activity on the lake as we followed the road around the east side of the lake a few miles to the Yacht Club. The club consisted of a single dark and dingy building which was a restaurant where you could eat inside if it was too cold to eat outside, overlooking the lake. The first thing you had to do when you arrived was to check with the boat captain to see if weather conditions were such that he can take you out for a boat ride. He looked at the flag on the pole and the sky out over the lake before he determined whether or not it is safe to go out in the lake that day. If so, we had to order our afternoon meal so they will be able to prepare it while we are out on the lake. They didn't have such thing as a menu so you just told them how many would be there to eat and you simply ate whatever they had. The bull rushes that grow around the edge of the lake used to make small reed boats are cleared away for about 30 feet of the lakeshore in front of the Yacht Club. There were a few boats tied up along side of the single dock but none of them were ever in use any of the many times we were there. The wooden boat that we rode in was a rather small inboard with a cabin in front that had undoubtedly been in service for too many years. The cabin covered about the front third of the boat and there were bench seats on both sides in back.

Lake Titicaca covers 3500 square miles, 12,600 feet above sea level and has a measured depth of 984 ft. Because it is such a large body of water, the temperature of the water is 55 degrees year around. It is the highest navigable lake in the world and it takes a steamer 14 hours to travel for Puno, Peru on the north end of the lake to Bolivia on the south end of the lake. Surrounded by snow capped mountains and terraces built by the Incas, up the mountains sides to grow agricultural crops made it one of the most beautiful places on earth. Both the water and the sky were a very dark blue which accented the surrounding snow covered mountains.

Often there was an Indian in a reed boat that met us out in the lake that took people for rides in his boat. I took some pictures of Edna and others riding in his boat. Sometimes he had a small boy, perhaps 6 years old with him and one time I saw a little fish about 4 inches long in his boat. I understand at one time this was a great fishing lake with large lake trout which are ideally suited to this clean cold water. That was before the Indians learned to fish with dynamite and now there are very few fish in this huge lake.

There are several islands in the lake that you can visit, including an island made exclusively of the bull rushes that surrounds the lake. This is the island where they actually build the reed boats. The long hollow rushes are bundled and laced together in such a manner that the bundles are again laced together in the shape of a boat. The boats made of the hollow buoyant reeds float high in the water and are usually propelled by a small white triangular sail which is adequate because there is usually a brisk breeze. We visited the lake often because it was it was one of the few interesting place close to La Paz. There was little to do in La Paz, the climate was not enticing and we had to make our own entertainment or go stark raving mad.

TIAHUANACO

Perhaps the place I found most intriguing was the ancient ruins of Tiahuanaco which was also located on the Alto Plano about 10 miles south of Lake Titicaca and about the same distance from El Alto Airport. Edna and I spent many Sunday afternoons exploring the ruins of this ancient civilization which was carbon dated from about 1200 BC to 1200 AD. Anthropologists believe that this ancient civilization consisting of an estimated 40,000 people was built on the south end of Lake Titicaca which forms part of the present boundary between Bolivia and Peru. The level of the 3500 square mile lake level has dropped to 12,600 feet above sea level which is now 600 feet below the runway at the EL Alto Airport. Anthropologists believe the Tiahuanaco was abandoned when the lake receded and the Inca civilization established its capital in Cuzco about a century before the Spanish Conquest in the first third of the 15th century. That is another story and I want to deal solely with my personal observations of the Tiahuanaco ruins. You could drive your car right up to the site and there wasn't any parking problem because you seldom saw anyone there. The first thing that attracted your attention was an area about 100 feet long and 50 feet wide that is elevated about 6 feet above the ground with the edges supported by a vertical stone wall. In the center of this elevated flat area called The Gateway to the Sun is a statue known as the Monoleto which is perhaps 5 feet high that is enclosed in perhaps a 10 foot square area that and is looking directly at Illimani through an open entry gate. The Monolito who was obviously one of their gods had a hex mark on it made by the Spanish conquers that would render this unchristian god harmless. There was about a half dozen steps just outside the of the large massive solid stone arch, which were also carved out of one solid piece of stone that was once about 8 inches high. Because of so much foot traffic, the portion of the individual steps where people walked was worn down to about half their initial height.

About 20 feet beyond the last step was another interesting area that they called the sunken sanctuary. It is a flat area about 20 x 30 feet and approximately 5 feet below the ground level with vertical stone walls around the parameter below ground level. Carved heads of people and various types of animals protruded from the vertical stone wall at various levels all the way around. There weren't any steps to go down into the sunken sanctuary but the flat area in the bottom was covered with green grass.

On the opposite end of the Gateway to the Sun was a massive stone structure which archaeologists believed to be calendar of some type, weighing an estimated 10 ton. It was generally believed to be orientated on the Sun but other scholars thought it may be the moon or Venus. It was generally believed that the prominent center figure represented September, which was the month for planting crops but they had never been able to translate the hieroglyphics so it remained a mystery. It is interesting to note that on September 21st, the spring equinox the Calendar was aligned so you could look through the arch at far end of at the Gateway to the Sun and the peak of Illimani is framed in the center of the arch. The sunken sanctuary which you couldn't see from the calendar and the Monoleto were also on this same geometric line.

One time when Edna and I were at Tiahuanaco, a Bolivian anthropologist who worked on the project was there and gave us a tour of the ancient city, pointing out and explaining the ancient ruins. We had not previously seen what appeared to be an amphitheater near the edge of the ruins. There was a row of large flat slaps of stone about 6 feet wide, 2 feet thick and 10 feet long laying flat on top of a small hill overlooking a valley that appeared to be an amphitheater. There were several of these stones placed end to end which had appeared to be to have anchors in them for 10 or 12 thrones where their royalty sat to view or direct ceremonies in the amphitheater. The ends of these blocks of stones were held together by a stone key cut into the blocks so they couldn't separate. Our guide explained to us that the closest place where such stones existed was about 3 miles from the site and they didn't know how they moved these and the other huge stones weighing up to 10 tons to the site of the ruins. Although no one knows how they moved the huge pieces of rock that weigh many tons, they speculate that this was on the lakeshore at that time and they brought them across the lake on a huge raft. Perhaps the raft was made of the bull rushes that grow in the lake that are still being used to make the reed boats that are so numerous on the lake. They are also used to make the floating island where they make the reed boats that are so common on the lake.

TIAHUANCO MUSEUM

One weekend when my boss from Washington and his wife were visiting La Paz, Edna and I took them up to Tiahuanaco to tour the ruins. We had wanted to see the old dilapidated museum but it was closed up and there wasn't anyone around. That day the caretaker just happened to be there doing some work and Edna with her fluent Spanish managed to bribe him into showing us what was left of the artifacts that they had uncovered when they excavated the ruins. Many of them had been stolen over the years and since they were unable to secure the museum, they closed it some years ago. There were still many items dating back to the beginning of the Iron Age, which we couldn't visualize what they had been used for. All the artifacts were lying on shelves, which were in rows down the center of the building covered by sand and dust which you had to clean off before you could see what they really looked like.

CARNIBVAL AT OROURO

Oruro, one of four major cities in Bolivia, like New Orleans or Rio de Janeiro, has a carnival celebration that lasts for several days just before the long Easter weekend was a special event that everyone looked forward to. Oruro is a city on the south east corner of the Alto Plano, 140 miles south of La Paz on the only flat, level highway in Bolivia. It is a tin, silver and wolfram mining center as well as a communication center with links to Chile and Argentina. It is also the junction through the mountain pass with mountain roads to Cochabamba and Santa Cruz.

The American Embassy is closed for the long Carnival weekend and embassy employees start making plans long before the event for transportation and hotel reservations. Housing was in short supply and one year someone reserved what appeared to be a second floor attic large enough for cots for about 20 people from our embassy. It was located near the square that you always find in the center of every city the Spanish ever occupied where all the activities would take place. There were bleachers all around the parameter of the square and the parade around the square went on for hours. The parade consisted primarily of what they called devil dancers and rented taxies where the family laid a bright colored blanket on the hood to display all their silver. The families took great pride displaying their wealth as they rode by in the taxi, displaying their family silver.

The devil dances walked down the street in gaudy wardrobes of various types which were obviously very expensive and all of them had a huge scary headpieces of various types painted in brilliant colors with horns like a Texas longhorn steer. They walked down the street between or beside of the rented taxies, occasionally stopping to dance with one of the ladies sitting on the bleachers that came out to the edge of the street. The ladies felt they were honored when one of the devil dances stopped to dance with them. Sometimes, one of the devil dancers had been partying so much that they lost their way and ended up in the bleachers but everyone knew they were just having to good a time and everyone was expecting it. Edna had her picture taken with one of the devil dancers and bought a gaudy headpiece with long horns that she brought back to the States with her but unfortunately it was damaged in shipment and she had to throw it away

CAR TOUR OF BOLIVIA

One long holiday weekend, Norm, Ann, Edna and I decided to take a trip to see some of the places we had never been. It was during the dry season when river bed had been graded into roads that you could drive on and rivers were shallow enough that you could drive across with your car. Regardless of that it takes a lot of planning. Gasoline is a problem because towns are few and far between and you may have to take an extra gas can along. Also in some places, you have to take your own food with you. It is like setting out on an exploratory expedition going to places we hadn't been to. We all wanted to see Potosi, which was still in the highlands where they had the mountain of silver that almost overnight made it the most populated city in South America. We also wanted to see in what they called a high valley like Cochabamba where they had what would be their version of our Supreme Court. We took my car and decided they it would be a slow trip but we wouldn't need to take any extra gas for my car.

The first day we had to make it to Potosi because there wasn't any place we could stay in-between. It was a challenging trip because they don't have road maps and the roads which are more like trails are not marked. The rule of travel in the Third World is if you come to a road junction; always take the most traveled road. Early in the day we came to a road junction where both of the roads appeared to be equally traveled. It didn't appear that it would be that much of a challenge because there was a church a short distance from the intersection where a group of Indians were preparing for some kind of a fiesta. All of us could speak basic Spanish but since Edna was really bilingual she was delegated to ask which of the two roads goes to Potosi. Initially, she couldn't find anyone that could speak either Spanish or English. She finally located a Catholic priest that could speak Spanish, who give her directions so we could get on our way. The road went directly across a rather wide river which obviously was not too deep because other cars had gone through before we arrived. We traveled for several miles down a road that had been graded in a dry riverbed. It was interesting to see quite a number of men shoveling sand through screens that had been propped up at about a 45 degree angle. These men were looking for gold pieces that had washed down from the mountains during the rainy season. Edna had purchased earrings, a necklace and a bracelet made of gold nuggets in La Paz.

We arrived in Potosi which is a very interesting little city located on the slope of what had been known as the "mountain of silver" late that day. The mountain had been honeycombed with tunnels through which miners had extracted pure silver which was shipped to Spain. It has been said that enough silver was taken out of this mountain to pave a road all the way to Madrid but any reasonable person would say that was going a bit too far. You could tell it was a very old town and the elaborate architecture of stately buildings with hand carved doors and artifacts from all over the world made you aware that it was built by people with money. We stayed in and old hotel which still had the splendor of the yesteryear.

The next day we explored a museum which was filled with exotic products of the world collected by the wealthy residents of the days when the mountain of silver was at the heights of its glory. Although silver and other minerals had been mined here before the Incas, it became one of the largest cities in the world after it was discovered by the Spanish Conquistadors in 1545. At 14,000 feet, it was the highest city in the world sitting on the east edge of the Alto Plano, claiming to have a population of 160,000. It was decreed an Imperial City in 1553 by the Roman Emperor and the King of Spain, who received one fifth of the silver extracted. With all the wealth, new residents brought in exotic products from all over the world on the back of mules or llamas and it became a city of culture and vice. By the Eighteenth Century the city was in decline because most of the rich silver deposits had been depleted and it was feared that the honeycombed mountain would collapse.

We spent most of a day at the Casa de la Moneda, which we would call the House of Money or simply a Mint. It was a large building in the city, 2 city blocks long and one block wide that had two levels, which opened out at ground level like we would call a walk out basement. When we entered the building on the upper level, the first thing that caught my attention was some kind of a wooden machine located in the far left corner of the building. The wood floor of the building was made of wood timbers about six inches thick and eight inches wide. There was a path from the entry door to the machine that was worn down about half the thickness of the floor timber where they carried the silver to the machine. Through a series of rollers it squeezed the silver down into sheets or plates that were the desired thickness of the coins they wanted to make. I spent considerable time carefully examining this ancient wooden machine. Except for a metal sleeve around each wood roller, the machine was all made of wood. The machine was powered by a large wooden shaft that came up from the lower level which turned all the rollers at the same time through a series of wood pegs which were like gears that converted the rotary motion from the vertical drive timber to horizontal drive that operated the rollers. We went down a flight of stairs to the lower level to see where the power came from to turn the drive timber. The vertical timber was resting on some type of some bearing on the floor and there were six or eight heavy wooden arms about eight feet long that were firmly anchored to the vertical wood drive. African slaves pushed these wooden arms around the circle to power the machine. The stone floor where they walked was deeply grooved from years of use. Also, on this level was a large area where they stamped silver coins out of the silver that they had rolled out to the desired thickness. The round stamp was made out of iron or steel so the completed coins which were a little larger than our old silver dollar had the picture, writing and date on them. They were ready to ship to Spain on a Spanish galleon after they were hauled down the mountain to the ocean on the back of a mules or llamas.

Sucre the legal capital where their Supreme Court was located was about 9,320 feet elevation and was about half day's drive from Potosi which was our next stop. It was founded in 1538, which was about the same time as Potosi. In addition to what we would call their supreme court, it is also a center of learning, churches and museums. The Quechua speaking Indians are the primary inhabitants of this area. It is a planned colonial city with wide tranquil streets, colonial architecture and famous Old World art collections. The well kept ornate Supreme Court building is an excellent example of colonial architecture of that period.

We returned to La Paz by Cochabamba where we didn't do any sight seeing as we had already been there on several occasions. Our tour in Bolivia would not have been complete without seeing this area which was not only the original development in Bolivia but all of South America. It all took place because of the mountain of silver in Potosi.

I came back to the U.S. over the Christmas holidays the first year I was in Bolivia to see my new granddaughter, who was only a couple months old. The next year which would be my last Christmas in Bolivia, Edna and I took a trip to see South America. We flew to Santa Cruz where we got a plane to Asuncion, Paraguay and took a bus to Foz Do Iquacu (pronounced E Wa Soo Falls) where Paraguay, Argentina and Brazil all come together. The trip that took most of the day went through the rain forests that were being cleared, using large bulldozers that uprooted the trees and left them in large rows so they could be burned once they were dry enough. The falls were in the shape of a horseshoe about a quarter of a mile wide and only 30 feet high but the falls extended all around the horseshoe, with water falling into the huge pool resembling a lake. The beauty of the falls came from its massiveness rather than its height. Also you could see all of it, from anywhere on the walkway that went around the lake it formed as well as the hotel on the high ground at the edge of the lake. We stayed at the hotel that night and caught a flight to Rio de Janeiro the next day, which was the day before Christmas.

We spent a couple days sightseeing in Rio and got to see most of the sites because Edna had been there before and knew what there was to see and how to do it. We would have liked to have gone to Buenos Aires which was Edna's favorite place to shop because it had had stylish shops that women couldn't resist. Unfortunately, Argentina was off limits to Americans at that time as they had threatened to kill one American a week and the American Embassy had forbidden us from going there using an official passport. Instead, we flew back to Asuncion, Paraguay where we were invited to dinner at the home of a retired employee of the American Embassy in La Paz. He had previously been assigned to the American Embassy in Ascension and married a woman from there that had property and political connection there, making it a good place to retire.

The next day we flew to Santiago, Chile which was a good place to purchase leather and copper goods. We each bought a leather jacket and some goods. Santiago is not on the ocean so we shared a taxi with two or three others and went to Valparaiso, taking about 2 hours driving from Santiago which was right on the ocean. In my discussion with our fellow taxi companions, I learned that many Swedes and Germans had worked their way to Santiago on cargo ships, liked it there and just didn't go back to their home country. We had a delicious meal of fresh scallops in a restaurant overlooking the ocean and went back to Santiago that evening. Unlike Areca, Chile about 100 miles to the north, where the ocean is exceedingly turbulent, it was very calm in Via Del Mar. Our tour of South America was completed and we went back to La Paz the next day

LP-9 VISITORS IN BOLIVIA

Unlike Vietnam it was a small embassy, I was fortunate in getting involved in embassy social activities and I participated in all social activities like when the U.S. Air Force Thunderbirds came to La Paz to put on an air show. When you are far from home it is always special to have family and friends visit. It is kind of an interlude between your past life and where you are now. Even so, you are there to do a job and all too often, you can't spend the time entertaining them that you would like to.

My first guest was a woman that I had worked with both in Vietnam and again Chicago. She wanted to go to Machu Picchu, a famous Inca ruins south of Cuzco in Peru. I told her I would also like to go there and if she could come to La Paz at a time when I could get away for a few days I would go with her. A local travel agent made the arrangements for us to take an all day taxi trip around the west side of Lake Titicaca to Puno, Peru on the north end of the lake where we stayed overnight The next day we took a train through the mountains to Cusco and the following day we joined a tour group train that went to Machu Picchu, toured the ancient ruins high on a cliff overlooking a river valley and returned to Cuzco. The train arrived in Puno just in time to take the overnight steamer ship on a 14 hour trip to a lake port near La Paz and the ferrorail from the port to La Paz. It was a tiring trip but there was much to see traveling through the high mountains and I was fascinated by the switch backs required to scale the mountain peaks.

Joy and her husband were my first family visitors and by that time Edna and I had become pretty well acquainted. Also, Edith was a world traveler, could speak the language fluently and knew her way around. She had been in Bolivia about 6 months longer than I had and knew where everything was and how to get there. I was happy to have them meet her. One of the unusual places we went for dinner was in what they called the Valley of the Moon. It was a little almost unknown restaurant on a trail less than a mile from the airport. The terrain was eroded like the surface of the moon, and you could sit at one of the two outside tables and look across the green valley at the snowcapped mountains. They brought out a little grill with red hot coals and a platter of all kinds of meat that you could cook yourself on the little grill

Later Joy came back by herself over our Thanksgiving holiday. She joined me on a holiday weekend trip to Cochabamba trip on the ferrorail which was like a streetcar with an engine that went through the mountains on railroad tracks. The single ladies at the embassy had their maids prepare all the traditional things we would have back home. We stayed at a house where CIA employees could go to get away for a while. Edna also had a formal sit down dinner for Joy at her apartment before she left.

When Jackie and her husband came it was in the middle of winter there and we were not able to get through the 15,000 mountain pass. We tried twice but the snow was just too deep to go down to the Yungas which is a semitropical area on the other side of the mountain. We did some sightseeing in the La Paz area but unfortunately it was at a time when I wasn't able to away very much. They went on to visit her sister, Joy in California.

My brother and his wife came down to spend a few days and I almost scared them to death when I took them up to the ski slopes at 17,000 feet over the I lane mountain road where you could see about a mile straight down because they don't have guardrails. We also went to the Yungas on the other side of the mountain where tropical fruit grew and to see the great Lake Titicaca.

A few months before I left, my former wife asked if she could stop on way to see my daughter, Joy in California. Edna and I had established a close relationship by that time and she wasn't very happy about it, but it didn't destroy our relationship. I think divorced parents occasionally need to talk about their family with each other because they will always be parents. It was shortly before I left to come back to the US and Edna had a very special going away party for me when I left Bolivia.

LP-10 PROJECT SUMMARY

I would be completing my 2 year tour of duty in Bolivia at the end of April. Even though the project would not be completed, my tour of duty could not be extended because I had to return to FAA which had only released me for 2 years. Also, the USAID money to fund the project would all be used up by that time. In the time remaining, I had to try to tie up some of the many loose ends so there would be some kind of a road map so they could complete as much of the project as possible after I left.

Even though I had previously had three and one half years experience working in the Third World and knew how difficult it was to get things done, this project was more than I could fathom. Because of bureaucratic delays, I didn't arrive on site until 3 days before I had to have new untried equipment installed and operating to establish a new circuit so commercial airlines could continue landing at La Paz. FAA had written the specifications and purchased the equipment which was designed to operate at 13,500 feet but it had it had never even been tested at that altitude. Transmitters had to be operated at less than half the rated power because at this high altitude the ventilating fans did not cool the transmitter tubes enough so they didn't melt the glass. Also, it wasn't known at that time that air is actually an insulator and the radio frequency energy arced across insulators and from internal wires to ground. Although I managed to get the critical circuit in operation, using lower power that didn't provide very reliable service, it identified one of several problems that unduly delayed the entire project. After two visits by the design engineer determined that problems were so severe that equipment could not be modified in the field. It would have to be returned to the factory in New York to be completely redesigned and remanufactured. Unfortunately, we had to provide continuous service even though it was inadequate and required excessive maintenance so all transmitters could not all be returned at the same time. At this point, just four months before I was ready to depart, only one third of the transmitters had been returned from the manufacturer. Although the equipment was guaranteed by the manufacturer to operate at an altitude of 13,500 feet, FAA had to pay the cost of transportation to return the equipment. As the FAA project engineer, I worked closely with what I would call the Chief of all Civil Aviation Operations. We had an excellent relationship and worked well together but unfortunately he had more duties and responsibilities than anyone person could manage. He supervised everyone in civil aviation in the entire country from the one English speaking air traffic controller required at the International Airport in La Paz to the field office chiefs at the other three airports. This included the so called electronic technical staff at La Paz which apparently never had any electronic training. He was a competent technician and it appeared that that he had to take care of even minor technical problems so he was spread pretty thin. With one exception, all the other technicians decided that they weren't going to get involved in the new installation unless they received a pay raise which wasn't about to happen because the military general that headed up the organization wasn't about to give it to them. The project was contingent on the Bolivian technicians doing the installation work so they would know enough about the equipment to maintain it once it was installed. If the technicians couldn't or wouldn't maintain the equipment, there wasn't much use installing it because obviously it would require maintenance. I tried to maintain it myself because of the nature of the equipment problems resulting from design problems. Also, time that I had to spend maintaining the equipment took away from the time I had to do installation and engineering work.

With only four months before I was going to leave, the communication station building which would be the control point for the entire project was not yet completed. I had completed the drawings for this building as soon as I arrived in Bolivia because it was the key point where all circuits had to be terminated. The equipment room for the new communication center was not completed until about 2 months before my departure. Without any technical support, it would not be possible to terminate the cables and wire the equipment rack where the equipment would be installed. I had been making an issue of the lack of technical support throughout the project and finally at this late stage of the game they hired five telephone technicians which were helpful in terminating wires and cables but that was the extent of their ability. Only one of the Bolivian civil aviation technicians at La Paz assisted in the installation of the system and would be able assist in maintaining it. This was quite a complex system and in addition to all his other work Ele couldn't do it himself. The military generals responsible for civil aviation had little interest in this project or civil aviation in general.

They didn't have an equipment room completed where we could install the electronic equipment or even terminate cables until about 2 months before I left but we did get the equipment racks installed and some of the equipment wired. The equipment room was constructed on top of the terminal building as an addition to the second floor. We previously had both the 10KW transmitters installed and in operation at significantly reduced power and the one that had been returned from the factory was now fully operative. When the other transmitter was returned, the installation was complete enough so it could be set in place and the prepared cables terminated. We also had our high power circuits to Lima and Buenos Aires and one of two circuits to Chile operating in addition to our three domestic airports even though there was still work to be done on all of them. We brought in four FAA installation technicians for the last 2 months in an effort to get as much done as possible, particularly at the 3 remote airports but there was just too much to do in too short a time. Money for completion of the project was all used up and they would have to complete the job after we left.

This project gives me some insight into why Bolivia is such an unstable country, having one coup after another. This project was delayed possibly 20 years by two coups, each of which set the country back at least 5 years. From my experience, two Bolivians can't work together so one can't learn from another. This is contrary to the philosophy of USAID which is based on training individuals so they can train others. I attribute much of the problem to the high altitude and the miserable cold climate where you don't even feel warm in the hot sun. I am readily aware that living in this oxygen starved air makes people irritable and there isn't any question that their minds don't work nearly as well as it would at sea level. The four airports that I was involved with vary from an altitude of 400 feet at Trinidad to 13,200 feet at La Paz and it was readily apparent that the technical ability of individual technicians decreased significantly at higher altitudes.

The country is also like a military dictatorship, where all top level government officials were educated in other countries by some type of a foreign assistance program. For example, the Bolivian general that was in charge of civil/military aviation was a Harvard graduate with no background or interest in aviation He was conspicuous by his absence as he was seldom seen at his office or anywhere else. Although Spanish was the official language of the country, the two Indian languages were spoken primary by the general population which was over 80 % Indian. When you got outside of the few small cities, it was difficult to find anyone that could speak any language other than their Indian language. For some unknown reason, it was not culturally acceptable to speak English even if they could. Often as soon as you got airborne when you were flying someplace, the man next to you would lean over close to you and say, "I speak a little English." Obviously it was a safe place away from everyone he knew to practice his English. Unfortunately, in today's world it is practically impossible to develop a country whose population can't read, write and speak English. This is probably truer in aviation than any other area because even before WW II when airlines started flying from one country to another, English was established as the international language for aviation. Every international air traffic control tower in the world is required to have an English speaking controller on duty. All air traffic control messages and other correspondence are in English. Likewise, all technical manuals and equipment instruction books that manufacturers provided for their equipment are in English. In order to become an electronic technician who installs or maintains electronic aviation equipment you have to know English. I suspect one of the reasons the electronic technicians refused to get involved in the installation of the new equipment was because of their inability to read or understand English. Unfortunately, the long term success of the project is contingent on the ability of these same technicians to maintain it using technical manuals written in English. This problem can't be solved by publishing technical manuals in Spanish because the Spanish speaking world doesn't have any creditable training in aviation electronics. For the last 50 years, FAA has provided technical training for all countries in the world but the students do have to speak English.

As I previously mentioned, the taboo against speaking English was apparent when I was trying to work through an interpreter to work out some problems on a complex project with the Bolivian general that was chief of Bolivian aviation. I had to be sure that we fully understood each other and didn't dare rely on my poor Spanish. I could tell by the look in his eyes that he understood every word that I said in English and said, "I see you can speak English." He squirmed a little and finally said, "A little". I later learned that the general had graduated from Harvard but didn't want to embarrass himself in front of his people by speaking English.

LP-11 RETURN TO CHICAGO

I had completed as much of the project as I possibly could and tried to leave it in such a way that others could finish it when necessary construction was completed and replacement electronic equipment arrived. In the few days left, I had to get my things packed and formally finish my official duties associated with the project. I was also honored with going away dinners given by Bolivian Civil Aviation and Edna who also invited all my Bolivian friends as well as those from the American Embassy. It was a sad day when

Edna took me out to the airport and saw me off to an unknown future. Edna and I had established a special relationship over these last two years and I knew I would see her again.

I would be returning to the FAA Regional Office in Chicago which I had helped establish after I returned from Vietnam a little over four years ago and even though I was well known there, I didn't know what my new job would be. It was never fun coming back from a foreign assignment because you had to find an apartment, get your household effects out of storage, buy a car and learn about all the changes that had taken place during your absence. Unlike when I was assigned to Chicago after returning home from Vietnam, it was more like a homecoming. I knew most of the people and they had arranged to have a vacant position for me so I didn't have to take someone else's job. My new job was one of the four management positions in the region that assisted the division chief in managing all the sectors in our large region. When sector manager's positions were vacated they were usually filled by someone in the type position. I had ordered a new Chrysler Cordoba which was ready to be delivered when I returned which give me some mobility from the start. Although I had previously worked primarily in the engineering area I was also pretty much at home in the management area and had a good overview of the operation. I knew most of the sector managers and had a good relationship with all of them.

I had only been there about a month when Edna sent me a letter from Albuquerque as she had been called home because her mother had a stroke. She had been there for some time and her mother was making some improvement. When she found what she thought was my office address, she sent me her home phone number so I called her and she came to see me. I had rented an apartment and got my household goods out of storage but I was far from being settled. We had a very close relationship but never had lived with each other or made any formal plans to get married but I had never forgotten how bad it was to be single in Chicago either. Edna was on emergency leave and had to go back to La Paz in a few days but she was eligible to retire. I bought her an engagement ring before she went back to La Paz, sold what she didn't want to bring back to the U.S. and retired.

When she came back in a couple months we went down to the nearest court house to get married only to find they were closed on Saturday making it necessary to go all the way to down town Chicago to get married. We both knew there was a religious problem and we couldn't be married in a church but nevertheless we wanted to get married rather than just live together. She arranged it so her family never got the opportunity to meet me because her two unmarried sisters would never approve of her marrying a Gringo that wasn't even a Catholic.

After being in the Foreign Service for over 20 years she had accumulated treasures from all over the world. When the truck with the lift-vans arrived a couple months later with all her earthly possessions, it seemed impossible that we could find a place for everything but we did. I was still pretty occupied getting started in my new job but Edna was egger to explore a new city with its tall buildings on the lakeshore and all the Catholic shrines. She was used to finding her way around by herself but one time she got into trouble. We lived out in the western suburbs and since I traveled some in my job, I showed her how to pick me up at the airport so she could have our car while I was gone. I called her when my incoming flight arrived and would be standing on the curb in front of the airline gate entrance where she would pick me up. Although we rehearsed it several times, she got tangled up in the many lanes of rush hour traffic and couldn't get near the curb so she pulled into the parking ramp. After awhile she made her way through the underground tunnel from the parking ramp to the main terminal and finally found me waiting for her on the curb. I asked her where she parked and she told me it was near the elevator. Unfortunately, she didn't know which one of the 20 elevators or on which of the many floors in the parking ramp that it was on. It took a couple hours to find our car and she had left the lights on. Fortunately, our car still started. It was quite an experience but after that she became a professional driver at O'Hare the busiest airport in the world.

LP-12 TRANSFER TO LANSING, MICHIGAN

About 3 months after we were married I was transferred to Lansing, Michigan to be the new sector manager. Although Detroit Airport had its own sector manager, field offices in the rest of the state had been divided between the Lansing and the Grand Rapids sector that covered the west half of Michigan. I had eight field offices on the eastern part of the state from Sioux St Marie on the north to Jackson in the south with my office being in Lansing. I had been back in the regional office long enough to realize this was not a prize assignment because it was well known that it was the problem sector in the region. When the Great Lakes Region was established before I went to South America, the Cleveland Area Office was in of the Eastern Region and all the other area offices were from regions that had more disciplined work ethics. The sector manager for Lansing was from the Cleveland area and he brought most of his office staff with him. The Lansing sector staff was used to two martini lunches which far exceeded the half hour allowed. Also since that time the Great Lakes Region got a new Mormon director who hired our new division chief that was also a Mormon. The sector manager that I was replacing had decided to take a similar job in Little Rock, Arkansas for some unknown reason and I was reassigned to take his place. I was directed to put an end to the sort of thing that was going on that gave the Lansing Sector Office a bad reputation. In other words I was sent there to clean up the mess which didn't make me very popular. Working through my assistant who was also one of the Cleveland group, I was able to make some headway but within a year he too found a new job back in Cleveland. When he left, my division chief knowingly appointed a former field office chief from my sector that was reassigned to a similar job in Chicago because he had an unacceptable relationship with a woman in his field office that everyone in the sector knew about. This was not going to be helpful in cleaning up the mess that I was sent there to do as he tried to gain popularity by joining the group that was causing the problem rather than the solution. Finally, unbeknown to me, he and one of technicians in my office had a confrontation over one of the ladies in my office and the Regional Office became involved. I no longer felt that I had my division chief's support and since they were reducing the number of sectors and one of the two in Michigan would be closed. When they consolidated my sector and the Grand Rapids Sector, I recommended they close mine which they did.

LP-13 TDY IN WASHINGTON

There wasn't any vacancy in the Region at that time and they sent me to Washington on TDY. Edna was delighted because she still knew so many people in the Foreign Service that passed through Washington coming and going from one post to another. Also Edna had worked In Washington for 3 years after WW II bringing home the American dead that had been buried overseas and two of here roommates still lived there. Since it was a TDY assignment we kept our apartment in Lansing because we didn't know what to do with all our household things and being on TDY we didn't expect to be in Washington for very long. Much to my surprise, Clint Murphy, Chief, Electronic Engineering Division who I had never met was my supervisor and had actually requested that I be assigned to his Division on TDY. We had a very long talk and he told me that I was going to be his Air Navigations Aids Engineering Branch Chief which I was not aware of. Although few people knew much about my career in my region, he knew that I had developed a new type monitor system for the capture effect glideslope; had built the longest range communication station in the world while I was in Vietnam; discovered why the communications transmitters in Bolivia that his Communications Engineering Branch wrote the specifications for wouldn't operate at high altitude and that I had done some work on Doppler VOR distributors which was still a current problem that needed to be dealt with now many years later.

Clint also spent quite some time outlining some urgent problems he wanted me to help with. He told me that he had assigned me to be his navigation aids branch chief because all our 1940 vintage air navigation equipment that established our present airway system was no longer reliable and had to be replaced. Also the manufacture of all radio tubes used in our present equipment would soon be discontinued because all new radio equipment being manufactured was of solid state design that does not use radio tubes. It was extremely urgent that we replace all our air navigation facilities with new solid equipment facilities before radio tubes were no longer available. We have been working for 2 years to develop specifications to purchase a new state of the art generation of solid state radio navigation aids and hadn't made much progress. The VOR/DME system is the international system and our new generation solid facilities must provide all the same navigation data to aircraft as our existing facilities but by utilizing other new technology such as uninterruptable power, computer and other digital technology, they will be more reliable and require fewer technicians to do a better job. Using a computer almost any number of these new facilities could be continuously monitored and controlled over telephone lines, several hundred miles from the facility. A technician at that site would also have the capability of diagnosing problems, making adjustments and recertifying any facility using the computer.

We also wanted technicians to be able to both diagnose problems and make adjustments with what resembles a laptop computer over a telephone line. If there is an equipment failure the technician can identify the plugin module required and even a warehouse man can replace it. He can call the technician who may be hundreds of miles away to make the necessary adjustments and recertify the facility. Instead of a technician having to visit each facility 2 or 3 times a week, someone would only have to visit it semiannually mainly to check the building and grounds.

He said 2 years ago he had relieved the branch chief to devote full time on this project and had since replaced several branch chiefs but hasn't made much progress and time was running out. Also this project requires considerable assistance from other divisions because computer, uninterrupted power and many other specialists are required to develop a finished product that all the many FAA organizations will sign off on. It should also be noted that we have to show the Congressional Budget Office how this project will be paid for by reducing personnel. He told me he wanted me to be both branch chief and manage the project at the same time as it is difficult to separate them. This would also be a new concept for FAA as the new package we would contract for would include installation in existing buildings collocated with some existing equipment. Also, the method of operating, adjusting and monitoring facilities remotely developed for this project could be applied to other remote facilities which will significantly reduce the technical staff required to maintain them while at the same time improve their reliability. This would be first of a new generation of facilities. I told Clint, "This is a real challenge but I would do the best I could."

I thought about where I would start for a couple days. I was not acquainted with the people that I would need to work with. I thought that I better meet these people on a one on one basis so I could also get their input and start developing a team effort. After I determined who the actual individual were that would be in charge of writing the portion of the specification for each in each engineering specialty, we worked as a team, each preparing their first draft on their proposed plan. Then we could sit down together and make the necessary adjustments so they were all compatible so they wouldn't conflict with each other. From time to time, we had to call in others with special expertise in other areas. For instance, we had to have a minimum of 4 KW solid state amplifiers for the TACAN transmitter and such a thing didn't yet exist. We determined that one company was in the process of developing such an amplifier and wrote into the specifications that an amplifier of this type would be required, leaving the door open for someone else to develop one.

I didn't have a very big staff in my branch and we were dealing with new technology that was somewhat foreign to all of us. For instance, most of us were competent electronic engineers who were familiar with radio tube technology. Now, we were dealing with solid state technology that not only replaced radio tubes but branched out in to computer type digital, reliable uninterruptable power or numerous other things. In other words, my primary job was to set up and manage a group of highly specialized engineers to come up with a finished product that had to be approved by about 20 independent groups like Research and Development, Flight Standards, Air Traffic Control Operations and last but not least the Congressional Budget Office.

One person that was indispensable to the entire project was my secretary. It was before the days of computers, now known as a (PC) and there was a an 8 inch high stack of paper which were our specifications that probably had to be altered many times to satisfy all the groups that had to approve of it. She was a young lady of about 20 that was an expert in operating what you would call the predecessor to the word processor. The machine had 2 cassettes in it, one that recorded what she typed and the other corrected or changed parts of it at some later date. I was fascinated by the machine but was overwhelmed with project I didn't have time to find out.

During my stay in Washington, I was sent to the International Air Navigation Conference representing the FAA. Edna went with me and we drove up to Atlantic City for the conference. It was just at the time, the gambling casinos were about to open and Edna had an interesting time checking out the new casinos that were about to open on the boardwalk. I was attending the conference which was during the period when we had just put up our first satellite. We all knew that this was the future of air navigations but even if the VOR/DME hadn't been the international system, we couldn't have prolonged the development of a new solid state system. This is also directly related to the global positioning system and at that time the U.S. Military wouldn't release the Vermeer control that would have made it usable for air navigation. Their main concern was that it was accurate enough to put a missile through a window half way around the world and this would put other countries in a position they could do the same to us. It was a nice trip that gave us the opportunity to get out of Washington for a week.

Most projects have periods where you are delayed waiting for something you can't do anything about and during one of these periods Edna and I went on a planned trip. We had ordered a new car through my son-in-law who was service manager at a dealership in Glendale, California before I went to Washington to be delivered to Lansing, Michigan. We took a trip from Washington to Glendale where my daughter lived, stopping at Edna's home in Albuquerque on the way. We left our old car for him to sell and flew to Lansing to pick up our new car and drive back to Washington. Unfortunately, the union that hauls cars from Canada was on strike and our car never arrived so we had to fly back to Washington without a car. Later, we flew back to Lansing on a weekend to do a number of things, since it was now obvious that my TDY assignment in Washington would be of long duration. We gave up our apartment, put our furniture in storage, picked up our new car and drove back to Washington.

When we returned to Washington, the project was going well. We had proceeded to the point where all the potential contractors were roaming around our office to pick up every scrap of information that might give them a head start over their competitors when the specifications were completed and logistics put it out for bids. It was quite a security problem and we had to make sure there wasn't anything in the waste baskets that would give them information regarding what the finished project might look like. One former Navy captain was there almost every morning and always made a point to tell us that he had to leave because he was having lunch with Tip O'Neal, the Speaker of the House at that time. That didn't help much because FAA is so unpartisan, that not more than a half dozen figurehead positions at the top are replaced when a president from another party is elected. We got approval of various phases of the project as went along so we wouldn't have an insurmountable problem when it was completed. The final approval by the Congressional budget was the last and most difficult hurtle. Two members of the Congressional Budget Office, Clinton Murphy and I sat in our service director's office and they grilled us on how we were going to pay for it. They refused to consider the fact that our air traffic control system wouldn't be able operate in 2 years because manufacturers had already stopped making some radio tubes and the 1940 vintage equipment was no longer reliable enough for today's requirements. The only thing they wanted to talk about was how are going to reduce the technical staff enough to pay for the new equipment. They didn't accept the point that in most cases someone would only have to visit most remote facilities twice a year rather than all facilities 2 or 3 times a week. Also, a technician at a computer hundreds of miles away can not only determine if there is a problem but in most cases can also make adjustments to fix it. Finally, our service director had to put his career on the line to make sure that he did what he promised to do. Clearing this last hurtle, we were ready to turn it over to logistics to put out bids to replace over 1000 VOR/DME and Military TACANs that we have in the U.S., Puerto Rico and American Samoa.

Many things were neglected while we getting the project underway and while I was waiting for bids to come in and I had time to do some of the thing that were put on hold. I needed to stick around until the bids came in so I could answer any questions or further clarify anything if necessary. I hadn't told them yet that I expected to leave as soon as the contract was awarded and go back to the Chicago Region where Edna and I could get household goods out of storage.

Our specifications must have been clear as we didn't get a single request for clarifications and after the $150 million dollar contract was awarded I told Clint that I was leaving. His assistant division chief just left and he wanted me to take that job but I told him I was going back my Region and start thinking about retirement. I enjoyed working with Clint but I couldn't see myself moving to Washington at this late point in my career.

BACK TO CHICAGO FOR THE LAST TIME

I still had some work that I had to finish in Washington but since we were going back to Chicago, I made a motel reservation for Edna and arranged for a rented car so Edna could go back and find a place for us to live. Since we had lived in the area the first few months after we were married, she was at least somewhat familiar with the area, so she could look around and find something she liked not any further than necessary from where I worked. She called me every night to tell me about what she found that day. After about 3 days, she was all excited about the apartment she found in Schaumberg where there was a ground floor apartment on a manmade lake with underground parking and 2 sliding patio doors. It was vacant and we could move in any time we wanted.

She came back to Washington and was looking forward to moving into our new apartment. By that time I had done about all I was going to do in Washington and called my Regional Office in Chicago telling them I was returning.

We had been living in a furnished apartment that we rented by the week or month so even though my Cordoba wasn't very big we got a top carrier and didn't have a trouble moving what little things we had accumulated during our almost year long stay. We had our furniture delivered about the time we got back to Chicago. I didn't like fighting my way to and from work on the toll-road but you have to expect that in Chicago. One of the branch chiefs retired and I ended up as branch chief for the evaluation branch. I had a staff of about15 technicians that did technical evaluations at various type facilities throughout the Region to determine they met FAA standards. About once every 2 months, we made a management evaluation at one of our many sectors. These in-depth evaluations were preceded by one or more technical evaluations at a couple of their field offices and our division chief came out on the final day to get an overview of their operation. It wasn't really the type of thing that hat I liked to as I would rather help someone than find fault with what they do.

During the year before I retired, Edna and I took a trip to Spain and Portugal that we had been planning since we got married. The Ambassador's secretary who was a good friend of Edna's in La Paz was now in Lisbon, Portugal had invited us to visit her and we rented a car and toured both Spain and Portugal. We stayed at a resort on the ocean in southern Portugal for a few days and proceeded down the coast through the fishing villages into Spain and spent a few days on the Coast of Del Sol on the Mediterranean. After taking a day's tour crossing over to Morocco at Gibraltar we proceeded up through central Spain to Madrid. Edna knew that a special friend of hers that had previously worked in Madrid for the CIA had gone down to Ecuador with another lady to write a book and she wanted to get her address. They said, "Just a minute and you can talk to her," which was a real surprise because Edna didn't know that she came back to work. She had just arrived, so she didn't have a house where we could stay as yet but she spent all her free time showing us around Madrid. I visited museums that Edna had already seen while she went other places she wanted to go. I also learned how bilingual Edna really was when she jabbered with taxi drivers in perfect Castilian Spanish. Her family was about a 5th generation

Spanish immigrants. Sometime after we left, Edna's friend was held up and almost killed when she drove her car to an American Base Exchange (BX). Some years later she called us when her and her new husband who was now an ambassador visited his family in Albuquerque and we had a chance to visit with them over the Christmas holidays.

RETIREMENT FROM FAA

I had been eligible to retire for a couple years and we decided to do it in the fall so we wouldn't have to tolerate another Chicago winter. We rented a U Haul truck and Edna found a couple of people that could load our furniture in the truck. We had also purchased a classic 1970 Cadillac convertible so we had 2 vehicles and had to tow the Cadillac behind the truck so we almost had our own caravan. Edna drove our car and I drove the truck over 1300 miles to Albuquerque where we put what we could in one of the three apartments that belonged to Edna and two of her sisters. Our furniture and other things we didn't have room for in the little apartment was stored until we sorted out what we were going to do. While we were deciding what we wanted to do, I got a call from the International Civil Aviation Organization (ICAO) with a job offer. This is one of over 100 United Nations Organizations and this one happened to be headquartered in Montreal, Canada. While I was a FAA Branch Chief in Washington I got frequent calls from them because although they were supposed to be the international authority their staff had little expertise and often called for advice on problems they couldn't solve. The technical assistance bureau had a British bureau chief and 65% of their employees were British even though at that time they didn't even have one of the top 10 airports in the world.

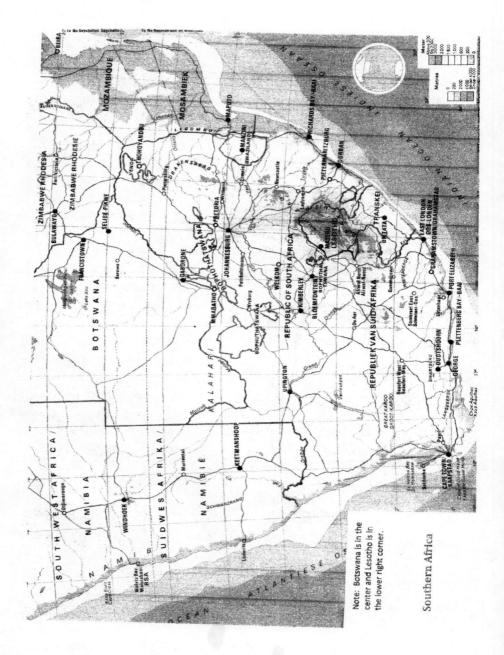

Note: Botswana is in the
center and Lesotho is in
the lower right corner.

Southern Africa

Two hundred Elephants go down to the river to drink and play every noon

The Graff can eat the leaves off the top of trees that the Elephants can't reach

This was taken from a lazy river that meanders through the enormous crocodile infested swamp near the village of Maun, in central Botswana.

VI

UN IN AFRICA

UN-1 INTRODUCTION TO THE UN & AFRICA

A man from ICAO called and asked me if I would accept a short one month assignment to Maseru, Lesotho. I asked him, "Where in the world is that?" They told me it was a small kingdom nation completely surrounded by South Africa. The Arab oil countries had boycotted South Africa because of their apartheid policy and since South Africa was the breadbasket of the southern half of the African continent they were concerned that they would close their borders, cutting off all food exports. Lesotho and neighboring Botswana imported everything except beef from South Africa and if they closed their borders, people in these countries would starve to death. The wealthy oil producing countries were going to build an airport in both of these countries so the necessary foodstuff could be supplied by air in event their border with South Africa were closed. The project had proceeded to the point that the Netherlands had prepared specifications for all communication, navigation and other air traffic control facilities for the new airport. They wanted me to go to Lesotho where I would review the specifications for these facilities for the proposed new airport. I told them that I would discuss their proposed assignment with my wife and get back to them in a couple days.

My wife, who had spent most of her life in the U.S. Foreign Service, working in many countries throughout the world was thrilled at the opportunity because she had never been to Africa. It was only a month's assignment so it wasn't a hard decision to make and I called them back and told them we would take the job. I didn't realize that we would have to spend a few days at ICAO headquarters in Montreal both going and coming but they were paying the bill and we had never been there so we didn't object.

Although I was pretty well versed on the technical aspects of ICAO, I knew very little about how the Technical Assistance Bureau functioned. In this case the bureau chief was British and even though they didn't even have one of the top 10 airports in the world at that time, 65% of all the Bureau employees around the world were British. Before I got alarmed, I found this was standard practice with all the UN Bureaus and it was common practice for bureau chiefs to hire most of their international technical staff from their home country. Qualifications were secondary to their country of origin. Also, at first I didn't attach any significance to the fact that all our airline tickets were on British Airways. Soon it became apparent that British Airways booked every ICAO flight which was obviously another perk that goes along with a country having the bureau chief. Also, we were routed through Europe with a layover in Switzerland and a stop in Kenya en route to Johannesburg where we had another layover before we proceeded to Lesotho on a smaller plane.

We weren't impressed with French Canadian Montreal because if you didn't speak French, you weren't welcome there and if you went to a restaurant you could expect to be ignored if you couldn't speak French. Also, it was kind of a dirty crummy place that you couldn't wait to leave. The airport which was built for the Olympic Games was about 50 miles out of town on a lonely highway. When we arrived at the airport in the late afternoon to leave, they were just opening the terminal building. The airport is only open two days a week when they have flights that come in. We waited in the empty terminal building for a couple hours for our British Airways flight to arrive. The Boeing 747 came in late and the few passengers deplaned but there seemed to be some delay in loading. Finally, they announced that there would be a delay because one of the engines had an oil leak but we would have to board the plane to eat dinner after which we would deplane and wait for instructions. We had mutton which was always the main course at the dinner meal on British Airways. All our baggage except our carry on had been loaded on the plane so those of us that had a carry on bag carried it to the hotel which was also built for the Olympics and it was quite some distance from the now dark terminal building. It was long past midnight when the clerk at the desk got instructions to assign rooms to us, now stranded British Airways passengers. We had specific instructions to be in the hotel lobby at 6:00AM the next morning when they would advise us of future plans. They told us that there would be some delay because they had to replace the engine that was leaking oil. They didn't tell us that they had to use a British Royse-Royce engine and since there wasn't one in Canada, they had to get one from New York. To make a very long story shorter, the engine was shipped by truck to the Canadian border but they couldn't bring it into Canada because they didn't have the necessary customs documents. After considerable delay, the engine was delivered in the middle of the winter and there wasn't a single building on the airport so it had to be installed outside in the subzero temperature. After more than three days, the new engine was installed and we left for Zurich, Switzerland where we had about a 6 hour layover. They put us up in a hotel but by the time they took us to the hotel and picked us up we only had about 3 hours sleep. It is a long way from Zurich to Nairobi, Kenya and we arrived there on the equator in the middle of summer. It was scorching hot and no one was allowed to deplane at Nairobi unless it was their destination and they had a visa. They didn't have any air-conditioning and we were on the ground for more than an hour with passengers hanging out the door and up and down the boarding steps trying to get a breath of hot air. About 100 feet away on the tarmac was another British Airways 747 that had been on the ground for about 3 days with all the passengers still aboard, waiting for a replacement Royse Royce engine because one of their engines had an oil leak. It was difficult to communicate with them because we were parked so far apart it was difficult to yell loud enough so we could hear and understand their British accent.

When we arrived at Johannesburg, we got our first introduction to apartheid and even though we were transit passengers en route to Lesotho, we had to go through immigration which delayed us to the point that we missed our flight to Lesotho and had to stay overnight. They had rooms on the upper floors of the airport terminal where we could stay and a restaurant where we could eat. We called Edna's friend Virginia, who worked in the U.S. Foreign service that was now Secretary to the U.S. Council in Johannesburg. She was not allowed to visit us at the airport terminal and we could not leave the terminal to visit her because we didn't have a South African visa but we could talk to her on the telephone. We did make tentative arrangements to get a visa so we could stop and visit her on our return trip. It was interesting to note that both Lesotho and Botswana airlines planes were parked far from the terminal and our luggage was lined up on the airport near the plane that we would be taking. All the passengers had to walk out to the plane and claim their own luggage which was sitting on the tarmac before they boarded the aircraft which was obviously for security purposes. Obviously, no one would put luggage on the plane that they were boarding that would blow it up.

UN-2 MASERU, LESOTHO

The Lesotho Airport resembled a cow pasture with sod runway that would only be suitable for small aircraft like the one we came in on. Language was not a problem as everyone could speak British English so we didn't have any problem getting direction to the small Quonset buildings that was the airport manager's office. He arranged transportation to take us to the only hotel in Maseru. Although Maseru was the capital of Lesotho, it was a small town with one street that went all the way through town. Our hotel was on the second floor of a building on this street near the edge of town. The entire country was nothing more than an island wasteland in the southern part of South Africa and there wasn't any industry but a few small fields where they managed to grow a few crops of something for their own use. Maseru was what you might call sin city as gambling and prostitution were there primary source of revenue. South Africa considered itself as being a very moral country and such things as gambling and prostitution were things that no one would even dare talk about but they weren't all that moral and enjoyed spending a weekend now and then in Maseru where nothing was off limits.

We left for Lesotho on fairly short notice and I didn't have time to get a haircut before we left so I asked Edna to find a barbershop where I could get my hair cut. I knew they did cut their hair because it was not unusual to see someone sitting on a chair in the shade of a tree along the road getting his hair cut. Edna walked down the main street asking people along the way where the barbershop was and everyone said it was further down the street. Finally she reached a small mountain at the end of the street and concluded they didn't have such a thing and none of the people she asked knew what she was talking about.

The day after we arrived I went out to the airport which was on the edge of town to try to get a handle on what I was here to accomplish. It was evident that the airport manager was less versed than I was on what the new airport project was all about. He had a pile of documents in the drawer of his file cabinet that he gave me so I could sort out what I was looking for. My mission was only to review the plans and specifications for the new airport so the only documents I took were those that involved that part of the project. The documents appeared to be an obsolete 20 year old set of Dutch specification for the VOR which is the principal navigation aid that would direct aircraft to that particular airport. My time was limited but just having completed the specifications for a new second generation VOR system for the entire U.S.A.; I was able to write new specifications from memory. My new specifications were for a more simplified system that would be more applicable for a Third World country where technical skills were limited. The function of a VOR is very sensitive to the site where it is located and I was also able to locate a site where a VOR should function without restrictions. The overall specifications for the communication/navigation equipment was a massive document and as familiar as I was with them it took me most of two weeks to write all new ones for my entire project. Outside of that, there was little that I could do except to make some general overall recommendations because the project was at such a preliminary stage that we didn't even know how the runway would be orientated, where the terminal building would be located or what it would look like. Under the circumstances there was little else that I could accomplish.

About a week after we arrived, a Canadian who was also there with the United Nations told us that the Hilton had just completed a new hotel which hadn't opened yet. He knew the Canadian manager and arranged for some of us UN people to move in before it was formally opened. It was a luxurious hotel built on the side of a mountain on the other end of the main street. They opened an upscale restaurant on the lower level overlooking the little city and were in the process of training the restaurant staff. American Thanksgiving was approaching and the manager decided to have a traditional Thanksgiving dinner to celebrate our holiday. Apparently U.S.A. is the only country that sets aside a day for thanksgiving and the Canadian manager was aware of it and wanted to serve a traditional Thanksgiving dinner. We invited those that we were working with to be our guest and all of us got an up front and personal look at how they think we celebrate this holiday. The hotel staff called Americans at the embassy and at USAID about how they go about preparing a traditional Thanksgiving dinner. They did a pretty good job on the dinner but the pumpkin pie was something else. I'm not sure who gave them the recipe but the pie was like a thin piece of leather that was hard as a rock. Somehow they may have got the our concept of Thanksgiving mixed up with Christmas because as you went down the wide stairway from the main lobby to the dining room, they had crates of turkeys and other birds stacked up on one side. At the bottom of the stairs they had one or two donkeys tied up eating hay. They made a great effort and we all appreciated it.

They didn't have any tours so we could see the countryside so one Sunday we rented a van with a driver who more or less acted as a native guide. Basically, it was a sparsely populated, hilly wasteland with small plots of land where people raised a few vegetables for their own use. The rural population lived in round adobe type houses with a thatched roof with perhaps three or four houses in close proximity to each other. We did see one place where there were paintings on the side of a cave that fascinated us. Our driver stopped by a shallow river where we had to take off our shoes and roll up our pants legs in order to walk across the little river with a rocky bottom. On the other side of the river which had cut deep into a stone ledge that overhung the river, there were pictures of what we would probably call a buffalo hunt. At least a group of hunters with spears was in the process of killing a beast that had some resemblance to a buffalo. It was our only outing in the countryside during our short stay.

It so happened that the United Nations, ICAO office in Montreal wanted me to return via way of Botswana where they were going to have a vacancy for a job like mine in the near future. They wanted me to take a look at it and consider the possibility of accepting the job there when it opened. Edna and I thought about it and decided as long as they were paying for the trip it was an offer we couldn't refuse.

UN-3 BOTSWANA

We flew directly from Maseru, the capital of Lesotho to Gaborone, the capital of Botswana on the South African border. Gaborone was a small town not much bigger than Maseru on the east edge of the great Kalahari Desert. The runway of the airport on the edge of town was along the side of a reservoir that was their only water supply. It was kind of like a dammed up river that never got full during the rainy season. There was only one hotel in what you would call the down town area along with two British banks because it was a former British colony. There was also a Holiday Inn on the edge of town in the vicinity of the airport. The only two restaurants were at the Holiday Inn and the hotel.

Botswana is a sparsely populated country about the size of Texas which is considered the most democratic country in the world. The head of one of the two black tribes who married a white British woman when he attended Oxford University in England was elected president in a free an open election and they had three children. The head of the other tribe was elected vice president and when the president died the vice president became president by an open vote of what we would call our congress. Although they had three diamond mines, raising cattle was the most sought after profession. The European countries had built an ultra-modern slaughter house in Labotse, a small town about 20 miles south of Gaborone that shipped most of their beef to Europe in refrigerated ships. Although it was primarily a black country, two of the government ministers like our cabinet members were white and they all made trips to the small villages and sat down with the men of the village for an informal meeting. Every man, regardless of how ragged and torn his clothes were would be heard and respected like everyone else.

The day we arrived we were given a room and free meals at the Holiday Inn. That night they had a reception for us at the British ICAO Director's house and all five of the UN ICAO group and their wives that we would be part of were there. It was a nice social gathering that introduced us to the people that we would be working with. The next day I had a long one on one discussion with the British UN Director who would be my boss and even though he was unusually guarded in what he told me, I came away with the feeling that many of the things he told me seemed to be somewhat guarded that suggested they might still be operating like a British colony. It was apparent that he didn't seem to be interested in my qualifications as he undoubtedly knew I was better qualified than any of the others his group. He seemed to have an unusual interest in my British connections and the fact that both my grandfathers came from either Wales or Northern Ireland. It also seemed to be significant that I still had relatives in the U.K. Apparently I would be OK.

The next day I had the opportunity to sit down alone with the man that I would replace if I took the job. We had an open one on one discussion of what the job really consisted of and what was in store for the future . . . He was a man of what appeared to be over 60 which is the mandatory ICAO retirement age so in this British controlled organization it was obvious that he was retiring. Although he was the aviation telecommunication engineer responsible for the entire country he seldom left his office and was less informed about the proposed program for the new airport and country wide aviation communications program than I was. Even telephone service in the capital city which he had nothing to do with was unreliable and there was there was unsatisfactory point to point radio communications with the outlying airports. ICAO had made me aware of the new airport and a major radio communications projects that would tie all their airports together. This would require writing the specifications and procuring all the equipment which they had set aside the money to accomplish several years ago. Obviously, they were looking for someone that could develop a complete telecommunications program, write the specifications, procure and install the new equipment and train a complete staff. It was apparent that it was a big job with many unforeseen obstacles to solve in a Third World country.

We stopped in Johannesburg and spent a few days with Edna's special friend Virginia on our way back to Montreal. I apprized ICAO of the problems and told them that I would have to think about taking the job when it was vacated.

UN-4 TOUR OF DUTY IN BOTSWANA

ICAO called me a couple months later to negotiate an agreement for a one year tour of duty in Botswana. I was aware that even though the salary and benefits they initially offered me was a lot as it was more than I was receiving from FAA when I was Navigation Aids Branch Chief in Washington. I also realized the British members of the team which had few qualifications were receiving more. Finally, we negotiated a satisfactory settlement and I received a job offer for two years rather than the one year previously discussed. Edna had been an international nomad so much of her life so she wasn't concern whether it was one or two years and I accepted the job. We had to go back to Montreal so they could ticket us on British Airways by the same out of the way route through Europe rather than take a direct flight from Johannesburg to New York. They had to punish South African Airways by giving the business to British Airways because of apartheid even if it takes a day longer and in either case you end up in Johannesburg where you had to spend an extra night.

We stayed at the Holiday Inn as we did on our previous stopover a few months earlier. It a was nice fairly large, two floor building and our room was on the main floor with sliding doors so we could look at the swimming pool in the courtyard. We didn't realize that we would be there for over a month and a half because there wasn't any housing available. Also, we didn't know that we would get free meals in the dining room all the time we stayed there. The food was good but after while Edna and another lady she met walked over a mile down town and bought something different for lunch for a change as I always came back to the motel for lunch when I was not traveling.

The first day I had to take a driver's test, driving on the left side of the road to get a government driver's license as I was in effect an employee of the Botswana Government. They paid me a small salary like I was one of their own citizens but my real salary and benefits came from ICAO. I was in a position where I could hire and fire employees and spend money for anything we needed. The only catch was the British airport engineer controlled all the money and he never told me how much I had. Not knowing, I just spent what I needed and he never questioned me but I wasn't used to that type of budgeting. I met all the local headquarters employees including two which were British Aid employees that were also supposed to be my employees at the airport that were being supervised by a British Aid worker. About a month later an engineering graduate from their local college showed up who was going to be my counterpart. Every UN/ ICAO employee was supposed to have a counterpart and we were there only to teach them the job that we were doing. If the other members of our ICAO Group had a counterpart they placed them in an office by themselves to make sure they didn't learn their job because if they did they would not need them anymore. I had them put my counterpart, Spike's desk in my office because I wanted him to learn my job because that was what I was there for. I had to buy a car so I could go to and from work and the first thing I had to do was teach Spike how to drive a car and get his license as neither he or any one on my technical staff knew how to drive.

Early in my tour a local employee of Civil Aviation took me around to see 5 of the 6 airports out of Gaborone so I would know how to get there and see what they consisted of. He had a 2-1/2 ton, Chevrolet truck with 4 wheel drive. All vehicles used to travel though the desert and on the trails were 4 wheel drive, had both an auxiliary 300 gal gas and water tank, 2 spare tires, fan belts and other equipment for emergency use. You had to use 4 wheel drive vehicle because the tires sunk down in the sand and the trails weren't marked so you were often lost in Lion country. If there was a fork in the trail the rule was to take the most traveled trail. The trails went through the Chobe Game Park which is lion country and even on the so called main roads you probably didn't meet more than 2 or 3 cars a day. We went north stopping at Selibe Pikwe, a cobalt mining town where we had a little air navigation facility and spent the night at Francistown which had the largest airport in Botswana. The next day it was an all-day drive to Kasane on the Chobe River which joins the Zambezi River that flows over Victoria Falls almost 100 miles to the north forming the border between what was Rhodesia at that time and Zambia. We stayed at the Safari Lodge on the Chobe River in Kasane. The wide river was unique because at one time there was a shift in the earth's surface. During the rainy season it flows southwest into the crocodile infested Okavango Swamps near Maun and during the dry season it season it flows east in to the Zambezi River and over Victoria Falls.

Kasane is located on the edge of the Chobe Game Park and Hunters Africa in Huston, TX has a hunting lodge there were they have a FAX that operates over a special telephone line direct from Victoria Falls. The following day we got up at daylight, got a sack lunch, made sure our gas and water tanks were full and headed out on the trails through the game park and a the Bushman village to Maun. It is a long hard drive and we couldn't stop to enjoy the herds of wild animals because you had to get there before dark. We didn't continue on to Ghanzi which is another day's drive further through the desert. We came back another way which was only 2 long days from Maun. You can't fly to Kasane but there is one flight a week from Gaborone to Maun and Ghanzi which are only on the ground for a few minutes and if you are going to stay there you have stay a week. We had navigation/communication facilities at all these locations so it was apparent that considerable time would be wasted traveling.

I had to see all these places in order to write the specifications for the communication system before bids could be distributed, contract awarded and the system installed. This would require more than one year of my 2 year assignment but fortunately each one would take time and there would be intervals between where I could do other things. I should be able to complete the specification and get the bids out soon because of my experience in Bolivia. I already knew what type of equipment I wanted and would write the specifications to accommodate that equipment. I was somewhat concerned about installing the equipment because I didn't have a staff with the necessary expertise and I couldn't do it all myself. I already found myself in a position where I had to do too much maintenance to keep the existing equipment in operation. So far I found that it was impossible to hire technicians with any usable skills. I was counting on the technicians that were graduating from the ICAO school in Kenya but I only had 2 years and they would have to be trained.

There were numerous other trips to various places and Edna could go with me if I didn't have to take 2 people with me because only 3 can ride in the cab of a truck. Edna really enjoyed these trips because sometimes when you are 50 or 100 miles from nowhere you see 4 sticks in the ground with a skin over them for shade and a child perhaps 8 to 10 years old with some carving of different types they were selling for almost nothing. She enjoyed buying things from the children. One time I was working in Francistown which is a typical African village for a few days and she was all excited when I came back to the hotel at noon because she found places where they sold animal skins and were actually carving ivory. She wanted to buy many things that interested her and wanted to know if we had room in the truck to bring them back to Gaborone. At Kasane, we went for a boat ride on the Chobe River in the evening and watched all the elephants and other game getting their last drink of the day. We were almost overcome by a group of hippopotamus that the boat driver didn't see until they got pretty close to us. There wasn't any tours available so Edna talked the owner of the Safari Lodge where we were staying into taking her on a tour of the game park while I was working. She was so impressed with the game park that we stayed over Friday night and I took her and Pule, one of our technicians into the game park and watched about 200 elephants of all sizes cross a small abandoned airport on their twice daily trip to the Chobe River. As we were driving through the park a park ranger stopped us on the park trail and Pule the technician I brought along, got out to see what was happening. The ranger told Pule that there was a pride of lions just in front of us and Pule was so frightened that he jumped in the truck through the window without opening the door. We also saw rare black rhinos and hundreds of other animals on our morning excursion, In Maun while I was working, she arranged a tour in the Okavango swamps to take a ride down the river in a dugout boat with a man pushing it along with a pole.

The swamps were famous for all the rare birds along the river and of course the crocodiles. (Recently, a crocodile had taken a German woman tourist when she went for an early morning swim. All they found was her clothes along the bank of the river.) They sent a sack lunch along for Edna and the boatman. Edna really enjoyed her stay in Botswana. Later when I had to take more staff along on in country trips I could no longer take her along but she always found something to do that interested her.

UN-5 MOVED INTO A NEW HOUSE

After about a month and a half we got word that our house was ready and we were anxious to move in. Even though we got free meals and lodging it was too long to live out of a suitcase. Unlike the U.S. Foreign Service the UN gives you a bill of lading to ship what they allow and their Administrative Officer doesn't give you any assistance in following up when it inevitably gets lost along the way. We had opted to ship a small amount by air to this landlocked country so we could expect it to arrive before our 2 year tour was over rather than take all the things we would have liked to. Our personal effects did arrive about the time we got our house but the new refrigerator that we had purchased to take with us looked like it had been dropped from 20,000 feet. We purchased it because refrigerators are very expensive in South Africa and it ended up that we had to buy a new one and for some reason the mover's insurance wouldn't pay for it.

It was a new house that no one had ever lived in with a combination living/dining room with a fireplace between. We didn't realize at that time that this was the only source of heat in this 3 bedroom house and it gets pretty cold there in the winter. There isn't any wood in the desert so we had to order coal from South Africa before winter. We did have to purchase some electric heaters but the British power company had a monopoly on electricity and it was very expensive. The house had what they called an American kitchen primarily because the money to build it was contributed by USAID to British Housing who apparently managed all housing and collected the rent monthly. The house was furnished with uncomfortable locally made furniture and had a cement floor with tile covering. It did have a solar hot water heater heated by panels on the roof that water circulated through. It was really quite a nice house for a Third World Country. It was on a large lot large lot located on a cul-de-sac near the Holiday Inn with a gate where the driveway was supposed to enter but there wasn't anything that resembled a driveway. Also, there was a building in back of the lot with a carport on one end and two little rooms with a toilet and shower in the middle. These were servants' quarters for a maid and gardener and they didn't have either electric lights or hot water. We hired a maid who lived in one of the rooms and we had to hire a gardener because the entire lot was overgrown with weeds 3 feet high but he lived somewhere else. The gardener cleaned up the lot, made a little garden in back, stole enough gravel from a pile outside our back fence to make a driveway, and planted a hedge around the perimeter of the lot. He also planted grass and flowers and a little cactus patch with some small banana trees in it . . . We still didn't have front or back steps so we bought pieces of slate, like flagstone and I made front and back sidewalks and a large slate patio in back where we had our evening meal and watched the sunset. I learned to do flagstone work from our Swedish neighbor next door. This turned out to be an expensive project because we couldn't get anyone to haul the construction material and Edna hauled it herself in many loads until the French Citron car we recently bought broke down. The neighbors out walking often stopped and commented on what a beautiful garden we had. Garden is the British word for yard but we did also have a vegetable garden in the back of our lot as well I also put electricity in the maid's house and both her and the gardener were happy and would sing as they worked.

UN-6 NEW TECHNICIANS

I started to get a technical staff and my workload became more and more difficult training new technicians in preparation for the installation of the new communications equipment that I had just wrote the specification for and was waiting for bids from the international community. I got two technicians we called Pule and Scientist that had just completed a 4 year course at the Nairobi ICAO technicians school and I also hired a Scott and an Indian technician that had been working in Africa. Edna could no longer go with me on in-country trips because I had to take 2 technicians along. Before long you all know each other well enough that you can talk about anything without offending anyone. When you drive for 2 days coming and going there is a lot of time to talk and a lot of things to talk about so you learn many things that you wouldn't otherwise.

A few days before we arrived in Botswana, two preteen boys' bodies were hung up on the limb of a tree and all their sex organs had been removed.

This opened the door for months of discussion on Voodoo, and medicine men that they refer to as traditional doctors exposing all their beliefs and practices. First, I asked them how you become a traditional doctor. There was clear agreement that it was like an apprenticeship since you had to work with a traditional doctor but there was some question regarding how long. There was also agreement that they had to sacrifice your first born child and the traditional doctor had unlimited power and could do anything they saw fit to remedy not just medical but social problems as well. For example, a night runner who may even be your husband or wife is one that goes out in the night and may kill or injure someone that is probably asleep somewhere in their village. I asked them how I would recognize a night runner if I saw one and they told me you couldn't because they don't have any face. There was some belief that night runners were agents of the traditional doctor who forced his will on those that were offending what we would call his patients. Everyone had a very deep fear of night runners.

Scientist, the technician that had been to the ICAO school in Nairobi was planning on getting married to the woman that he had been living with for some time. First he had to go to the elders of his remote village and tell them that he wanted to get married and needed to get their approval. It would take some time because they would have to investigate and have a number of meetings together to decide whether or not the woman he wanted to marry was a night runner. They hadn't reached a decision yet and he was still waiting.

The sex organs from the two preteen boys that I previously mentioned were removed because the traditional doctor obviously needed them to make some powerful medicine. There was also other less harmless thing that their patients could give them as payment for his services. For example, when I was working at Kasane or when Edna and I went to the Indian Ocean they wanted us to bring back a bottle of water from the ocean or the Chobe River so they could give it to the traditional doctor to make powerful medicine. We had to put a little sand in the bottle so the water would be happy.

On these long trips over the bumpy gravel roads or trails with a Toyota Land Cruiser we also had prolonged discussion regarding about such things as them living in a country where they were free. We spent many hours on this subject over a period many days. I started it off by asking them if they thought they were better off living in a country where they have freedom and rights to do anything they could afford as compared to the black people in South Africa. It was a lively discussion that went on for weeks. There were pro and cons regarding whether the black people in South Africa were better or worse off than they were. They all conceded the black people in Botswana had more freedom and rights but on the other hand they didn't have the necessary resources to utilize these rights. For example, a maid in Johannesburg has to come in from the ghetto in the morning but she gets paid three or four times as much as a maid in Botswana. Men in the farming area which is the breadbasket of South Africa lived in better houses, operated large farm machinery and have better housing and schools for their children. After prolonged pro and con discussions, they were all happy where they lived but the rights they had were of little value because they didn't have the money to take advantage of them. Overall, they concluded it was better to be black in South Africa than Botswana but they all liked what they had and what they were doing and wouldn't want to change even if they could.

When I was on a weeklong trip to Kasane with the Scottish technician I had recently hired, I got a serious infection with considerable blood in my urine and I went to a little clinic where they had two French doctors. They diagnosed my case as malaria and give me some medication which didn't provide any relief. We hurried up and did most of what we came for before we departed on the 2 day trip back to Gaborone. There was one doctor in Gaborone that apparently had some medical training but he said I would have to see an urologist in South Africa. That night, Edna called her friend Virginia who was secretary to the US Council in Johannesburg. Virginia made arrangements for me to check in to a hospital where I would be able to see the best urologist in Johannesburg. We drove to Johannesburg where I was hospitalized for a week and Edna stayed with Virginia. The urologist thought it was a kidney stone and did some surgery but finally concluded it was a virus that settled in my bladder. I stayed in a ward with seven South Africans for a week and was impressed with their medical care. It just goes to show how far you are out of reach of medical care in Botswana. They did have a kind of a hospital in Gaborone but we were afraid to use it even if it was before anyone knew about the AIDS epidemic there. Both Edna and I later got a yellow fever vaccination there as it was required for us to go to Swaziland and we were later concerned when the AIDS epidemic broke out a couple years later.

After I had the opportunity to work with Spike, Pule and Scientist for a few months, I had a better idea of what their capabilities were and what additional training would be most useful. Scientist and Pule had spent 4 years in a technical ICAO school for aviation electronics in Kenya but they really didn't have any experience working on equipment. Hopefully they had learned enough theory to be able to absorb both the theory and hands on training in both communication and the Visual Omni Directional Navigation facility which is the universal international navigation system. Spike was a graduate of the local engineering college and his job would be management of the entire national program but he didn't have any training or experience in management or how the facilities that he would be responsible for operated. With a new airport being built in the near future we needed to get a training program underway as soon as possible. I proposed a training program where all three of them would go to our FAA school in Oklahoma City which is really the only school in the world that trains international students. All three of them would take the communication & air navigation courses and since Spike's job was to manage their national program, he would also go to a short school for upper level managers and spend some time at what we call a sector office to see how everything worked together. I recommended they send him to Minneapolis for the later where my friend and former coworker was the sector manager for the state of Minnesota which would be somewhat equivalent to what he should be trying to set up for Botswana. I talked to USAID in Botswana and they agreed to fund my proposed training program. It had to be scheduled and didn't start for a few months. Spike passed all the courses but I was extremely disappointed when Scientist and Pule failed the air navigation facilities course because this would be a very important facility when they built their new airport. Also, it didn't say much for the ICAO school in Nairobi

UN-7 FEMALE TECHNICIAN ARRIVES

One morning when I got to work there was a young woman in my office waiting to see me who said she had just completed the ICAO school in Kenya and was reporting for work. I was not aware that there was a woman in the same class as Scientist and Pule, nor the fact that she got pregnant and lost a year so she just graduated. She said her name was Babitse and her husband who was also going to school in Kenya had been designated the Architect for Botswana when he graduated. Unlike the other two technicians she had graduated from a technical school in Gaborone before she went to school in Kenya. I was surprised to see a woman in that type job because women didn't do such things in Botswana. After making some inquiries, I found that she had been selected to go to that school by someone from the Philippines that previously had my job several years ago. It was a controversial selection but her name could have either been a man or woman's name and government officials didn't recognize that they were approving a woman. Now that she had completed the school there were other hurtles in the way to obstruct her. One was that they would not approve my request to send her to the local school where Scientist and Pule went to learn how to drive a car and get their license. I solved that problem as I did with Spike by teaching her myself and she took her driver's test to get a license in her native village. Since the other technicians got some state side training, USAID also approved similar training for her. She came to visit Edna and me in Albuquerque a couple years later when she was going to school in Oklahoma City. She was pregnant with her second child at that time but she was the only one of the three technicians that passed the navigation aids course.

All of us UN employees were considered government officials and were always invited to special government events. In one case Botswana President, Sir Seretse Khama hosted the President of Mozambique and they had a huge outdoor welcoming celebration in the capital grounds. There was an abundance of food, drink and complementary speeches to welcome the leader of this communist country. UN employees were filling high level government jobs and were also part of the welcoming committee when high level guests from other countries came to Botswana.

UN-8 PRESIDENT'S FUNERAL

The funeral of President, Sir Seretse Khama was a more solemn occasion which was attended by leaders of most of the world countries. It had been customary for the US to send our Vice President to represent the US on such occasions but President Carter sent Andrew Young, Ambassador to the UN to head up the US delegation. Botswana considered it an insult to send a black man to head up the US delegation to their president's funeral Also, President Carter was the laughingstock of the world and degrading to the US when he sent a few helicopters out in a sandstorm to rescue our US hostages in Iran. The world news media played up the story for several months that," US, the most powerful country in the world was unable to rescue a few diplomatic hostages from the US Embassy". That was the beginning of America's downfall and not a pleasant time to be an American.

UN-9 VACATION TRAVEL SOTHERN AFRICA

Sometimes I was in traveling for two weeks and we worked long hours and weekends as well so I got pretty stressed out. It was a stressful job and sometimes I just had to get away for a few days so occasionally Edna and I took a little trip just to get away. We made monthly trip to Rustenburg, South Africa; noted for their platinum mines, where we did our monthly shopping. We also went to Pretoria and Johannesburg on several occasions and had a couple weeklong trips to the Indian Ocean and one to Swaziland. We also made a trip through what is now Zimbabwe to Victoria Falls with a Canadian couple that had later joined our UN Group. It was a little scary because the new Black Government had just taken over the country, changing its name from Rhodesia to Zimbabwe and there was still a civil war going on between two black tribes to see who was going to govern it. We purchased quite a lot of wood carvings on the Zambia side of the bridge between Victoria Falls and Zambia. We came back through Kasane where we stayed overnight at the Safari Lodge where I frequently stayed.

We made a weeklong trip to Durbin and stayed at a motel under a huge lighthouse on a bluff overlooking the Indian Ocean. Durbin is populated primarily by East Indians that were brought in more than a century ago as laborers. The motel was owned and operated exclusively by Indians and they didn't have any black laborers. There are three classes of citizens in South Africa: The white Europeans which are primarily Dutch, the East Indians which have fewer rights than the whites but more than the blacks. South Africa is a bilingual country where the evening TV news on TV in Afrikaans (Old Dutch language), the 10:00 news will be in British English. The next day the times will be reversed. We had a wild ride on our return trip, even though we left early in the morning we went through Johannesburg during the evening rush hour on the way back. Edna was diving in the 6 lanes of traffic at about 70 miles per hour to keep from getting run over and I was trying to navigate, looking for our road to turn off. Because of apartheid it is almost impossible to find a motel or a fast food restaurant along the way so we were trying to cross the border into Botswana before it closed at 8:00 PM. If we didn't make it, we would have to come back about 100 miles to find a motel. We did just make it and Gaborone is almost on the border so we were home.

During our two year tour in Botswana we took a two week vacation starting at Port Elizabeth located at the south east tip of the continent on the Indian Ocean. We spent most of a week at Jeffery's Bay, a small town on the ocean located a few miles west of Port Elizabeth where we stayed at a hotel where they also served three meals a day as part of a package deal. We chose this location because this was a rest type vacation and there wasn't anything to do there except swim in the ocean and pick up shells which we brought back to the States with us. We followed what they call the garden route along the ocean all the way to Cape Town We found a hotel in down town Cape Town which was centrally located and we had good access to the small city. Table Mountain is supposed to be the key tourist attraction so naturally it was our first destination. People in South Africa are very friendly especially to Americans. We were outside looking for a taxi to take us to Table Mountain and people waiting on the corner asked us if they could help us. I told them we wanted to go to Table Mountain and they said you can take a bus from here directly to the mountain and they helped to make sure we got on the right bus. It was a double decked bus and both black and white people were getting on and off the bus. We were on the upper deck so we could see better and after all the talk about busses for blacks and busses for whites we noticed the few people in the upper deck were all black except us. We thought we might be on the wrong deck but we noted there were both black and white people on the lower deck so we forgot about it. The bus stopped at the base of the mountain and we had to go up by cable car. It was a an excellent view of the city and you could see all the way down to the cape which was about 50 miles to the south.

Later when we were exploring the down town business area we run into what appeared to be like a very large McDonald's restaurant with blacks and whites randomly seated around the tables so there wasn't any evidence of all these apartheid problems we are beat over the head with by the news media back in the States. The next day we drove down to the Cape of Good Hope which is about 50 miles south on a narrow strip of land with ocean on either side. At the end of the road is a hill with a radio and light beacon tower on top. This is where the Atlantic and Indian Oceans meet and the water is so turbulent that it looks like it is boiling. It is easy to believe the mariners' stories about this being the most turbulent water in the world. It is also understandable why so many ships sunk going around the cape from one ocean to the other. We returned to Gaborone on a road straight from Cape Town across the desert through a Black Homeland on the South Africa/Botswana border. In the middle of the barren desert, there was a one or two acre plot of land covered with foliage with rows of windmills in a grid formation that pumped the water to irrigate the entire vineyard. It was a nice, much needed vacation and I was ready to get back to work.

Edna and I also took interesting night train trip from Gaborone through the bush country to Bulawayo, Zimbabwe. We had a roomette but you couldn't get out the door because the aisle was packed with sleeping people. We saw the sunrise and sunset which seems to be more beautiful in Africa than anywhere else. We met Edna's friend, Virginia in Bulawayo and she went with us to Victoria Falls the next day. After staying there a couple nights, we spent a couple days at a lodge in the Wankie Game Reserve. Although we had seen so much game in the Chobe Game Park we didn't expect to see so much more at Wankie. One of the tour busses in Wanke was striped like a zebra and we could drive right out in the middle of a herd of zebra and apparently they thought we were one of them. We later took a car trip with our Canadian friends that had now joined our aviation UN group. That time we came back by Kasine and stayed at the Safari Lodge where I stayed when I worked up in that area. Both times we walked the iron bridge across the Zambezi River below the falls into Zambia where you could buy almost any type of wood carvings at a very reasonable price. We bought all we could carry across the bridge. Both were nice trips with special friends.

UN-10 RADIO BEACON CONTRACT

Before I came to Botswana Civil Aviation, they had purchased five radio beacons which were installed at airports which were quite far from Gaborone by a contractor from South Africa but only one of them operated and that wasn't reliable. I had more work than I could do and since I hadn't generated this problem and the director hadn't even mentioned it to me, I hadn't got involved. Civil aviation hadn't accepted the new facilities from the contractor as yet so even though it fell under my jurisdiction it wasn't yet my responsibility. One day our ICAO British Director asked me if would sign a document to accept the contract so they could pay the contractor. I told him no because only one of the five radio beacons operated at all and that one wasn't reliable. He said OK and dropped the subject. A few weeks later while I was on a two week trip to our remote facilities with a couple technicians, unbeknown to me the director had one of the British Aid Program technicians sign the accepting documents. Still unaware that we had accepted the contact as being completed, I got a call from one of the two British banks in Gaborone advising me that we had overdrawn our letter of credit which I wasn't aware even existed. Our office was near the bank so I went right over to the bank to see what this was all about. The banker gave me a copy of the contracts, a separate one for each facility which I had never seen, with an adding machine tape stapled to the stack of contracts. He didn't give me a copy of any letter of credit but I had enough to see what these contracts were all about. I went back to my office and carefully scrutinized these contracts for the first time. Finally, I found what the problem was obviously. Each of the contracts which were almost identical was on a separate sheet of paper with one exception where the same information was on two pages. The adding machine tape included the subtotal for the first page of the 2 page document as well as the grand total on the second page. The error was obvious so I went right back to the bank and pointed out their error, the banker thanked me and I left without even suspecting any wrongdoing. I wasn't aware at that time that we had formally accepted the contract and thought it had to do with us not having enough money in the letter of credit which I still hadn't seen to pay off the contact when it was accepted.

I had just completed the specifications for quite a large communication equipment contract and advertised for bids internationally a few days before the contractors sales representative from the company that installed our radio beacons showed up unannounced to have lunch with me. That in itself is not unusual but I didn't realize he was talking about the radio beacon contract they had previously installed which was unsatisfactory rather than the communications equipment contract that I hadn't yet awarded. When he said, "You know you have to pay off to do business with Botswana". I was offended because I thought he was trying to bribe me into awarding the new contract to them. I went on to explain that I had just written the specifications and awarded a $150 million dollar contract to modernize the FAA navigation system and I don't get involved in payoffs. Sometime later I found that his company wasn't even interested in bidding on the communications contract and he was talking about the radio beacon contract that they still hadn't got paid for.

A few months later after their yearly change in bank managers, I got another call from the bank and again explained their error to them. This was a wakeup call that indicated to me that this wasn't just an innocent mistake. It was almost impossible to hire competent technical help and I had hired the Scottish technician that actually installed the equipment in the radio beacon contract. On day when we were alone, returning from one of our remote facilities, I ask him point blank, who is it that is supposed to have got the payoff on the radio beacon contract you installed. "Oh," he said, "the Director of Civil Aviation, of course." I had suspected that was the case but had never heard it from someone that was personally involved that actually knew.

The ICAO Director of Civil Aviation had slipped away quietly a few weeks ago without a going away party and another British member of our all British team had quietly been selected to replace him. We were very good friends and socially involved. I wrote up the incident and give it to him with full documentation and he took it to the permanent secretary of our ministry in the Botswana Government. He called me in with our new director in to insure me in no uncertain terms that such a thing never happened and he never wanted to hear anything more about it. I am not easily intimidated so I also sent a letter to the United Nation officer that drives around in a limousine with flags on it like an ambassador and supposedly supervisees all the many UN organizations like ICAO that serve some kind of a function in Botswana. He also threatened me to keep quiet about such things and thought it probably never happened. This just threw more gas on the fire and I sent fully documented letters to President Carter's Ambassador to ICAO in Montreal and to Andrew Young, Ambassador to the United Nations. Neither of them apparently cared and didn't bother to even acknowledge receipt of my letters. It is understandable why the UN is a complete failure.

Now that I suddenly inherited these 5 beacons and didn't have any skilled technical help my work was cut out for me. The beacon at Maun that made up a key section of the airway from Johannesburg, over Gaborone to the Atlantic Ocean would be my first priority. Because of apartheid South African Airway couldn't fly directly across Africa to

New York and had to fly straight west until it was over the ocean before it headed north to New York to avoid flying over any of the hostile countries. It was a 16 hour flight with a one hour fuel stop at a tiny island in the middle of the Atlantic. Edna and I took this route when we came home for Christmas one year.

Maun was inaccessible and I had to either fly there and stay a week or spend two full days going and two more returning home if I drove. It was a difficult problem that nobody had been able to solve so I decided to spend the whole week there. The beacon worked flawlessly the week that I was there and I begin to suspect power problems. Maun was a fairly large town and unlike most little African towns had its own power plant so you should be able to expect fairly reliable power. Regardless of that they used large diesel engines that had to be rotated periodically for maintenance purposes or an engine added or removed to accommodate changes in power requirements. I had previously worked at a small hydroelectric plant with only two turbines one day a week to give the regular operator a day off and was aware of some of the pitfalls of mechanically adding or removing generators from on line service. You have to adjust the speed of the generator you are putting on line so it is exactly the same as the on line generator and throw the switch to engage it when the phase is exactly in sync. If you don't follow that exact procedure there will be a spike or surge on the power line Equipment using vacuum tubes was quite tolerant of small surges but transistor equipment couldn't tolerance any line surges and the $20 transistors would burn out even when there was small surges.

When I got back to Gaborone, I discussed the problem with the British Power Company and since they didn't have any experience with transistors they thought that I didn't know what I was talking about. Regardless of what they thought, I ordered some surge protectors for the equipment from Chicago and when they were installed we didn't burn out any more $20 transistors. Getting radio tubes, transistors and other supplies had initially been difficult and time consuming, They were ordered by the Botswana Government through the British High Commission in Gaborone and the British Government procured them from the U.S. which might take as much as a year to get them and the cost was 2 to 4 times what it was on the U.S. market. I had a catalog from a Chicago radio parts store that I brought with me and one day I called the Commercial section of the American Embassy to see if they couldn't set up an agreement where I could order directly to get supplies for the Botswana Government. It turned out that they did and I was able to order by telex and material would arrive by air in a few days. This was how I got the surge protectors for the radio beacons.

We also took a car trip to Swaziland which is also an independent country that borders the northeast corner of the South Africa. It is the home of the Zulu tribesmen. They are very tall, well-built men and are noted for their ability as guards. The two countries are separated by a long hill that runs as far as they eye can see and as soon as you go over the ridge it seems like there is a misty rain as far as we went on the other side of the ridge. The entire country is large fields of pineapple. It was an interesting country where the natives lived in round adobe houses with thatched roofs and we purchased a few high quality baskets that were made there. A few years after we were there one of Edna's friends that she was in the Foreign Service was sent there as the U. S. Ambassador so we later heard a lot about it from her. Traveling by automobile was quite expensive because all gasoline in the southern part of Africa was made out of coal in South Africa because the Arab oil countries boycotted them because of their apartheid policy. This was the same reason they were building airports in Lesotho and Botswana so they could supply them by air if South Africa closed their border. South Africa was self-sufficient but none of the countries they supported had that capability. Actually, South Africa is the breadbasket for the southern third of the continent.

UN-11 PROJECT SUMMARY

Both Edna and I enjoyed this interesting diverse country, the friendly native population living in a free society, and our association with people from all over the world that were our neighbors. Although I was satisfied that I did the job that I was sent there to do, I was extremely dissatisfied to find that the United Nations and its family of organizations are not only dishonest but definitely of negative value to all the organizations in all countries we pay so generously to serve. They come into a country paying incompetent people absorbent salaries to teach host country personnel skills they don't know themselves. If they do know they refuse to teach them to anyone else because their services would no longer be required. Just to site one example of how it works, the Canadian government sent an individual to Montreal University where he got a master's degree in metrology to become Botswana's head of meteorology. When he returned to Botswana, they sat him in a back room at meteorology while the uneducated meteorologist worked under a UN chief that was supposed to be teaching him his job. He had no intention of training a man that was better educated that he was to take his job. Finally, when I complained that I was the only one that had a counterpart in civil aviation they transferred him to civil aviation where he was supposed to be groomed to be the director of civil aviation. They sent him to England to school for air traffic controllers and by the time he returned they had made arrangements with USAID for him to get another Master's degree at Emory Riddle University in the USA in aviation economics. When he returned to civil aviation in Botswana they put him in a little inside office where he didn't have any access to what was going on. In the meantime, the director that got the contract kickback left unannounced and another UK member of our group was selected for the job but the over educated Botswana citizen still sit alone in his little office. I complained long and loud and when the new director retired, after I left he finally became director of civil aviation. I was the only one of us five ICAO employees in Botswana that had a counterpart in my office and an organized training program so he would be prepared to take over my job.

After I left, I learned that they sent my counterpart who already had an engineering degree in Botswana to a full 4 year degree course in England. The only difference was his education was paid for by Botswana rather than Canada or the U.S. It is also interesting to note that his Botswana degree was taught by British teachers. He didn't have any need for another 4 year engineering degree and since they were building a new airport this was where he should have been to get some on the job training. Summing it up, I consider the entire UN to be dishonest and of negative value to the countries it is supposed to be serving. It is a burden on countries like the US that pays such huge taxes to countries that use it as a piggy bank to employ their incompetent citizens. It is also an injustice that retards the progress of countries they claim to be serving. I could have stayed a few more months until I reached the age of 60 but after I discovered all the graft and corruption and the leader of my group actually getting a contract kick back I couldn't get out soon enough. Also, it was very upsetting to find the problem extended all the way back to Washington. I could have stayed and collected the big money but under the circumstances I elected to go home, when my tour was completed.

This is the house I built in Redwood fall, Mn in 1953 after work at night, on weekend's holidays and vacations. I could only afford to buy one board at a time and my growing family needed housing.

I built this retirement house on Clam Lake near Siren, WI after I retired in 1983. This house burned after my wife died and I had major surgery in 2007.

VII

FINAL RETIREMENT

RT-1 TRIP HOME TO USA

After an exciting but stressful two years, we took a leisurely trip back to Albuquerque. We stopped in Colombo the capital of Sri Lanka for a few days and continued on to Jakarta, Indonesia to visit Edna's friend Beverly who was still in the Foreign Service. She

Suggested that now we are down in this part of the world we should go to the island of Bali which is a jewel out in the Indian Ocean. We spent several days there watching the catamarans glide out over the endless blue Ocean. We purchased quite a few quality wood carvings there at a very reasonable price. We also went to see native dancers and took a tour of the mountainous area created by the volcanoes that formed this beautiful island. As we went up the mountain roads we met small groups of perhaps a half a dozen men with their dragon which they had to take to some religious shrine to have it blessed periodically. Their dragons were mostly a mixture of bright red, green and yellow cloth with one man being able to look out the eyes of the head and the other three filling out the body and back of the dragon. We flew back to Beverly's place which on the second floor of the main street in Jakarta.

We had both spent quite a lot of time in Hong Kong and since it was one of our favorite places, we stopped for a few days just to get one more look. We enjoyed a good old big Mac hamburger which we had never been able to get in our travels. While we were there China was just opening up to the outside world and we decided to take a three day tour, going over on the hydrofoil and coming back on the train. It was our first look at how fast China was developing into a new major country with construction going on everywhere. We visited a hospital, commune and a school with our guide that was once in a labor camp but now things had changed and she spoke very good American English.

We went from Hong Kong to Hawaii and visited Edna's cousin on the island of Oahu. We stayed at his house and he took off a couple days from teaching to show us around. Neither of us had visited the battleship Arizona which is now a memorial for those killed when the Japanese bombed Pearl Harbor starting WW II.

When we got to Albuquerque in the spring of 1982, we were ready to retire, buy a house and settle down. It was a good time to buy a house because during the Carter Administration interest rates had soared to over 20% and new home builders had only been able to get a 5 year mortgages when they built their house. Now many could not qualify for a new mortgage and had to sell their house on a depressed market at bargain prices. We stayed in a motel for more than a month while we were looking to determine what area of the city and what type of house we wanted. We had saved our money and were able to pay cash for a house so once we found the house, we were anxious to buy.

RT-2 NEW HOME

We bought a house with the same floor plan as a house that we looked at shortly after we were married but weren't ready to settle down at that time. It was a nice house but the backyard needed a considerable amount of work so we made that our summer project. It sloped down from the back of the house to the back of our lot and there was a pile of volcanic rock that we had to do something with. We finally decided to go all out and terrace the back yard using the volcanic rock to build a wall across the lot so it was level both above and below the wall. We got a large semi-truck load top soil which had to be hauled from where it was unloaded in our driveway to the back yard in a wheel barrow so we could have a reasonably flat area further back from the house. We also decided to put in a hot tub which was buried down to ground level where we put flagstone around it. Once we got to that point, I went out to a sod farm and got loads of free rolls of grass that they throw away if there is a weed or any flaw in the roll. They are happy to have someone get rid of it for them so they don't have to haul it away. We ended up with a beautiful back yard with green grass, a fish pond, volcanic rock wall, a stone barbeque grill, and a waterfall with a little river where the water flowed from the waterfall to the fishpond. We were proud of it and went on to buy 5 undeveloped lots in the mountains.

RT-3 BUILD LAKE HOME

While we were in Africa, I had my daughter buy us a lake lot back in Wisconsin near where I was born and raised until I was drafted into the military in WW II. That winter I went up to Wisconsin where most of my family still live and I bought a winterized cabin that was just 300 feet from the undeveloped lake lot we purchased while we were in Africa. This was the only lake cabin in a new area that had previously been a farm but now was a heavily wooded pine forest where we would build a winterized cabin where we would spend our summers.

The next spring we went up to Wisconsin for the summer and started making plans for our new house. We incorporated a lot of things we like liked about New Mexico architecture like a cathedral ceiling and I drew up the house plans. We had to start by cutting hundreds of trees and we learned a lot about red tape regarding zoning and permits for such things a water well and septic system. Before we left to come back to Albuquerque that fall, all we had actually accomplished was to put in a well, septic system and to pour the concrete slab for the floor of the house. Edna and I worked on it together and it was convenient being close enough to the cabin we bought that we could use a cordless telephone and utilize the electric power from our cabin.

We worked hard but it was a good summer where we socialized with my former high school classmates. They also became Edna's special friends and Edna being a gourmet cook did a lot of entertaining. We finished our new house and socialized with my high school classmates and during the winter months went on tours in Mexico with my high school classmates. One winter we went to the Gallopades Island off the coast of Ecuador where Edna had always wanted to go.

RT-4 MEDICAL PROBLEMS

We both had some major surgeries during the period from 1989 to 1992 but recovered quite well and life was good until Edna was diagnosed with gastric cancer in 2005. I can best explain that difficult period by enclosing a group e-mail that I sent to all our friends and relatives that were inquiring about Edna's health problem. Every time her situation changed I sent one e-mail to all that previously inquired. After Edna died and I was hospitalized my daughter did the same for me.

Note: I just sent this E-mail to those that I had their E-mail address on 10/21/07.

Dear Friends and Family,

Now the dense fog of many months is starting to lift, I have reread all your e-mails, cards and letters; I am struggling to get a letter together to thank all of you. First, I want to express my thanks and deepest gratitude to my daughters that have seen me through it every day of this long difficult crisis. I couldn't have made it without them and I am very proud of them both. As for the rest of you, I am overwhelmed by your cards, letters emails and prayers and want to express my deepest gratitude to all of you.

I would like to write a brief summary of this two year crisis which hopefully once written will clear my mind so I can get on with my life as I have been able to do on previous crisis. We need to go back to November and December 2005 when I had my 4th and 5th back to back cancer surgeries for this same problem. Although we normally go back to Albuquerque in October, doctors were reluctant to release me by the end of January. It was important that we leave as soon as possible because Edna was having an anemia problem like she had previously had a number of times in the last few years. It was serious enough that doctors were sure it was internal bleeding but it healed itself before they could find out what caused it. We hurriedly went back to where her healthcare providers were and again the problem had corrected itself. Again they made an all-out effort to find the problem and discovered she had a large malignant tumor in her stomach. Two thirds of her stomach was surgically removed and after a recovery period her cancer doctor put her on oral chemo. This went well and her doctor let her come back up to Wisconsin for 3 months before he had to take a series of test to see how she was getting along. The summer went reasonably well but before the 3 months was up she had vaginal bleeding and we hurried back to Albuquerque where they had set up an appointment with a gynecologist. He found that she had a large tumor in her abdomen and scheduled surgery. In the meantime her cancer doctor completed another battery of tests and declared her cancer free a week before surgery

We were shocked to find that her abdomen was full of cancer. She was in the hospital for a short time and a nursing home for a month and under hospice care for a week at home before she died. I was her caregiver for that awful week when I heard a hospice nurse asked her if she wouldn't like to join Jesus and get rid of her unbearable pain. She said, "No my husband needs me." She was fully aware that I had to have major surgery which was long overdue. After two sleepless nights, I met the hospice nurse with bed sheets under my arm that I had just taken out of the dryer. She could see that I really had it and said, "Let me take over, take this pill, lie down on the couch, go to sleep and you can't drive a car until this afternoon." She called an ambulance and they took Edna down to the hospice where she died that night, on March 3rd 2007. I called her sister, Lupe who was there when she arrived but Edna was unconscious at that time.

Edna and I had both written a letter and signed it outlining what we wanted done after our death to avoid disagreements at that time. Her sister was in charge of her Memorial Service and she would be cremated. Her remains would be entombed at Ft. Snelling National Cemetery where I would eventually join her. I tried to expedite getting the essential things done to close her estate because I had to go Minneapolis where my surgery needed to be done as soon as possible and I probably wouldn't be back in the near future. In the middle of April, I drove to Minneapolis taking Edna's remains with me, stopping at the VA Hospital to schedule treatment and cancer surgery of my left lower jaw.

My house is 100 miles from the VA hospital and I made many trips back and forth before surgery on May 29th. The last two weeks before surgery, I had to go to the VA Hospital twice a week so they could drain the puss out of the cancerous tumor in my jaw. My daughters and I had planned to have another memorial service for Edna where her friends could celebrate her life and have a luncheon at our house like they did in Albuquerque. My health continued to deteriorate and I couldn't wait to have her remains laid to rest at Fort Snelling before I had my surgery. One day when I had a doctor's appointment at the VA, my daughter Jackie joined me on her lunch hour to arrange for her entombment and mine when God decides that time has come. I stayed with my daughter in Bloomington the night before surgery and went to the hospital early the next morning. Both of my daughters were there during the 10-½ hour operation and time in the recovery room late in the evening.

I was very heavily medicated and wasn't aware of anything thing that happened for about a month but I was irritated that I couldn't talk because they had opened up my trachea so I could breathe when the swelling in my head closed up the air passages. Jackie was overwhelmed with her job, family and coming to see me every day so her employer let her go on part time for a month or so. One day I was moved to a nursing home where they didn't have the necessary facilities to care for me and I was back in the hospital the next day. A week later, they sent me back to nursing home but I was never comfortable there and when I started radiation therapy, a taxi picked me up early every morning to take me back the hospital. I had lost a lot of weight before Edna's death and had continued to lose weight because I was not able eat or drink. They again admitted me to the hospital where they put a feeding tube in my stomach. I am still fed through a tube and will continue to be until the swelling in my face and jaw caused by the radiation gets back to normal. I am now 4-½ months out of surgery, 2 months out of radiation therapy and one month out of the hospital. Joy came back for another week when I was released from the hospital to get me moved and settled in my lake house so I could take care of myself.

I had a nurse and two aids that came twice a week and a housekeeper that came once a week. I am still not able to eat or drink by mouth or drive a car but I am on the mend. My recovery appears to be on track and it is time for me to get on with the rest of my life!

(End of E-mail)

RT-5 HOUSE BURNS

A couple months later on December 27th my house burned when it was -35 degrees and I spent the next 9 months in a motel while they were building me a new house. 2007 was a bad year and it also became apparent that I would probably be on tube feeding the rest of my life because a section of my jaw bone had been removed and the lymph nodes they removed resulted in the lymph fluid pocket in my cheek, tongue, lip which are paralyzed.

My daughter, Jackie drew the plans for my new house and purchased furniture and appliances when they were on sale and didn't have them delivered until the house was finished. She is not only an interior decorator but shopped for best prices on building material. An additional $25,000 for fill dirt was required because of a new flood plan building code; the insurance company paid for almost everything including my 9 months in a motel.

I managed to get most of the landscaping done but there is still much to do the following spring. Regardless of having a shining new house, it will always be a lonely place because Edna and I always enjoyed being together and I am lost without her. My new house is larger and is sitting on 4 feet of fill dirt because of new flood plain building code requirements. It has a better view of the lake because it's higher elevation and all the large windows on the lake side.

Edwards Brothers, Inc.
Thorofare, NJ USA
December 22, 2011